10-13-09

OSHKosh '09

To Bob, with best Regards, HAPPY

Flying.

SCARFACE 42

OshKosh 2008

SCARFACE 42

Robert W. Robinson

SCARFACE 42

United States Marine Corps
Air/Ground Support "In Close"

Robert W. Robinson

Cataloging -in-Publication

Robinson, Robert W.
    Scarface 42 / by Robert W. Robinson.
    p. cm.
    Includes bibliographical references and index.
    LCCN 2007907453
    ISBN-13: 978-0-9797704-0-1
    ISBN-10: 0-9797704-0-8

    1. Robinson, Robert W. 2. Vietnam War, 1961-1975--Aerial
operations, American. 3. Vietnam War, 191-1975--Personal narratives,
American. 4. Military helicopters--Vietnam. 5. United States. Marine
Corps--History--Vietnam War, 1961-1975. I. Title.

DS558.8.R63 2008   959.704'348'092
                                    QBI07-600324

Published by
Tailwind Publications LLC.
P.O. Box 1222
2220 West Harbor Drive
Bismarck, North Dakota 58502-1222
701-258-6337 or 701-226-6337

Printed in the United States of America by
Sunray Printing Solutions
25123 22nd Ave
St. Cloud, MN 56301
www.sunrayprinting.com

Cover design by Brad Ryti.

Cover photo by Barry Pencek with
digital editing by Brad Ryti.

In memory of
my father

PFC Robert E. Robinson
Killed in Action
Northern Germany, World War II
22 May 1922-01 December 1944

Dedicated to those who have sacrificed their lives
so that others may live in peace.

Acknowledgements

MANY YEARS AGO, while attending a military school at the Air University at Maxwell Air Force Base in Montgomery, Alabama, I gave a speech about events that had recently occurred in North Dakota. At that time, I was a member of the North Dakota Army National Guard and the state had just experienced a series of natural disasters. I was the Aviation Facilities Commander and had been actively involved in several activations to provide air support.

After I finished my speech, a colonel from the Pennsylvania National Guard asked, "Robby, have you ever considered becoming a storyteller?"

Well, I can tell a pretty good story, but when I began writing this book, I realized I am writing challenged.

As this book progressed and actually started looking like a book, my lovely wife Linda, a former English teacher and my editor, began systematically tearing it apart and making corrections. Without her help and patience, this book would never have come to print. She has my eternal gratitude for the hours and hours she spent working on this project. (After reading this paragraph, with tears in her eyes, she said, "Thank you. Now let me fix it.")

I also would like to thank all my former comrades-in-arms for their contributions and sharing of information. I would like to thank the following for their assistance in reviewing the book, providing information and/or answering questions pertaining to events in which they had been involved. Gen Mike Williams, United States

Marine Corps (Ret.), LtGen John E. Rhodes, United States Marine Corps (Ret.), Col Barry Penchek, United States Marine Corps Reserve (Ret.), Col William "Bill" Hartbarger, Tennessee Army National Guard (Ret.), LtCol Pat Owen, United States Marine Corps (Ret.), Capt Perry Unruh, United States Marine Corps (Ret.), SgtMaj Larry Groah, United States Marine Corps (Ret.), John Upthegrove, Mark Byrd, Brad Ryti, William "Bill" Beardall, Theodore "Ted" Soliday, Deane Swickard, Robert S. "Skip" Massey, Sid Baker, Pat Dumas, Mary Ann Kelly, and last, but not least, all my friends and relatives whose encouragement kept me going on this project.

Contents

Preface

In 1949, as a five-year-old child on my grandparents' farm in North Dakota, I had a rare opportunity. After being snowed in by a severe winter storm, my other grandparents who lived in the nearby town of Washburn hired the local pilot to fly out and pick me up in his Piper Cub outfitted with snow skis.

Seeing the snow-covered countryside from 1000 feet on the short trip to town, I was hooked on flying. There was no doubt in my mind about what I wanted to do in life. When in the country, I spent hours staring at the sky watching migrating ducks and geese fly by on their journey south. When in town, I spent hours at the airport watching planes come and go, dreaming of someday being "up there."

In the seventeen years following that day in 1949, general aviation evolved from piston engines to jets. I really did not pay much attention to the flying contraptions called helicopters—few were ever seen in the North Dakota skies. Later, while I was a student at North Dakota State University in Fargo, the United States went to war in a place called Vietnam. By the fall of 1969, I was there flying helicopters.

My experiences in Vietnam were not much different from those of any other pilot or crewmember, but I did have the privilege of flying with the finest aviators and air crewmembers in the military. Scarface Squadron had an *esprit de corps* that is hard to explain. They worked hard, played hard and never forgot their mission of protecting and supporting the grunt on the ground. This is not my story; it is the story of Scarface, HML-367 United States Marine Corps.

Following my departure from the Marine Corps, I read many books about the war in Vietnam but noticed few had been written about Marine Corps aviation. I decided to pursue a part-time project that ended up consuming many years. Digging though military archives looking for after-action reports, squadron command chronology reports, interviewing fellow squadron mates, and listening to tape recordings of events and missions helped restore my memory. The interview process was particularly difficult because, to paraphrase Confucius, for each teller of the story, there was another point of view. After more than thirty-five years, no two people remembered the same event in the same way. All events in this book are real. They are presented as best as my research and memory could provide. All missions which were recorded on tape are presented as recorded. The communications and call signs which were not recorded are presented according to best recollection of those interviewed and myself.

In order to provide a pictorial view of the war for the reader, I have placed as many pictures of the event I was writing about with the event itself to give the reader a better understanding and visualization of the action.

Marine helicopters went where the action was. Our squadron helicopters and those from other squadrons were involved in heroic events daily. The events presented are only a microcosm of their involvement in the war in Vietnam.

SCARFACE 42

I

Mr. Secretary

If there must be trouble let it be in my day,
that my child may have peace.—*Thomas Paine*

SEPTEMBER 15, 1967. Somewhere over Wisconsin at 30,000 feet, the Boeing 727 leveled off. By that point in the flight, at least four people had walked back to the row of seats in which I sat and offered their seats in first class to the man sitting on my right. Each person addressed him as Mr. Secretary, and each one had something nasty to say about the inconsiderate airline on which we were flying. I was beginning to get an idea that this guy must be someone important.

As the flight continued, I diligently studied the handbook the United States Marine Corps had sent me on how to prepare for Officer Candidate School (OCS). I was happy that I had worked hard during the previous six weeks to get into shape and to prepare myself for the challenge ahead, yet I was apprehensive about my immediate future. The handbook presented a summary of academic and physical requirements expected of us in the three-month program. The thirty push-ups and sixty sit-ups were going to be a piece of cake, but the seven pull-ups were going to give me trouble. Unfortunately, the handbook had arrived only one week prior to my departure and I had not been able to work on pull-ups.

Glancing at the pile of papers the gentleman next to me was reading, I noticed United States Department of Agriculture letterhead. I looked at him and saw a long scar on the side of his face. I had seen him on television many times and remembered the scar.

1

Now I understood why several first class passengers had offered him their seats. He was Orville Freeman, the United States Secretary of Agriculture. He continued reading his papers, and I went back to reading my handbook.

When the flight was about forty-five minutes out of Washington, D.C., I summoned enough courage to ask the rugged-looking member of the President's cabinet a question about lodging for the night.

"Sir, I'm on my way to Quantico, Virginia, for Marine Corps Officer Candidate School." Making an unsuccessful attempt at nonchalance, I continued, "Could you tell me where there I can find a decent hotel near the bus depot?"

The Secretary looked at me, a smile breaking. He paused before setting his papers down.

"Really? I went through that establishment myself about twenty-five years ago. Orville Freeman is my name," he said, offering a firm handshake.

"Pleased to meet you."

The Secretary shuffled his pile of papers into a neat stack and placed them in his briefcase.

"Let me give you a couple of pointers," he said recalling his first day at Quantico. "Don't get there too early. When I reported to Quantico, I got there bright and early. I must have been the first one to show up that day. I wandered around until I found the check-in area listed in my orders."

He remembered seeing a gunnery sergeant and foolishly asking him where he needed to check in. Giving him a once over, the gunny told Freeman he was early, but said he would take care of him.

"The next thing I knew, I was scrubbing a barrack's floor in my suit!" the Secretary said, a smile crossing his face. The corners of his eyes creased, and he smiled again as he recalled the gunny going out to look for more candidates in need of help checking in.

"Before the day was over, I had plenty of company. I think your best bet is to show up later in the day and be as inconspicuous as possible for the next three months."

We continued our conversation until the plane began its descent. The approach was a cliffhanger. Thunderstorms were pounding the D.C. area. Though it was dark, I could see heavy rain as lightning flashed. The turbulence concerned me. After a "three-bounce" landing, I was happy to be on the ground, as was everyone else.

As the other passengers were getting out of their seats, Secretary Freeman looked at me. "Wait until everyone gets off, and come with me," he said. "I'll have someone get your bags."

Exiting from the rear stairs, I looked around. We were alone on the tarmac except for the ground crew unloading baggage. The Secretary's chauffeur walked up to us. He greeted the Secretary and took our baggage claim tickets. Mr. Freeman and I walked into a parking garage where I saw nothing but limousines. It was apparent this part of the facility was reserved for the government's executive fleet.

While we stood by the limo waiting for our luggage, Secretary Freeman told a few more stories about his Marine Corps experiences. The chauffeur returned with our luggage, and we climbed into the limo. I had never been in a limousine, and I was awed. Not only was the limousine roomy, it had two phones! Secretary Freeman told me his chauffeur had made a reservation for me at a hotel, and they would drop me off there. During our ride to the hotel, the Secretary pointed out some of D.C.'s landmarks.

When we arrived at the hotel, Secretary Freeman did not seem to be in a hurry. We continued our conversation for about fifteen to twenty minutes while sitting in the limo in front of the hotel. As I was getting out of the limo, he gave me his private secretary's name and phone number and told me to give him a call if I had any problems. Needless to say, I was impressed.

The desk clerk and the night manager behind the registration counter eyeballed me as I walked into the hotel. I approached the counter and gave the desk clerk my name and told him that Orville Freeman's chauffeur had made arrangements for me. Their distrust was clearly evident. Though the chauffeur had told them the Secretary would pay the bill, the manager started giving me the third degree. After going through my story with them, I finally said that I had planned on paying my own bill anyway. Suddenly, their attitudes changed, and they checked me in. I guess they thought I had been trying to take them for a ride.

The hotel was old, but the room was adequate. After getting settled in, I did some sit-ups, push-ups, and pull-ups. I struggled to get the seventh pull-up on the door trim. I was nervous about the whole thing and wondered what I was getting myself into. I questioned my confidence in being physically prepared for this adventure.

After a restless night, I hung around the hotel until late morning before taking a cab to the bus depot. Heeding advice received from the Secretary, I elected to take an afternoon bus to Quantico.

It looked as if the bus was full of new candidates headed for the same destination. The atmosphere was one of nervous anticipation. I introduced myself to the guy sitting next to me. He looked as nervous as I did, and I figured we were headed for the same place. I was right. His name was Larry Grasman. He had come from northern Michigan. He and I became friends and worked side by side all the way through OCS and flight school.

We arrived at the Marine base about 3:00 P.M. and were immediately sent to the in-processing center. Though I had never been in jail, I felt like I was in one. I thought I knew what a convict felt like the first time the door slammed behind him. The other candidates and I were being shuffled around as if we were a herd of cattle. No one had a name other than "candidate." The building we were shuffled into for processing was old, and the room was a large open bay. Someone else had total control of my life.

After filing through the processing line, getting orders stamped, being fingerprinted, and answering at least 200 questions, we were put in a holding area. Everyone was eyeing the drill instructors (DI), wondering which one he would be assigned and trying to determine which one looked the meanest. About the time we started thinking that maybe DIs were human and could not be as bad and nasty as we had heard, someone nearby told a joke, and a small group around him laughed.

"You had better shut the fuck up, or I will tear out your tongue and stuff it up it your ass," a skinny DI with a booming voice shouted.

The silence was sudden.

Welcome to the United States Marine Corps, I thought.

That evening I learned what it was like to be on my hands and knees in my sport coat scrubbing the barracks floor. I also learned what it was like to stand at attention and look at the tonsils of a screaming DI and to do more push-ups than I could count while listening to him say things about how badly my mother had screwed up.

The next three months were the most challenging of my life. Marine OCS was designed to weed out candidates who could not meet the required physical and leadership standards. Many did not make the five-week cut and were sent to Parris Island, South Carolina, to start over at enlisted boot camp.

The three months of training included hikes through the Virginia hills with full packs, rifle, and helmet. The hikes ranged from two to twelve miles. Our first hike was going to be a "piece of cake." It was not! The two-mile "hill trail" damn near killed us all. The DIs did not think the nearly vertical hill, which seemed at least as high as Mount Everest, should slow us down from our near-double-time pace. Bodies were falling out of formation everywhere.

Those who endured the constant mental pressure from the DIs along with academics, leadership development, bivouac exercises, and torturous physical demands earned the brown bars of a second lieutenant. I was proud to be among them.

As newly commissioned aviation candidates, we were being sent to Pensacola, Florida, for flight training. Because of a backup at the training facility, we were forced to take thirty days of leave. During that time I joined my wife Linda and son Jay in North Dakota and enjoyed the Christmas holidays at home. The ground officers or 'grunts' stayed in Quantico to attend the six-month-long Officer Basic School.

Shortly after the new year, my family and I arrived in Pensacola in our loaded-down Buick convertible. We were all excited. Being a part of the Marines was going to be a new experience and a new way of life. We found housing, and I checked into the Marine Detachment at Pensacola Naval Air station.

"Lieutenant, welcome to Pensacola," the salty looking gunnery sergeant said, as I handed him my orders. He looked them over and stamped them with three different rubber stamps. "Report to Building 5240 tomorrow at 0800 hours for orientation and in-briefing."

"Sounds good to me, Gunny," I replied.

I showed up bright and early the next morning along with about thirty other new students. Most were graduates of my OCS class, and I teamed up with several friends.

Shortly thereafter, a lieutenant colonel walked into the room, introduced himself and welcomed us all to Pensacola. He spoke about our futures in the Marine Corps and the flight training program. He followed that with a clear warning about drug usage, assuring us of a quick end to an aviation career for those caught using.

Because of continuing backups in the training program, it would be several months before we could start flight training. In the interim, each of us was assigned a collateral duty. Finally, on April 1, 1968, I got a flight training slot and was told to report to ground school at Saufley Field north of Pensacola Naval Air Station (NAS). I was ready to get this show on the road.

After two weeks of ground school, the actual flight training began. We learned the basics of flying in a T-34 Mentor which was a fixed wing, military-converted Beech A-36. The aerobatic aircraft had tandem seating and a 235-horsepower engine. Following that, we entered the advanced phase of flight training in the T-28 Trojan, another tandem-seated fixed-wing aircraft. The Trojan, also fully aerobatic, had a 1450-horsepower radial engine. The advanced program consisted of advanced aerobatics, basic instruments, and formation flying. After formation, we were ready for carrier qualification.

Carrier qualification in the T-28 was, without a doubt, the highlight of flight training. Students scheduled for carrier qualification were put in groups of four. For two weeks, the four of us in my flight group drove sixty miles west of Pensacola to an outlying airstrip near the Mississippi border. The runway markings and wires on the airstrip simulated a carrier deck. Practice landings were made in a procedure called field carrier landing practice (FCLP). We practiced landings with the help of a landing signal officer (LSO). A experienced carrier pilot, the LSO would talk us through the landing from his position on the ground at the end of the runway. Each student was assigned to an instructor pilot (IP) who flew the first few flights with him until he learned the procedures.

After two weeks of making downwind approaches at exactly eighty-two knots—not eighty-one knots or eighty-three knots—my flight group and I were finally ready; we could make precision landings to a twenty- to thirty-foot area marked on the runway. I was selected as the flight leader.

With butterflies in my stomach, I taxied my flight to the active runway. We lined up in formation for take-off and received our clearance. I took off first. As soon as my wheels were in the air, my number two started his take-off run. Numbers three and four would follow suit. An IP followed as our chase aircraft to make sure things did not get out of control.

The flight joined up on me, and we headed out over the Gulf of Mexico looking for the carrier *Lexington*. The *Lexington* had an air direction finding (ADF) beacon, and I homed in on it. About twenty minutes and sixty miles later, there it was.

T-28 used by the navy as the primary fixed-wing trainer for students going into helicopters and multi-engine aircraft. This aircraft was being flown by Lt. Ed Egan and was headed for carrier qualification in the Gulf of Mexico. Picture provided by Ed Egan.

From two thousand feet, the carrier resembled a postage stamp. My heart was thumping! I established radio contact with the ship and was cleared to enter the traffic pattern for the break. As I brought the flight over the carrier deck at 800 feet, I did the traditional "kiss off" to my wingman and made a sixty-degree bank breaking off to the left and entered the downwind. Each of the other three planes would break off at three-second intervals. On the downwind leg, I pulled out the landing checklist—even though I had memorized it—to make damn sure I read and completed each item as required. I was not going to screw up and forget something. Landing checks complete, I opened the canopy. A second confirmation that the landing hook was down was completed abeam the stern of the carrier. I reduced power and started my descent as I turned to the base leg.

Midway through my base leg, I picked up the "ball" off to my left (the reflection of an aircraft appears as an orange ball on a huge mirror placed at the stern of the carrier). The ball moved up or down on the mirror indicating the aircraft's position in proximity to the proper glide slope. In addition to having the ball as a reference, I also had the LSO talking to me. He did not need to see the ball to ascertain if I was above or below glide slope; he was an expert. He was also the most important person in my life at the moment.

On final approach everything was looking good, but my heart was still thumping. The LSO was not barking at me. I went through my procedures mentally, *Airspeed, eighty-two knots. Ball centered. Hook down. Check list complete . . . Hook down. Two hundred feet to go.*

The stern of carrier was coming fast. One hundred more feet to the carrier. Six lights flashed green. I rotated the nose of the aircraft to its landing attitude and pulled off all power. Slam! The T-28 hit the carrier deck at eighty-two knots. The hook grabbed the number three wire, and the aircraft came to a stop in about thirty feet, reminding me why it was important to have our shoulder straps in the locked position.

I was so excited I almost took a whiz in my flight suit! Looking around I saw a member of the deck crew coming to the front of the aircraft. He directed me for immediate take-off. I had to get moving, right then! My wingman was turning on final approach.

I was surprised by the difficulty I encountered in getting the aircraft into position. It felt as if the plane was slipping and sliding on the *Lexington*'s oily wooden deck. Once lined up for take-off and given clearance, I held the brakes and powered up the engine to maximum before releasing them. The aircraft moved down the short runway. The water was coming closer. Afraid to look at the airspeed, I rotated the nose fifteen degrees above the horizon, and the T-28 flew off the deck as it had hundreds of times. To my relief, it did not sink after it left the deck.

Three of us completed our five qualifying landings and formed an orbit north of the carrier while the fourth pilot in our formation made two more landings after missing two hooks and having to go around. When he completed his five landings, he joined up. With congratulations from our flight instructor who had been watching closely from his high perch, we headed home. It was a proud moment for all of us.

After carrier qualifying, we proceeded to advanced instruments followed by introduction into *helicopters*! Most of us were disappointed we had to fly these noisy, goofy-looking machines. After all, we had had high hopes of flying jets.

After two months of helicopter transition, the Marine Corps felt we were coordinated enough to chew bubble gum and walk down the street at the same time and gave us our wings. On April 9, 1969, in a small reception room at Ellison Field, Florida, my wife Linda pinned the Naval Aviation wings of gold on my chest. I was one proud marine!

Author being presented his wings. Attending are his wife Linda and son Jay.

The day after graduation Linda, Jay, and I headed for the West Coast for UH-1E Huey transition at Camp Pendleton. I would be flying the Huey in Vietnam. Following qualification, my orders were to report to the 1ˢᵗ Marine Air Wing, Da Nang, Republic of Vietnam. The Western Pacific (WESPAC) orders were no surprise.

I was happy to have been assigned Hueys. Their mission was "slicks" and gunships. Unarmed "slicks" had utility missions supporting "grunts." The missions ranged from hauling VIPs, medivac, and delivering chow, to anything in between.

After transition, I took leave in order to move Linda and Jay to Crookston, Minnesota, where Linda would teach senior high school English.

On my twenty-fifth birthday, I kissed my family goodbye at Minot Air Force Base near Minot, North Dakota, and climbed aboard a C-141 transport which flew to Travis Air Force Base near San Francisco where I reported for transportation to Vietnam.

UH-1E configured as a gunship. Photo by Bill Daugherty.

II
<u>Vietnam</u>

AUGUST 31, 1969. "Gentlemen, the captain has turned on the seatbelt sign for our descent to Da Nang Air Base. Please fasten your seatbelts. Place your seats in the upright position and stow your trays."

The ensuing silence in the aircraft was almost deafening.

Oh, shit, I'm finally here, I thought, and I suspected every marine on board had the same thought. Two years of training, and this was it.

Shoreline east of Marble Mountain on the southeast edge of Da Nang. Photo by Charles Maddox.

As the shoreline came into view, the knot in my stomach got bigger, and I could taste bile in my throat. The concern evident on my face was reflected in nearly all of the faces of the marines nearby. The exception was Major Howard Henry. On his second tour, he seemed unconcerned.

I had crossed the Pacific sitting in the seat next to Major Henry. I liked him. He was fun to be with and had a story or joke about everything. Sitting with him had made the long flight enjoyable.

As we descended from altitude, the shoreline became distinct. The South China Sea was dark green. Waves splashed along the long sandy beach for miles. Inland from shore, the terrain was flat with rice paddies everywhere. Mountains covered with dark green jungle could be seen off to the west. I looked for signs of war but did not see any. I did not know what to expect. Most first-tour guys had heard stories of having to dive for cover after getting off the plane.

The pilot of the big stretch DC-8 made a tactical approach to the airfield, staying high until the last minute, then making a steeper descent than I had anticipated.

Despite its unusual nature, the landing was uneventful. I watched with amazement as we taxied to the reception area. The field was alive with activity as marine and air force fighters landed and departed one after another.

Our aircraft taxied to an area where several commercial airliners had parked. As it stopped, I looked out the window and saw soldiers with large duffel bags standing in a containment area looking as if they were headed back to the "world" (the U.S.A.). I cannot say I was envious, because I was about to start an adventure! I was both scared and excited, but looking forward to it; I knew the twelve months ahead would be the best and the worst of my life.

As we disembarked the aircraft, the hot, stifling Asian air blasted my face. Sweat began to form before I reached the bottom of the DC-8's departure stairs. We headed to the reception area. Departing troops were packed up and in line. They were happy campers, and more than once we heard them hoot, "You'll be sor-rrrry."

We rode shuttle busses to the central processing center where all on board would be assigned to a unit. Standing on the wooden deck outside the processing center, I could not help but notice the helicopter traffic flying by: just about all of them were CH-46 Sea Knights. The Plexiglas had been taken out of the passenger windows, and the aircraft frames were tube-like with dual-rotor heads. They looked like flying coffins.

As I stood looking, a sudden explosion about 400 meters to my left sent up a mushroom of white smoke. A marine sleeping of the floor of the deck jumped about two feet in the air, coming down with his M-16 in the ready position. For some reason, I did not fear any danger. I could see that a small building had just blown up. The cause was a mystery to me. I stood there like an idiot just watching. After observing a considerable amount of commotion without any gunfire, I proceeded to the in-processing center. Once inside, I spotted a sign hanging above a counter that read 1st MAW (First Marine Air Wing) check-in.

Anxious to find out where I was going and to which squadron I would be assigned, I dragged my heavy duffel bag and stood in line for what seemed like forever. Knowing I would be assigned to a UH-1E Huey squadron, I was hoping for HML-367 out of Phu Bai or VMO-6 at Quang Tri. The other Huey squadron, HML-167, was at Marble Mountain, and I had heard it was primarily slicks. The other two squadrons had gun ships. There was no doubt in my mind that I wanted guns. I did not have a big urge to go out and kill anyone; my motive was personal: I wanted the ability to shoot back.

"Lieutenant, I'm going to assign you to HML-367 at Phu Bai," said the major behind the counter. His voice sounded as if he was making his 8,000th assignment of the day. I was just another number to him, but my assignment was just what I had hoped. I had heard nothing but good things about HML-367, which was located about sixty kilometers north of Da Nang.

Major Henry was assigned to VMO-2, as he knew he would be; it was the Marine's one and only Cobra squadron. We shook hands and wished each other luck. He headed for Marble Mountain a few miles away. I would stay at the Da Nang air base for the evening.

The night was restless, the air hot, humid, and fetid because of the lack of sanitary facilities. I was convinced the base was going to be under attack any minute. My only weapon was the K-Bar (large knife) I had tucked under my pillow.

After a long night, I climbed out from under the sheets and greeted my first morning in Vietnam before hitching a ride to Marble Mountain, the Marine helicopter base. I searched for a helicopter going to Phu Bai. After checking with three or four squadrons, I found a CH-53 Sea Stallion from HMH-361 going north. I grabbed my gear and climbed on board. The flight took me northeast of Da Nang, past Monkey Mountain and over the Hai Van Pass, a narrow mountain range that met the sea north of Da Nang. Once over the pass, the topography changed. Rice paddies dotted the flat terrain and small fishing boats filled the bays. Thirty

Phu Bai Air Field. Picture by John Rhodes.

minutes into our flight, we made our descent into Phu Bai. We could see a desolate looking military installation. The runway was surrounded by tin Quonset huts and wooden shacks. There was no green, just brown and silver. The provincial capitol, Hue City, could be seen about five kilometers to the north. After landing, the huge helicopter taxied down the ramp and came to a stop.

"Here you are, lieutenant," the crew chief shouted over the noise of the helicopter, "Your squadron is over there." He pointed to a tin shack housing UH-1E Hueys at the end of a row of revetments.

Thanking the crew chief, I climbed out of the noisy green monster. I had no idea that the crew chief I was thanking had only a few hours to live. The CH-53 did not return to Marble Mountain. It departed for Quang Tri after dropping me off. An hour later, it departed Quang Tri for Marble Mountain. The scattered wreckage was found three days later; four crew members and one passenger died that day.

At Phu Bai, I headed for the closest shack to get directions. Dropping my bags at the door as I entered, I walked over to a seasoned gunnery sergeant who stood behind the counter studying an aircraft log book. He did not even look up as I came in.

"Gunny, where's operations?"

Looking up, he paused, and, after giving me a look identifying me as a fucking new guy (FNG), he directed me to operations. I dragged my heavy bag over to the next building, dropped it outside the door and went in. The operations officer, a lieutenant, sat behind the desk with a flyswatter in his hand, counting off confirmed kills with each swat.

"Hi, you a new guy?" he asked, looking up.

"Yup. Bob Robinson," I said, reaching out to shake hands.

"Ed Watson. Glad to meet you. Welcome aboard. You go by Bob or what?"

Home sweet home at Phu Bai. Photo by Perry Unruh.

"Most call me Robby," I replied.

"Great, Robby it is. I'm the duty officer today. Let me find you a bunk and get you settled."

"Sounds good to me."

Watson took me to a tin Quonset. "Here's home," he said as we walked up. I was surprised to see an air conditioner sticking out of a window by the door. Next to the entry was a small pond with sand-bags around it. Several ducklings were having a great time splashing and swimming in the pond. Once inside, I found an empty cubicle.

Usually ten pilots were assigned to each Quonset. The sleeping area was divided into five cubicles on each side with lockers and blankets as dividers. A small walkway in the center led to the doors on each end. On the south end was a small kitchen area with a refrigerator, cabinets, and a poker table.

"Not bad," I said to myself. After all, I had been expecting a tent.

The afternoon began with an introduction and briefing from Major Adams, the S-1 (administrative officer). Normally the executive officer or the operations officer would in-brief new pilots, but they must have been flying.

"Lieutenant, you have just joined the finest helicopter squadron in the Marine Corps," the major said. "We do not strap into helicopters; we strap them to us." He went on to explain the squadron's mission. Supporting the grunts was our first priority, followed by covering transport helicopters with the "best damn gun cover in Vietnam." Along with guns, the two-fold mission provided VIP transportation with slicks.

I learned most of our work would be north along the "Z" (DMZ or demilitarized zone). I would probably fly left seat for the first three months. It would take about that long for me to get a feel for the mission, to learn the area of operation (AO) and how to keep my butt out of trouble.

1Lt John Upthegrove checking out the ducklings. Photo by Perry Unruh.

"I want you to take the next three days to acclimate. Get your maps together. You'll have some time to meet and get to know the rest of the squadron. We work hard and play hard. We expect a lot from our officers and enlisted men. Welcome aboard. You're going to like it here."

After he covered squadron policies and procedures, we went to the CO's office and met LtCol William "Bobby" Wilkinson. The colonel, like Adams, was proud of the squadron. He gave me the standard "pep talk."

Introductions to leadership completed, Watson introduced me to the pilots who happened to be in the ready room. After meeting them, I knew that what I had heard about this squadron being good was correct.

Several pilots I had known at Camp Pendleton were assigned to 367. Lt Roland "Scotty" Scott and Lt. John O'Meara, the best of buddies, had been with the squadron for about three weeks, and if these two were not in trouble, they soon would be. Lt Richard "Rich" Bennett was also there. A "baby face" lieutenant, he did not look over eighteen, yet he had done everything from auto racing to being an extra in a Frank Sinatra movie.

The "Sac," Lt Frank Sacharanski, showed up a few days after I did and checked in. Carrying a duffel bag and a flight bag, he wandered into my hootch. I was in the kitchen assembling maps. Looking up, I recognized him as an acquaintance in flight school.

"Hey, Sac, welcome aboard." I noticed he had a bandage on his forehead. "What happened to you?"

"You would not believe it, Robby. I could not catch a hop on a helicopter up here from Da Nang, so I hitched a ride on the back of a 'six-by.' The 3rd Marines had a convoy headed this way, so I said to myself, 'What the hell. It will give me a chance to see the countryside.'"

"Sure," I replied. "Now, what happened to your head?"

Somewhat reluctantly, he answered. "When we started going up a big pass—I think it was called the Hai Van Pass—a bunch of kids on the side of the road were watching the convoy. One of the little bastards had a sling shot and shot a dart that hit me in the head. I hope it was not poisonous."

It took me a couple minutes to pick myself up off the floor and regain my composure.

"I suppose you're going to be put in for a Purple Heart for that one."

Walking off, looking for an empty bunk, he grumbled, "A guy could get killed around here."

In the days following, Lieutenants Mark Byrd and John Hartline also checked into the squadron. It seemed like old home week as they were friends from Camp Pendleton.

A few days later, it was time for my first combat mission. I was assigned copilot with 1Lt John Upthegrove, a tall broad-shouldered marine with a quiet disposition. He been in country about six or seven months and knew his way around I Corps well.

The briefing in the ready room was at o-dark-thirty (dark and early). Upthegrove briefed the flight. We were going north to Quang Tri to pick up Colonel Hershey, a brigade commander. Our mission was to fly him and his staff to his field units. The mission would take most of the day. A single slick mission, we would not have gun cover.

I was directed to conduct the preflight inspection. Upthegrove still needed to do the paperwork and check out the aircraft logbook.

By the time I rounded up my gear, maps, and weapons and got to the aircraft, the crew chief was already there. He had put his M-60 machine gun under the back seat. The rotor blades were untied and turned, ready for start. I did a thorough preflight inspection with a flashlight. By the time I finished, Upthegrove was strapping into his seat. I hustled around the aircraft to the left seat and jumped in. The crew chief was standing to the right front of the aircraft with a fire extinguisher. He was waiting for the start signal from Upthegrove.

We completed the before-start checklist. Upthegrove raised his right hand and made a circle with his index finger indicating he was ready to hit the start switch. The start was uneventful. The crew chief strapped in. All check lists completed, we received our clearance from Phu Bai tower to taxi to the runway for takeoff.

I tried to get my bearings as we taxied to the runway. Both UHF (ultra high frequency) and VHF (very high frequency) radios were busy. While working my maps and frequencies, I followed everything that was happening. My situational awareness was maxed-out.

Approaching the runway, we received clearance for takeoff. Upthegrove looked as if he did not have a care in the world.

The sun was rising as we headed north. We soon saw Hue City, the provincial capitol and a site of fierce fighting during the '68 Tet Offensive. Upthegrove pointed out the Citadel, which had been a point of heavy combat during the offensive. Crossing the Perfume River, which was black in color, I observed half of the population of the city out taking their morning dump. I could see how the river got its name. We continued over the city and picked up Highway 1.

Once we passed Hue City, our Huey never got above 100 feet. Upthegrove explained that the standard practice on flight altitude in areas of small arms fire was low and fast, below 100 feet and at least ninety to 100 knots. We were advised never to give the enemy a chance or the time to take aim. The other option would be to fly above small arms fire at 1500 feet above ground level (AGL) or higher. All aircraft needed to receive clearance through controlled fire areas where artillery fire could create a danger or fast movers might be working out. We used rivers (blue line) and roads (brown line) for navigation and clearances.

Clearing Hue City, Upthegrove called for clearance. "Red Devil, arty. Scarface Five Eight, requesting clearance low level, brown line Hue to Dong Ha."

The Citadel in Hue City. Photo by John Rhodes.

"Roger, Scarface, cleared as requested. Red Devil out."

We flew along Highway 1 as low as we safely could. More than once, we scared the hell out of some poor peasant in a rice field or riding a bike up the highway. Our policy was to stay to the right of the highway. This prevented running into some other crazy S.O.B. doing the same thing in the other direction. Even the army followed the rule.

After landing at Quang Tri, we refueled and then flew to Dong Ha where we picked up our passengers (PAX). Hershey briefed Upthegrove. We taxied to the runway and received takeoff clearance from the control tower. Our first stop would be LZ (landing zone) Fuller, commonly known as Dong Ha Mountain.

As we headed west, I searched my map and found the firebase. It was on top of Hill 544, coordinates YD 014594, about twenty-four kilometers west of Dong Ha. Shortly after takeoff, I could see the mountain.

Upthegrove called the unit on our medium frequency radio (FM) and received an LZ briefing. The brief included information on winds, obstructions in or near the landing zone, and enemy information such as the last time they took fire and its direction. He added that if we were to take fire, it would probably be from the west.

I copied the information I felt was important. Upthegrove called for smoke.

Looking ahead, I saw green smoke rising from the top of the mountain. Upthegrove verified the color and wind direction. Verification of the color was very important. More than once, the VC (Viet Cong) had also popped a smoke to lure an unsuspecting helicopter into a trap. As I had not known what to expect, I was relieved when I heard they had not received any fire for several weeks. For all I knew, we would take fire everywhere.

The LZ was smack-dab on the top of the mountain. Upthegrove set up his approach to the pinnacle which was at an altitude at least three times higher than I had ever gone into. The sides of the mountain were almost vertical. The winds bounced the aircraft moderately as we got closer. As Upthegrove slowed the aircraft for landing, concern raced through my mind. *What would we do if we*

Popping smoke. Dong Ha Mountain. The Rockpile. Photo by Bill Daugherty.

Ch-46 departing Dong Ha Mountain.
The Rockpile is seen below. Photo by Bill Daugherty.

suddenly had an engine failure or lost rotor RPM because of altitude and temperature, I wondered, while looking for an escape route. I knew the best approach had an "out" in the event of an emergency, but the only "out" here was to make a sharp turn and avoid the side of the mountain.

Despite my anxiety, Upthegrove made an excellent approach. We landed without incident on the LZ, a pad only large enough for one helicopter.

Hershey departed after telling us he would be back in about thirty minutes. We shut down the aircraft. Just feet away, a 155 mm artillery was firing a support mission. An OV-10 was marking the hits and adjusting.

The Rockpile, a significant landmark and radio relay point for reconnaissance (recon) teams, was across the valley to the southwest. True to its name, the 230-meter-high formation looked like a pile of rocks. Upthegrove was quick to point out a very small landing pad. Landing on it was no piece of cake.

The Rockpile. Photo by Bob Houston.

Thirty minutes later we were headed north toward the DMZ. The marines had several firebases to the north. All were located on the highest mountain or hill in the area. Hershey wanted to look at a recently abandoned firebase located in the "boonies" north of the Rockpile. The 3rd Marines had flattened everything to the ground before they left the area. Only a few pieces of wood and some garbage remained. Approximately twenty-five little people wearing round peasant hats and black pajamas were rummaging through the debris. They were not carrying any weapons. I wondered how they had gotten there. I thought I had just seen my first Viet Cong. They waved and flashed big smiles as we passed by. Their smiles were not convincing. "Who else but VC would be out here in the middle of nowhere?" I asked myself.

Leaving the area, we headed south to Vandegrift Combat Base (VCB) and landed on one of the two landing zones located next to a grunt headquarters. While waiting for the "heavies" to do their work, I could not help but notice the surrounding terrain. It was beautiful. East of the valley lay mountains covered with lush green vegetation and heavy jungle. The air was calm and quiet. No heli-

Landing pad with "free parking" on top of the Rockpile. Photo by John Rhodes.

copters were flying. Everything seemed peaceful and quiet. I wondered what this place would be like without a war going on.

Hershey and his staff finished their business at VCB. After a few more unit visits at other locations, we dropped them off at Quang Tri before heading home down Highway 1 to Phu Bai.

This was the first time I had flown in nearly six weeks. I had just flown eight of the eighty-five hours of flight I was to get during my first month in country. I was bushed.

III

<u>SDO</u>

LIEUTENANTS IN THE SQUADRON had the opportunity to serve as a squadron duty officer (SDO). The SDO was the squadron point of contact in the event something out of the ordinary should happen after hours. Every night, the SDO reported in at 1700 hours.

My first night as SDO started out quietly. My duty NCO challenged me to a game of ping-pong. Having been a good player in my younger years, I accepted his challenge. The first game was a wipe-out. He seemed to be enjoying every minute of it. He absolutely waxed my ass. I took the defeat in stride and foolishly agreed to another game. Midway through the game, I was again being beaten to a pulp when we heard gunshots on the flight line.

"Oh, oh!" I said as I ran to my locker and grabbed my "burp gun," slapped in an ammo clip, chambered a shell and headed out to investigate. Not knowing what was happening, my NCO and I worked our way through the aircraft revetments to the end of our flight line where two guards were posted in a bunker. Listening and not hearing any more firing, I called out to the guards.

"This is the SDO. What's going on?"

"Sir, they have the situation under control down the flight line, the next bunker over," one of the guards responded.

Wanting to find out what was going on, we headed toward the next bunker. It was dark. As I got closer, I could see the silhouettes of several people. Again, I called out.

29

"Guard, this is the duty officer. What's going on?" I was a bit hesitant about going any farther. I did not want to be mistaken for a "gooner."

Seeing me, they shouted back.

"Sir, we have three prisoners over here."

"I'm coming over," I replied.

Walking to their position, I could see the prisoners standing next to the two marine guards. As I came up to them, I could see they were also marines. "Okay, what the hell is going on here?" I asked, approaching the prisoners.

"Sir," a guard replied, "these guys were sneaking back from the army side. I think they went to the massage parlor over there. They are juiced up, but are not giving us any trouble."

As guard finished, the SDO and the sergeant major from the squadron next to us came over. They took a look at the captured commandos.

"Lieutenant, these marines are mine," the sergeant major said with a chuckle. "I'll take it from here. It looks as if these guys do not have enough to do."

Walking back to the ready room, I chuckled thinking about what the "Top" would conjure up to teach the three the wisdom of their exploits.

As the SDO, I also had the duty of waking up flight crews. While making my rounds at 0500, I came to Major Hornsby's hootch. A large man, Hornsby was our aviation maintenance officer. He probably ended up in helicopters because he could not fit in the cockpit of an A-4. With an explosive temper, he was not known for his pleasantness. His hootch, a wooden shack, had an entrance all its own. When I tried to enter, I was stopped at the stoop; the door was stuck. I gave it a good Marine Corps yank and whatever was holding it was pulled right out of the wood.

The noise awakened him. Knowing he was awake, I called out, "It's 0500, sir." My job was done, and I decided to get the hell out of the area. As I was leaving, I heard words that made me believe I had made a wise decision. Fortunately for me, he never said another word about it.

IV

<u>Medivac</u>

IN MID-SEPTEMBER, VMO-6 was notified it would be redeployed to Okinawa. The squadron stood down on October 2nd, and departed for Okinawa on October 20th. Our squadron assumed responsibility for VMO-6's missions after their stand-down. We often stayed at Quang Tri for medivac standby, and we were also available for other gun missions as needed. Our twelve-hour shifts ran from 0700 to 1900 and 1900 to 0700 the next morning.

Early in October, I was assigned Quang Tri medivac with Upthegrove as the flight lead and Captain C.T. Brown on our wing. We got the night shift. Our quarters were Quonset huts with six bunks and a small table on which a radio was placed. Other than that, they were bare. Playing cards was our favorite entertainment, and many hours were spent playing gin rummy for a penny a point and ten cents a set. One night, I was about ready to lay down my cards when the radio came alive.

"Medivac, stand-by. Medivac, stand-by. We have an emergency medivac!" Dropping our cards, we scrambled to our feet, grabbing our gear as we gathered around the radio.

We received the situation. A marine unit west of Dong Ha was taking fire and had wounded. Several required emergency medivac.

After copying the coordinates, call signs, and other pertinent information, we hustled to the flight line. The aircraft preflight and run-ups had been completed before we went to the standby hootch. The aircraft were ready to go. Within minutes, our Hueys and the two CH-46s started their engines.

Upthegrove got clearance from Quang Tri tower, and we taxied to the runway. Our flight was cleared for takeoff. We were the first off with the CH-46s right behind us. The flight of four aircraft headed west toward the lights of Dong Ha. The ceiling was low, and it was dark. The situation was tense!

A marine unit was in a firefight about twenty kilometers west of Quang Tri, just south of Highway 9 and a couple of klicks (kilometers) east of the Rockpile. Four of the wounded marines were classified as "emergency medivac," and two others had been classified "priority medivac".

Direct Air Support Center (DASC) had initially reported the unit was receiving small arms and mortar fire from the east of their position. They were getting fire support from two tanks located north of their position on Highway 9.

The weather was not looking good as we passed Dong Ha. Flying at the base of a ragged, broken ceiling, our radar altimeters showed 600 feet AGL. We could see stars through breaks in the clouds. Below the clouds, the visibility was relatively good, and lights occasionally provided a reference to the ground and surrounding area. We followed Highway 9 west and saw flares dropping and tracers from the action ahead.

Upthegrove called on the Fox Mike (FM). "Charlie Mike, Charlie Mike. This is Scarface Five Eight. Over."

The reply was immediate. "Scarface Five Eight, this is Charlie Mike. Go ahead."

"Roger, Mike, this is Scarface Five Eight inbound with a flight of two guns and two 46s. What is your situation? Give me a briefing. Over."

Charlie Mike called back with his brief. The unit's situation was bad. They had a probe on their perimeter and had been taking small arms fire. They had had sappers in their concertina wire. They had six wounded: four emergency medivacs and two priority medivacs. A flare ship, call-sign "Basketball," was on station. The unit was located on a north-south ridge with the enemy fire concentrated on the east side. He felt the medivac aircraft should try to land west of the ridge, keeping him clear of enemy fire once on the ground. Because the LZ was on a relatively steep slope, there was concern the medivac would not be able to land. The wind was calm. Any fire would come from the east.

Upthegrove acknowledged the brief.

"Are there any friendlies outside your compound? Over."

"Negative, Scarface," Charlie Mike replied.

"Roger. We'll be at your poz in about ten minutes. Over."

Charlie Mike closed off, sounding calm despite the situation.

Looking ahead to the west, we could see Basketball on station. He was still dropping flares. My adrenalin was building. This was my first night-time "shoot 'em up."

About five kilometers out of Charlie Mike's position, Upthegrove called the lead CH-46 and told him to hold his flight to the east until we took a look at the situation.

"Wilco," he replied.

We were kept busy dodging descending flares and ragged clouds as we proceeded inbound.

Upthegrove had Charlie Mike talk us over his position. The flares lit the area enough for us to see the terrain and the ground. Though there was light, there was no color. It looked as if we were looking at a film negative. Once overhead, we had Charlie Mike turn on a strobe light to confirm his position. The unit was still taking fire from the east.

Making sure the lead Sea Knight had the brief, Upthegrove called, "Chatterbox, this is Scarface Five Eight. Did you copy the brief?"

"That's affirmative, Scarface," he replied. "I'm going to go with his suggestion of the west LZ. I'm inbound. Have him turn on his strobe in the LZ now and pop smoke on my call."

"Roger, Chatterbox. I'm going to work over the east of their position starting now."

Chatterbox Lead started inbound from his orbit area. Upthegrove rolled in firing rockets parallel to and below the ridgeline providing a margin of safety for the friendlies. The first set of rockets departed the rocket pods and headed toward the gully. The flash made as they left the pods surprised me. Because I had closed one eye in anticipation of the rockets firing, I did not lose my night vision.

Upthegrove's armament selector was set on "two." Each time he punched the button on his cyclic, one rocket from each side fired. Four rockets exploded just outside the wire before he switched to his four fixed machine guns. I worked the two in the turret from my TAT-101. Each gunner put his M-60 fire right in the wire. Green tracers were coming our direction as we pulled out of our first run. The VC fire was answered by a flow of red from our wingman. Upthegrove pulled up the nose of the gunship, and we climbed to what I thought to be five or six hundred feet. He executed a sharp pedal-turn to the right, bringing the nose of the helicopter back into another gun run just as our wingman was at the bottom of his gun run. Brown was taking fire as he pulled out.

Rolling in, we concentrated our fire using eight M-60s to blanket the area in the draw from where the enemy fire was coming. Climbing out of the second run, Charlie Mike called that we were taking fire. Looking back, I could not see any tracers. Brown was now in another gun run. He called saying he had the tracers and was concentrating his fire on their position.

Upthegrove called for smoke and a strobe on Chatterbox's request as he arrived overhead. With help from Charlie Mike's strobe light, the smoke was spotted, and the CH-46 pilot started his approach. He made a circling descent to the west of the unit's position. Our two gunships maintained a barrage of fire down the ravine during his approach.

Chatterbox elected not to use his landing light until he was almost on the ground.

As he slowed down and got lower, he called, "This is not much of a zone; real steep. I'm going to give it a try. Looks like I'm only going to be able to put my left rear wheel down. Have them load through my side door. Watch out for the blades."

He came to a hover and tried setting the left wheel on the slope. The situation turned bad. "Oh, shit! I just had a blade strike. I'm out of here."

One of the rotor blades had made contact with something on the ground or with a tree branch immediately throwing rotor system out of balance and causing severe vibrations.

Despite the impact, Chatterbox Lead reached altitude. Leveling off, he called Upthegrove.

"Scarface Five Eight, this is Lead. My aircraft appears to be in good enough shape to make it back to Quang Tri. Chatterbox Two, you've got it. See you later."

We were down to one medivac aircraft. It looked like the only choice we had was to have him go in on the east side of the ridge.

Just when Upthegrove was ready to have Dash Two go in, a new voice came over the FM. "Charlie Mike, this is Puff. Can I be of any service to you?"

Upthegrove and I looked at each other. "Where in the hell did he come from?" we both wondered. "Puff" was the call sign for "Puff the Magic Dragon," an air force C-47 gunship loaded with mini-guns and fifty caliber machine guns.

"I wonder who called him," Upthegrove said. Returning Puff's call, he gladly accepted his offer to help and briefed him on the situation.

Just then, Basketball called, "Scarface, this is Basketball. I'm going to have to leave. I'm bingo fuel."

"Roger, Basketball. Thanks for your help."

Upthegrove was not concerned. Puff had flares on board and would help out if needed. Wanting to give Puff a good mark of the

VC position, Upthegrove called, "Puff, I'll lay down two Willy Petes. I want you to put your fire right between them. Over."

"No problem. Just make sure you move out of the way."

"I'm going to move the medivac aircraft to the west before we mark the target," Upthegrove answered. "Chatterbox Two, move west of the zone, and we can get this show going."

"Roger," Chatterbox responded.

After he moved, Upthegrove rolled in firing two Willy Petes, one on each side of the ravine.

"Puff, do you have the smoke?"

"That's affirm, Scarface."

"Good, put your fire right between them," Upthegrove responded.

As we moved out of the way, we looked back toward the ravine and saw a solid stream of tracers coming out of the sky. None of us had ever seen anything like it. All of Puff's fire was right on target between the smokes.

After Puff started working out, Upthegrove had Chatterbox Two start his approach to the zone. Again, the only reference was the strobe light. This time the descent was to the east of the ridge. Chatterbox was careful not to get into Puff's line of fire. The new LZ was on a slope. Flares were still lit, and we could see the CH-46 making his tight right-hand spiral descent without position lights or the landing light. Reaching fifty feet AGL, he turned on his landing light. Once in a hover, he decided to touch down on his nose wheel only and load through the side door. He made a skillful landing. The wounded were loaded. Puff had taken care of the situation: The '46 had not taken fire, and the situation was under control; the display of firepower was awesome.

Puff pulled off station and was orbiting when our wingman called, "Five Eight, it's over. Let's go home," he said. He seemed to have forgotten who was the flight leader.

Upthegrove, asserting his leadership role, paused for a few seconds before calmly answering, "I think we need to stick around for a little while. If things start getting hot we will just end up coming back."

Brown did not respond.

Puff departed for another mission, and the flares burned out. We continued to orbit the area for about fifteen minutes with no further incidents. Finally, with our fuel and ammo low, we decided to call it an evening.

As we departed, Upthegrove called Charlie Mike, "We're out of here. Call if you need us again."

"Thanks, Scarface. Charlie Mike out."

Our flight headed back to Quang Tri. We were not called again that evening.

The next morning, while on another mission, we passed Charlie Mike's position. My curiosity got the best of me. I gave them a call.

"Charlie Mike, Scarface Five Eight here. How are things going this morning? Did we get any confirmed last night?"

"Yeah, Scarface. You guys sure raised hell with Charlie. We got nine confirmed in the wire plus a lot of blood trails. Thanks again for your help, Scarface."

Continuing our flight, we turned south by the Rockpile and headed toward VCB. Flying copilot for Lt Perry Unruh, Lt Mike Williams was on the radio calling Vandegrift tower for landing clearance. They were in a Huey about a kilometer ahead of us. As I was getting ready to make our call for landing clearance, we heard Vandegrift tower reply and give Unruh clearance to land on the north pad. Not seeing his Huey, tower called, "I do not have you in sight . . . are you low level?"

"That's a negative, tower . . . I'm fifty feet," replied Williams. A Naval Academy graduate, he was the squadron comedian. He had elected to join the Marine Corps rather than to go navy. It's probably just as well he did, because at five foot nine with a stocky build, he bore a striking resemblance to the Marine Corps bulldog. He had grown up in Baltimore and could keep the whole squadron howling for hours listening to stories of things that happened at the butcher shop where he worked before going to the Academy.

We were standby guns for the rest of the day, and we had no significant events. Our only activity was to expend our ordinance at a suspected enemy position north of Quang Tri near the DMZ. We still had a couple of rockets left after finishing.

"As long as we are by the Z, let me show you something," Upthegrove said, as he turned the gunship east toward the ocean. When we reached the coastline, he turned north into the DMZ.

"Do you see that compound up ahead?"

I looked ahead a couple of kilometers and saw what looked like a small fort with a huge North Vietnamese flag flying high above the center of the compound.

"Yup, I got it."

"Good. Do you think we can get that flag?" Upthegrove asked mischievously.

"We are not going to go up there are we?" I replied with nervous apprehension. "That's North Vietnam!"

"Naw," Upthegrove replied. "We're just going to give them a little something to think about this afternoon." He lowered the nose of the gunship and started a dive. When the airspeed increased to about 100 knots, he brought the nose of the aircraft above the horizon and fired our remaining rockets toward the compound. The rockets arced up over the DMZ and came down on the other side of the compound.

"Damn! One of these days, I'm going to get that flag," he said turning the Huey back toward Quang Tri.

We landed at Quang Tri and headed for the refueling pits.

"After we refuel, we're going to go to the army re-arming point to get some flechettes," Upthegrove informed me.

The marine supply system was very good. We could get just about anything we needed in flight gear and ammo, but some rockets were not available. Because we got only the basic 2.76 rocket, we were forced to improvise. Whenever we got near an army re-arming point, we would re-arm there. They had flechettes, a rocket that was not available at our rearming points. Flechettes were filled with several thousand 2-3 inch darts. Fired at the right altitude and angle, a flechette would put a dart in almost every square foot of an area the size of a football field. They were great for prepping a landing zone prior to insertion of troops or for use against personnel, and, if the zone was booby-trapped, the chances of detonating the trap with flechettes were good. Against personnel, a single dart was deadly.

On the way back to home plate from Quang Tri that day, we flew over several bodies of water inhabited by waterfowl.

"Are you hungry for duck?" Upthegrove asked. "Let's see if we can get one for Thanksgiving."

"Sounds good to me." I replied. Duck for Thanksgiving would be a nice treat as the food at Phu Bai was close to being only good enough to gag on. We decided to try duck hunting with flechette rockets.

Spotting a flock on a body of water below us, Upthegrove rolled in. Each time we rolled in, the flock took flight just about the time we shot off a rocket. We were able to see the pattern of the flechettes as they hit the water and adjusted accordingly.

After five or six rockets were expended, we finally had one duck down and made an approach to where our future dinner lay, but one problem remained. How could we get it out of the water? We solved that problem with the aid of our crew chief.

Upthegrove made an approach to a hover over the water. With his gunner's belt attaching him to the helicopter, the crew chief was suspended below it. Skillfully, he scooped up our feathered treasure, and we were on our way laughing and joking about our future meal.

I must admit this was one expensive duck. I do not know what a flechette cost, but this duck had cost the United States Government at least five rockets.

Thanksgiving snack. From left to right: 1st Lts. John O'Meara, Robert Barnes, Charles Paraguey, John Upthegrove, Cpl E.R. Haines, 1Lt Mike Williams, GySgt C.E. Hattis, 1Lt Steve Murray, and 1Lt Roland Scott. Four gunships, one confirmed . . . duck. Photo by Perry Unruh.

V
Ringneck Down

A COUPLE OF DAYS LATER, northwest of Dong Ha and near the southern border of the DMZ, an OV-10 piloted by Capt G.L. Medford of VMO-6 was working with a recon team. The team had enemy movement and reported sitings of several bunkers. Medford had several flights of fast movers (jets) on station and was working with Lovebug 556, a flight of F-4s dropping snake (speed-retarded bombs) and nape (napalm). After making three passes under heavy fire, their ordinance was depleted. Medford called in his second flight, Ringneck 558, which consisted of two A-6 Intruders. Major P.M. Busch was the pilot and flight leader. 1Lt R.W. Hargrave was his bombardier navigator.

Medford briefed the flight on the target and marked the bunker complex with a "Willy Pete." On his first pass, Busch unloaded ordinance while taking heavy fire. Shortly after his pull-out, the aircraft took severe hits and the two crewmembers ejected. Within seconds, the A-6 exploded into a ball of flame.

Medford and his AO spotted both chutes as they deployed. Watching their descent, Medford issued a Mayday call requesting a helicopter to retrieve the downed crew. The crewmembers appeared to have landed approximately 400 meters apart with a ravine between them.

After making a low pass over the downed crew, it was obvious they had been injured during the ejection and by the rough terrain in their area of impact. There was also a possibility they had been wounded by enemy fire.

VMO-6 OV-10 Bronco. Photo by Ashley Shoop.

1Lt John Rhodes was the flight leader of two slicks assigned to the regimental headquarters in Quang Tri for the day. Lt Mike Williams was Rhodes's copilot and his crew chief was Cpl Dan Hessen. Rhodes was inbound to Quang Tri reporting to DASC when he heard the Mayday call. Wanting to help, Rhodes told his wingman he would respond to the call and instructed him to continue with their original mission.

Answering the Mayday on guard frequency, Rhodes identified himself as a single Huey slick and informed Medford he would respond to the request. He then contacted Dong Ha DASC and requested the coordinates.

DASC gave Rhodes a heading in the general direction as well as coordinates: AT943635, northwest of Dong Ha near the DMZ.

As Rhodes approached the site, he saw smoke rising from the burning A-6. After making radio and visual contact with Medford, Rhodes and his crew were directed to the general area of the downed crewmen.

Following a low-level search the parachutes and one crewman were spotted about two kilometers from the aircraft. The chutes stood out in sharp contrast to the terrain. Medford gave Rhodes a situation brief and departed the area to refuel and re-arm. Rhodes made several low passes over the immediate area searching for a place to land.

While searching, Williams and Hessen discussed the situation. Agreeing that someone needed to get on the ground, they volunteered to get out.

Unable to find a suitable LZ, Rhodes decided to do whatever was necessary to get the injured personnel out. They needed to be taken out immediately. Their Huey had taken heavy small arms fire during their low-level search for an LZ, and he knew the NVA below would be after the downed aircrew.

Rhodes set up an approach to Hargrave, the downed bombardier navigator. The hillside below them was covered with small trees and vines. It looked precarious, but it was worth a try. Rhodes told Williams and Hessen he was going to get as low as he could and both of them could jump out and get to the downed aviator. Rhodes's plan was to hover down the ravine to an area with a clearing he thought would be good enough for landing and wait there for the crew to bring the airman down. They would have get the other man afterwards.

As the Huey neared the ground it became apparent the area was not going to work. There was no way Rhodes could touch down. Hovering above the foliage would put the Huey too high for Williams and Hessen to jump. Looking it over, he decided to take a chance at getting lower. He hoped the aircraft would not sustain too much damage from a blade strike while cutting its way down.

Rhodes continued his descent. The rotor blades began striking the trees and brush as the Huey descended to a point just barely low enough for the crew to jump. The brush was small and damage to the aircraft was not severe.

After the crew hit the ground, Rhodes hovered down the ravine toward the area in which he thought he could land. Unable to land,

Rhodes slowly flew the Huey toward Major Busch, the downed pilot. Focusing the search near Busch's chute, Rhodes spotted him lying on the ground. While circling the area searching for a spot to set down, Rhodes spotted movement of a small ground force of NVA about one klick away. They were heading toward the crash site.

Looking back at Busch it was obvious he was unable to walk. Rhodes changed his plan and hovered over to him.

The foliage was about the same as it was on the other side, possibly a bit thinner. The hillside had a moderate slope. The injured pilot was down but conscious. Finding an area not too thick with brush near him, Rhodes came to a hover. He started his descent though the trees and brush. Both the main rotor and the tail rotor were sustaining damage. The Huey shuddered as the rotor blades struck the small branches. The aircraft was developing a severe 1:1 vertical beat—the helicopter bounced each time the rotor made a rotation. To complicate matters, the tail rotor damage from hitting the foliage was causing rotor pedal vibrations. Rhodes was in danger of losing his tail rotor and all directional control. Reaching the ground, he set the helicopter down on the slope. It was a precarious landing.

Major Busch began crawling to the aircraft, but Rhodes could not get out to help him. He needed his hands and feet on the controls to hold the Huey on the slope.

Busch reached the aircraft, but because of leg injuries, he could not pull himself into the cabin. Looking back, Rhodes could see him struggling. His body was only halfway in the cabin. He needed help. With both of his hands and feet busy holding the shaking, shuddering helicopter, Rhodes put his left knee against the collective to hold it in place, freeing his left arm. Reaching back, he grabbed the pilot's harness and yanked in an effort to get his waist above the floor. Unable to get enough leverage, he failed in the first few attempts. After a few more yanks, Rhodes and Busch got their coordination together and Busch made it to the floor of the cabin. Finally aboard, he crawled to the center of the cabin and wrapped his arms around the jump seat as Rhodes took off.

Radioing his crew on the other side of the canyon, Rhodes informed them he was going straight to Charlie Med at Quang Tri. He told them he would be right back and would try to get a CH-46 to pick up the other crewman.

Unaware that his crew had not heard his transmission, Rhodes departed the area. Not knowing where Rhodes was going, Williams and Hessen assumed he would come back and started carrying Hargrave up the steep incline hoping to find a better area for loading him into the Huey.

A Ch-46 showed up overhead as they ascended the hill. Knowing it would have a hoist, they stopped where they were. They were exhausted from the climb and were not sure they could have carried Hargrave any farther.

Shaking and shuddering, the wounded Huey made it to Charlie Med. Rhodes dropped off his passenger and headed back to retrieve his crew and the other wounded marine. Enroute to the area he could see the Ch-46, call sign "Cattle Call Six," hovering over the rescue site. He had lowered a litter basket and was hoisting Hargrave aboard. The skipper and his wingman were orbiting the rescue scene providing gun cover.

After the Medivac bird departed, Williams and Hessen, still on the ground, started worrying about the NVA. They figured they would be trying to get them, and Hessen had an M-16 and Williams had a mud-filled stub-nosed .38.

Rhodes arrived shortly afterwards. Williams and Hessen were happy as hell to see him coming. With his crew still on the ground, contact was made. Rhodes told them to go about 100 meters up the hill to an area which appeared suitable for landing.

The slope was too steep for a landing. Carefully, Rhodes hovered above the slope, low enough for Williams and Hessen to do a pull-up on the skid and climb aboard. They flew the aircraft back to Quang Tri where it was inspected for damage. The skin had been knocked off the main rotor blades in several areas. The tail rotor blades were bent outward at the root and inward at the top to the extent that there was only $^{1}/_{2}$-inch clearance between the tip and tail boom at full deflection. The aircraft was left at Quang Tri and eventually trucked back to Phu Bai for repairs.

VI

<u>Arc Light</u>

ABOUT THREE WEEKS INTO COUNTRY, I was scheduled to fly a slick with 1Lt Steve Murray. Our mission was to fly to Quang Tri and pick up three generals. Two CH-46 chase birds were assigned in the event we were shot down or had to make an emergency landing. With three marine generals aboard, it would not look good to lose them.

We departed Phu Bai and arrived at Quang Tri with time to spare. After refueling, we moved to the VIP pad to pick up our PAX.

"Holy shit! Look at all those stars," Murray said as the three walked to the aircraft. A lieutenant general (three star) led the pack followed by a major general (two star) and a brigadier general (one star). We were definitely carrying some heavyweights. I wondered what was up.

"Lieutenant," the brigadier said, handing Murray a map. "We are going to observe an Arc Light at the coordinates marked in red. Do you think you can find it?" he asked arrogantly.

"Yes, sir," Murray replied. "I'm familiar with that area. It should not be a problem."

"Good. Then let's get going."

"This guy is a real prick. He must want that second star real bad," I said to myself.

We got our takeoff clearance from the control tower and departed Quang Tri westbound. Abeam the Rockpile, we hung a right to the north and found our area about six kilometers north, near the DMZ.

We set up an orbit with the two chase birds southwest of the designated target. Murray was in communication with them. He warned them not to wander off. All we needed was to have an aircraft wander into the strike zone. Our concern was that the B-52s hit their target. We were only a kilometer south of the impact zone and sure as hell did not need any miscalculation at 35,000 feet.

As Murray was warning the chase birds, the brigadier came over the Intercommunication Control System (ICS).

"We've got six stars back here, and I do not even see an M-16 in here," he barked. "What are we going to do if we get shot down?" Before Murray could answer, he shouted. "What's all the talking about up there? I want radio silence. Where in the hell did you learn radio procedures, Lieutenant?" On and on he went. This guy was not only a prick, he was a certifiable prick. I decided it was best to keep my mouth shut. Murray and I stole a glance at each other every once in a while. I could tell our thoughts were the same.

The sky was clear. Visibility was unlimited. After thirty minutes of orbiting, we could see the jet streams of the flight of B-52s coming from the east. They had launched out of Guam. As they got closer, I double checked our grid coordinates to make sure we were not too close or over the target area. All the while I tried to ignore the constant complaining of the one star in the back. I could not figure out why the two or three stars did not just rap him along side of his head and tell him to shut up.

The B-52s were over target on time. Their bombs hit the ground. It seemed like our helicopter shook from the impact. I had never seen anything like it. A whole grid square blew up. All we could see was dirt and dust in the air for about 100 feet up. I barely heard the one star in the back yelling for us to watch our flying and leave the arc light watching to them. What an asshole!

After the dust settled, I was amazed at the destruction. The entire area was pitted with bomb craters.

Devastation caused by B-52 Arc Light. Photo by M. McElwee.

The generals had us fly over the area and do a reconnaissance to look for any damage to enemy positions. After giving it a good "look-see" we headed back and dropped them off. The two star and three star both thanked us as the one star stomped off without saying a word. Later he filed a complaint to the Wing about radio procedures. It must not have gone far as no one ever heard any more about it.

VII

Scarface Down

IN THE AFTERNOON OF OCTOBER 10, John Rhodes, our crew chief Corporal Everett Sims, and I were sitting by our Huey on the tarmac on LZ Owl at Dong Hoa. We were trying to find a little shade from the brutal sun. Our mission was 101 VIP slick. We had just landed after transporting a brigadier general from LZ Owl to Vandergrift and picking up a lieutenant colonel; they wanted to go to a unit at grid XD984543. We completed the mission and returned the lieutenant colonel to VCB before returning to LZ Owl with the general. We were now standing by.

While we waited for him to finish his meeting, a CH-46 landed next to us. The crew chief jumped out and ran over to us.

"Did you guys hear one of your birds got shot down?" he asked, his voice full of anxiety. "We heard your Six come over guard. It sounds like his wingman just went in."

Rhodes jumped into our Huey and turned on the battery and radios. After a few minutes, he stepped out. "Grab your stuff! Ed Bauernfcind just got shot down."

"Did the crew get out?" I asked, interrupting.

"They have three of the crew out but still have one trapped in the aircraft and can't get him out without a torch. They do not know who it is."

"Is the guy on the ground alive?" I asked, interrupting again.

"I don't know," Rhodes answered. "They didn't say. A small grunt unit they were supporting is providing security. We need to go over to Quang Tri to pick up a torch and a Seabee and take him out to the site."

Rhodes, Sims, and I jumped in the Huey and started up. DASC passed on the coordinates. The crash site was at coordinates YD 064640 west northwest of Dong Ha. We flew to the Seabee compound about five to ten minutes away. There we found a Seabee waiting with an acetylene bottle and a torch. The Seabee, Sims, and the equipment took up most of the space in the back of the Huey. The equipment must have weighed 250 pounds. I think the Seabee did as well.

I could tell he was thinking, *I really do not want to do this.*

We departed and headed west out of Quang Tri. The area of the incident was northeast of the Rockpile, about a twenty-minute flight.

Approximately ten kilometers from the site, Rhodes called and made contact with the Skipper, the on-scene-commander, and informed him we were inbound with the equipment. He asked about the situation and requested a zone brief.

The Skipper reported that they had a reaction force on the ground and that there had been no further contact with Charlie, though they were definitely in the area. The downed aircraft was in an upright position in a gully. The grunts would not go near it because the engine was still running. It was at full throttle, and they thought it was going to blow up. One crewmember was in the aircraft. The LZ was going to be tight. It was on the side of a hill with a slope too steep for landing. Rhodes would have to hover on one skid to unload.

Rhodes informed the Skipper that he had a good copy on the information. We had him in sight and were ten minutes out.

We could see three gunships in orbit over the crash site. At least we would have plenty of gun cover if we took fire. As we approached the site and flew overhead, we could see the Huey

Downed Scarface Huey on lower right. Photo by John Upthegrove.

crunched in the bottom of a ravine. Apparently the tail rotor had been shot up just as they were in a pedal turn to return to target. Their airspeed must have been too low. It appeared they did not have full control of the aircraft before impact. At least they were upright, and we were not taking fire. At least, not yet.

Directly over the LZ, Rhodes did a power check to see how much power was available. He pulled power until the engine was putting out the maximum available torque for the altitude and temperature. Going into the zone, he would be watching the power closely.

The Echo-model Huey was extremely underpowered, and this type of situation could cause major problems. If we needed more power than we had, we would lose rotor RPM. Rhodes had to be prepared to abort the approach.

With the power check complete, Rhodes started our approach. The Skipper was not kidding about the zone being tight. The vegetation was heavy, but once overhead, we saw the aircraft wedged in the ravine. Our LZ was a small hole requiring a vertical descent.

Rhodes brought the aircraft to a hover. With barely enough power, the Huey struggled. As we descended vertically into the LZ, the entire crew watched the blade tips and tail rotor, ready to give Rhodes a warning should they get too close to the trees.

After a very short discussion, we decided that Sims, the Seabee, and I would get out to see if we could get the crewmember out. There was no way we could take the 250-pound acetylene tank and cutting equipment down that embankment!

As the Huey settled into the LZ, our adrenalin started pumping. Rhodes hovered with the right skid on the ground, all the while keeping an eye on the rotor blades which were turning dangerously close to the side of the sloping hill. Sims and the Seabee jumped out the right side and unloaded the cutting tools and acetylene tank. I unstrapped and opened my door. Climbing out of my seat with the finesse of a raging bull, I proceeded to put my full weight on the collective, using it for leverage on my jump. Fortunately, Rhodes was a strong man. His collective just went from weighing nothing to about 150 pounds. Had it slipped out of his hands, or had he not held it right where it was, the helicopter would have rolled down the hill, and I would have been the first victim.

Airborne, my head snapped. I had forgotten to unhook the intercom cord. Consequently, I got a whiplash, just as our instructors had warned in flight school. Rhodes held the aircraft in place despite the fact I had nearly killed both of us. After a jump of about six feet, I landed on the slope with a tumble. Rhodes, assuming I was clear of the aircraft, took off.

Recovering after my John Wayne escape from the Huey, I looked around. I could hear the Huey's engine. It was still running and still screaming at full power. Sims and the Seabee were already going down the hill.

I looked around to get my bearings and an idea of the friend-lies' location. On the other side of the ravine, a grunt was signaling for me to talk to him on the radio. Another grunt, about thirty meters from me on my side of the ravine, waved me over. I ran over and grabbed his radio.

"This is Scarface on the ground. Over."

"Roger, Scarface. This is X-ray Zulu Six. You had better get down there and tell those guys that the aircraft could blow any minute now. I've seen it before. Over."

"Roger, X-ray Zulu. What's the situation down there? Over."

"We have one person still in there. Like I said, I've seen them blow when the engine is going like that, so you had better get them out of there now! Over."

"Roger, Scarface. Out."

I started running down a small path leading to the bottom of the ravine. All of the grunts were well north of my position. I was suddenly aware that there were bad guys in the area. I reached down and unhooked the strap over the hammer of my .38 pistol so I could draw it if I needed it.

As I reached the bottom of the ravine, something did not feel right. Looking down, I saw that I had unhooked my holster. Rather than unhooking the hammer guard, I had unhooked the snap that held the gun-slinger type holster to the belt. My pistol and holster were just about at my knee and out of the belt.

After straightening out that problem, I continued to the bottom of the ravine and then up the ravine toward the crew and Huey. A shallow stream ran along the center of the ravine. As I got closer to the Huey, I could see the stream had changed color. It was a pink-ish-red from blood. My stomach was getting queasy. My mind was racing. The two crewmen were already at the aircraft. When I was about ten meters from the Huey, the noise from the screaming engine was deafening. I hesitated for a split second. *If this thing blows,*

I'm dead! I thought, with fear taking over, but then I felt a twinge of guilt for being such a chicken shit. *The hell with it,* I thought, as I ran up to them.

Looking in the crumpled aircraft, I could see the copilot, 1Lt James "Jim" Rhodes was still strapped in. There was no question in my mind he was dead. There was no way we could get him out through his side door. A large tree was leaning against it. Without discussing the situation, we started breaking away the pieces of Plexiglas still in the left front window. We could see that the only way to get Rhodes out would be to lift him through the front. Leaning into the cockpit, I looked down to see if I could turn the throttle off and stop the damn noise. Both collectives were broken off. Rolling off the throttle would be a waste of time. Had I been thinking clearly, I could have just turned off the fuel switch, starving the engine of fuel.

1Lt James Rhodes, Killed in Action. March, 27 1945—October 10, 1969.

We pulled Rhodes out of the cockpit and carried him about twenty meters from the aircraft before stopping to rest. We took off his bullet bouncer, making him about thirty-five pounds lighter. As we rested beside his limp body, I could see a jagged cut about eight inches long on the side of his throat. A piece of Plexiglas must have broken off and somehow made the cut during impact.

LCpl "Danny" R. Hesson
Killed in Action 10 Dec.1948-10 Oct.1969.
(No picture available.)

Jim Rhodes was not a large man, but his lifeless body was hard to carry up the ravine's steep incline to the LZ.

Once back at the LZ, I went over to the radioman and made a call, "Scarface Three Two, this is Scarface on the ground. Over."

"Go ahead, Scarface," John Rhodes answered. "Is he alive? Over."

I could hear the tension in his voice. "Negative, Three Two," I said sadly. "We have the body in the zone and are ready for pick-up. Over."

"Roger," was his somber reply.

LCpl Manley Siler, Killed in Action.
20 Nov.1948-10 Oct.1969
Picture furnished by the Permian
Vietnam Memorial.

I walked back over to the LZ, sat down next to a bush and proceeded to "lose my lunch."

The grunts must really think I'm a wimp, I thought. I did not care.

We loaded the body aboard the aircraft. I climbed in the back with the other two. We left the acetylene tank. Rhodes took us out of the area. I came up on intercom from the back and told him I really did not want to climb up front. I felt totally wiped out. He did not have a problem with me staying in the back. He headed to "Charlie Med" at Quang Tri.

En route we learned the aircraft's crew chief, Lance Corporal Manley E. Siler and Gunner Lance Corporal Danny R. Hessen had also been killed. Bauernfeind was still alive. He was broken up, but it was thought he would survive. The flight had started out as his first HAC (Helicopter Aircraft Commander) hop. Following normal policy, Jim Rhodes, an experienced copilot, was scheduled with the inexperienced HAC.

This incident was an eye opener. Until now I had been having a good time doing hot-shot flying and shooting up the countryside. Overall, I had been enjoying my tour. The reality of losing friends or getting killed myself was always on my mind but, like for most people, reality does not set in until it happens.

VIII
Prairie Fire

MISSION 72, PRAIRIE FIRE was a Scarface-assigned mission. Because of the jungle terrain, aerial reconnaissance was not effective along the Ho Chi Minh Trail. Army Green Berets were assigned to complete covert activities utilizing specially trained teams.

Code named "Studies and Observation Group" (SOG), a much more politically correct name than what we called them. We referred to them as "Special Operations Group." These SOG teams carried out reconnaissance in Laos and Cambodia throughout the year. Our squadron was involved daily.

The multi-service mission of army, marines, air force and ARVN (Army of Vietnam) forces supported the insertion and extraction of reconnaissance teams in Laos. A team normally consisted of two army Green Berets and six indigenous Montagnyard tribesmen from the mountain highlands. All American participants needed security clearances, and each had to sign a statement committing him to secrecy with a penalty of a $10,000 fine and/or jail time for leaking any information about the project.

The controlling Green Beret headquarters for I Corps was Combat Control North (CCN) located just south of Marble Mountain Air Facility on the outskirts of Da Nang.

Prairie Fire was a SOG-controlled mission. Teams inserted into Laos would stay for about six days monitoring NVA movement along the Ho Chi Min Trail. The marines would function as flight/strike commander and provide gunship cover for the mission. The army would normally provide the UH-1 slicks and AH-1 Cobras. The air force would provide a fixed wing O-2 on station to coordinate air strikes if needed. On occasion, the Vietnamese would provide slicks using H-34s.

Because of the need for secrecy, all aircraft call-signs were changed for the mission. Our squadron changed to "Eagle Claw"; the army Huey slicks became "Gnat," and the army Cobras became "Dragon Fly." On occasions when the ARVN CH-34s worked the mission, they used "Kingbee" as their call sign. The air force would provide forward air control support flying the O-2 Cessna

Skymaster. Their pilot's call-sign was "Covey" and his observer's was "Fat Capper."

Early every morning, all Prairie Fire helicopters launched for the SOG Mobile Launch Team Two Headquarters (MLT2) located

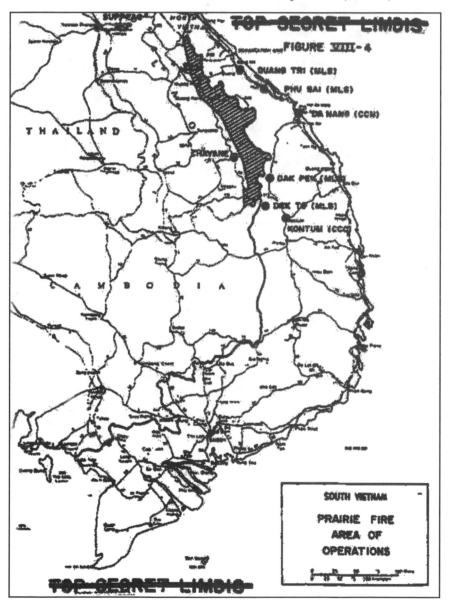

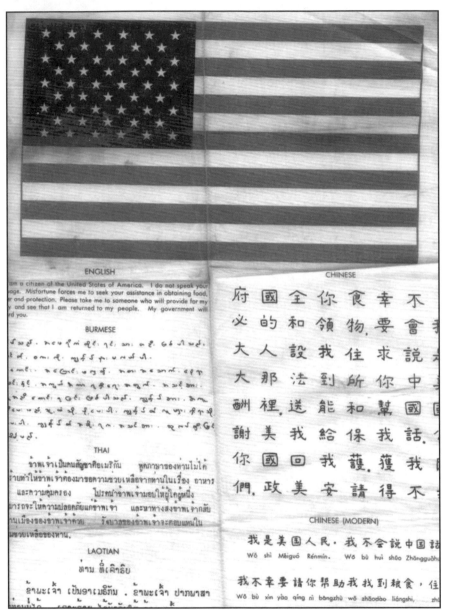

Blood chit carried by air crews when flying Prairie Fire
missions in Laos and Cambodia. A blood chit guarantees a
payment for assisting American soldiers.

approximately eight kilometers west of Quang Tri where they were briefed for scheduled insertions or extractions. If none were scheduled, they would be placed on stand-by for emergency extractions.

The MLT2 compound had a large helicopter pad and could safely park up to eight or ten helicopters. Also on the compound were several wooden buildings separated by a wire fence from an area housing the Montagnyard tribesmen.

I enjoyed looking at the army Cobras while on stand-by. They were awesome machines. One Cobra provided more firepower than two marine Hueys. Because of the Cobra's superiority, I wondered why the marines were involved; this was definitely an army mission. I figured it must be a political thing since the army was working in the I Corps—an area which had been designated as the marine's responsibility.

The normal mode of operation for a mission was to depart MLT2 and head west along Highway 9 to the Rockpile, then to continue west into Laos, or to go south to Vandegrift before heading west and flying over the abandoned site of Khe Sanh before entering Laos. Once in Laos and close to the area of insertion, the marine gunships normally did a low-level reconnaissance of the area and looked over the landing zones. Usually, several LZs were picked, and slicks would carry out a couple of false insertions. They would make their approach into a landing zone and sit on the ground for about two long seconds before lifting off without inserting a team. The deceptive maneuver would be carried out in two or three zones to throw off any observers the NVA might have in the area, and they were almost always watching. The idea was to get the NVA who might be watching headed in the wrong direction.

Laos was a beautiful country. Unlike Vietnam, where the landscape was pockmarked by bomb craters, the lush vegetation was unscarred. Despite its beauty, sightseeing was not an option. Everything was business here, and tension was always high. When things went bad, they really went bad. Not only were there a lot of bad guys with really big guns, it was a long walk home.

When a team came into contact with the enemy and was being pursued, the resulting problems were huge. On one occasion, a team was so far out that the extraction team would have only a few minutes on station. There were also times when an air force CH-53, known as the Jolly Green Giant, had to be called out of Thailand for the extract.

The Montagnyards usually wore NVA uniforms and carried Soviet-made AK-47s. This, on occasion, caused consternation for the crew picking them up, especially if the Green Beret with them was not seen.

On one occasion, while flying a team back to MLT2 after an extraction, the slick called Eagle Claw Lead and told him they were carrying a pretty good crowd in the back. He asked just how many PAX he should have picked up. Eagle Claw Lead responded that there were seven on the team inserted. A long pause followed. "We have eight," said the slick's pilot. The team, all dressed in NVA uniforms and toting AK-47s, had neglected to tell the crew that they had a prisoner.

On November 10, 1969, the Marine Corps Birthday, I was flying Prairie Fire with Major Lively, our Executive Officer. It was the first time I had flown with him. A former jet jock, he did not have a lot of helicopter time. He and I were the flight lead with Upthegrove on our wing.

We did our morning brief and preflight and launched for another low-level flight up Highway 1 to the MLT2 landing pad. Shortly after landing, the day's briefing took place. It was going to be a busy one. Three insertions, all relatively close to the Laos/Vietnam border and west of the DMZ, were scheduled. The mission required two trips. Three Huey slicks were assigned to the mission. Two of the slicks would each carry a team of eight—six indigenous troops and two Green Berets. The third slick, the chase, would be available for rescue operations. Due to the nature of the mission, we would be at our maximum gross weight, plus some, depending on how much extra ammo and grenades the crew chief and gunner had sneaked onto the aircraft before we left.

Shortly after our brief, we launched and headed along Highway 9 until we reached the Rockpile. We continued to the LZs.

Once in the area, two false drops were made before the first insertion. The second insertion was only a kilometer from the first. Both were without incident, and we departed to refuel and pick up the third team.

Our flight and the chase slick decided to refuel at Vandegrift while the other two slicks and Cobras headed back to MLT2 where they would pick up the third team and refuel at Quang Tri. The plan was to meet just east of the Laotian border and south of the DMZ in an hour and a half.

As our flight back reached the Rockpile, we spilt up. The guns and our chase turned south and headed for Vandegrift while the rest of the flight kept going east toward Quang Tri.

We launched after refueling and taking a break for our lunch of C-rations. Our flight headed west to Khe Sanh and then north toward our rendezvous point, a spot beyond Hill 880. We entered our orbit to wait for the rest of the flight.

Suddenly, without warning, our Huey's nose yawed sharply to the left and the entire aircraft shuddered. The engine flamed out and rotor RPM warning horn blasted in our headsets.

Lively was on the controls. Immediately after the initial yaw and resultant shudder, he lowered the collective putting the aircraft into autorotation. It took a second or two for me to realize what had happened. Lights were flashing. The engine out horn was blasting in my ear, and we were going down hill. The engine had just quit! We started to fall out of the sky like a Coke machine.

I am going to die, no doubt about it was my immediate thought.

Fortunately, we were about 1500 feet above the ground over a relatively flat valley. The valley floor was covered with elephant grass rather than the usual dense jungle. As we came falling out of the sky, Lively turned the aircraft to the west for landing.

By this time I had regained my composure and realized that I had emergency procedure duties to complete. I pointed to what looked like a good flat area over to the right. It was into the wind which would help in giving us lift for landing on the bottom.

Lively made a Mayday call as he made the turn to the right. Reaching over I pulled the handle to release the rocket pods to make the Huey lighter, but the pods did not fall. We were still coming out of the sky like a rock. Our airspeed was good at eighty knots. The engine-out horn was still screaming in our ears. I did not have the composure to turn off the switch.

As we passed through 100 feet AGL, Lively reduced the airspeed by bringing up the nose of the aircraft. He continued slowing the aircraft until we were about five feet above the elephant grass and the groundspeed came to zero. He leveled the helicopter horizontal, and I braced myself for impact. Everything was looking good.

Lively did almost everything perfectly. Unfortunately, neither of us realized the elephant grass was five or six feet high. We were ten feet above the ground instead of five and in a vertical descent. I braced myself for a hard landing. Lively pulled the collective up as high as it would go giving us maximum pitch, but there was not enough to stop our descent. We hit with a thump! A sharp pain shot through my back.

We were on the ground and alive. My first priority was to get out of the helicopter. Reaching over, I pulled the emergency exit handle located by the door. I pushed and the door promptly fell off. Burp gun in hand, I climbed out. The four of us formed a hasty perimeter around the downed Huey. Just west of our aircraft, our wingman Upthegrove made a low pass over the area. A call came over my emergency PRC-90 (survival radio).

"Eagle Claw Lead, this is Two. Over. What is your situation? Over."

"Eagle Claw Two, this is Eagle Claw Lead," Lively responded. "Everyone is okay on the ground. I don't hear any enemy fire in the area so we seem to be secure for the moment. Are you in contact with anyone for getting us out? Over."

Upthegrove continued making low passes over the area looking for enemy activity. Not seeing any, he called again. "Eagle Claw Lead, this is Two. I have a Gnat slick about ten klicks south of our position inbound. Over."

A few minutes passed with nothing happening. It did not appear we would come under attack and have to fight our way out. The crew chief looked over the aircraft searching for bullet holes. Finding none, we assumed the problem was mechanical. That provided some relief.

Lively called Eagle Claw Two and told him to have the pick-up aircraft orbit for a while. The M-60s, KY-28 radio, ammo, and anything else we could carry had to be removed from the aircraft. After unhooking the M-60s and KY-28, Lively instructed Upthegrove to send in the Huey. The army Huey was right there and landed nearby. After loading our weapons, ammo, and radio, we were off and on our way back to MLT2.

Unloading our gear, we thanked the army for the lift and climbed into Upthegrove's Huey for a ride home. The third insertion was cancelled and we headed back to Phu Bai.

As we taxied to the ramp at Phu Bai, Upthegrove got a call from tower telling him he would have to return to Quang Tri to escort a security team and show them the crash site. A reaction platoon was being sent to secure the aircraft until a CH-53 could be sent to external the Huey home. The platoon would have to spend the night in a relatively open area deep in "bad man" country. I did not envy the platoon or Upthegrove. He and his crew had already put in a twelve-hour day.

Upthegrove dropped us off. Having enough fuel to get to Quang Tri, he headed back north. After refueling at Quang Tri, he joined the flight transporting the reaction platoon and led them west. It was now dark, and he had to go low and use his search light to locate the downed Huey. Having a good knowledge of the area, he found it after a short search. He directed the army Hueys to a suitable landing area.

The marine birthday party was underway when Lively and I returned to Phu Bai. We joined it but did not have enough energy left to do much celebrating. Nonetheless, I did my best. By the time Upthegrove got back and made it to the club, he and his copilot were among the few sober guys in the place. Even the squadron's most laid back and conservative officer, Captain C.C. Mannschreck, was dancing on a table.

A CH-53 externaled the Huey to Phu Bai the next day. A thorough inspection was conducted. The skids were spread from the impact. The fuel control on the engine, the cause of the failure, had to be replaced. Aircraft BU154960 was fixed and flying again within a couple of weeks.

IX
RT Mississippi

1Lt Mark Byrd looked at the scheduling board and saw he was scheduled for Mission 72 in the morning. Byrd, not a big drinker under any circumstances, decided not to hit the club at all that night. The next day might be a busy one, and he wanted to be ready. According to the board, his assignment was to fly as copilot to 1Lt J. "Herb" Brown on the wing of the flight leader 1Lt John Rhodes. 1Lt John Hartline would be Rhodes's copilot.

Early the next morning, the mission's crew met in the ready room at 0600. The weather was marginal with gusty winds and low ceilings over Phu Bai intensifying the already dark sky.

Rhodes briefed the flight. The crews headed out to the flight line for preflight and start-up. As Rhodes and his crew got to the air-craft, the crew chiefs and gunners were finishing the task of mounting the M-60 machine guns and placing extra cans of ammo and grenades needed for the mission.

The preflight was completed on time, and the crew strapped the Hueys to their backs. The aircraft were cleared for start. Brown had a normal start, but the controls seemed stiff. After rolling the throttle to full RPM, he pulled the collective to lift his aircraft to a hover. Because the controls were nearly frozen, the Huey was hovering at one foot. Brown realized he had screwed up. The hydraulics were off! Someone had accidentally left the hydraulic switch in the "off" position, and Brown had not caught it during his start-up checks. He struggled with the Huey as it lurched around in the revetment. Pushing as hard as he could on the collective and fighting with the cyclic, he tried to maintain a hover and get the aircraft back on the ground before it hit the revetment. The Huey bounced as it hit the ground. Brown recovered the aircraft without further incident.

This is no way to start the day, Byrd thought as the Huey settled.

The flight did their radio checks and taxied out to the runway before taking off with Rhodes in the lead. When the flight arrived at MLT2, the army Cobras and Hueys were already on site. Envious of the rotor brakes on the marine helicopters, the army crews watched as the Eagle Claws shut down. Required for shipboard operations, the brakes on the Eagle Claw helicopters allowed the rotors to come to a stop with a pull on the brake handle. The army pilots had to wait several minutes while the free-wheeling blades on their helicopters slowly turned down before finally coming to a stop.

Rhodes proceeded to the operations shack and received the morning briefing from a young Special Forces captain who looked no older than twenty-one or twenty-two. The captain gave him the current situation, the locations of the teams in the field, and the plan for the day.

As he came out of the shack, Rhodes called the crews over and informed them they would be on stand-by. After that, the crew settled in, either catching some zzzs in the crew shack or making small talk with the army crews.

At about 1500 hours, Byrd, sitting on a stump playing his harmonica, looked up and saw that Rhodes and the flight leaders had been called to the Operations shack. Something was up!

After they entered the shack, the captain, who had briefed Rhodes earlier in the day, walked to a large map covering most of the wall and pointed to an area in Laos, west and south of their location. Recon Team Mississippi, consisting of two Americans and six indigenous members, call sign "Hay Eater," was in contact with the enemy and needed an emergency extraction. The weather was still bad with high winds, scattered thunderstorms, and intermittent showers. Also, there were no landing zones in the area. McGuire rigs would be needed to pull out the recon team. The McGuire rig, an extraction device, allowed the Huey crew to drop up to three ropes through trees. The person being extracted would sit on a canvas belt about as wide as a deflated fire hose and place the straddle rope between his legs to prevent him from falling out. One wrist would be placed in a wrist loop sling. Ammo cans with rocks in them were sometimes attached so the ropes would fall through the jungle better.

Rhodes briefed the marine flight crews. The army counterparts did the same. Following their briefings, all crews scrambled to their aircraft.

The lead Cobra pilot-in-command, Chief Warrant Officer William "Billy" Hartbarger, started his engine. While still sitting on the pad, he called his unit operations notifying them they were launching and might need a backup. After several calls and no response, another pilot from his company monitoring the frequency called and offered assistance.

"Griffin Two One Three One Charlie, this is Cobra One Three. Can I relay for you?"

"That's affirm, One Three," Hartbarger replied. "Tell Operations we just launched on a Papa Foxtrot, and it sounds like it may get pretty hairy. I may be calling one of you for back-up."

"Roger, Three One Charlie. We are free. You got trouble?"

"Negative. We are just leaving Quang Tri at this time. It could be big."

Once again Two One Three One replied, "Is this something worth watching?"

His voice edged with sarcasm, Hartbarger answered, "Well, I don't know. Have you ever made a landing zone with seventeen-pound warheads?"

Sounding puzzled, One Three called back. "Is that what you are going to try?"

"That's the best we can do," Hartbarger answered.

One Three called back in disbelief and asked again, "What are you going to try and do? Make an LZ?"

"That's affirmative. They ran into some stuff they did not like, and they have to get out." Before Hartbarger could say more, another company aircraft jumped into the conversation.

"One Three, this is Three Four."

"Go ahead, Three Four."

"Roger, I have 76 ten-pounders if you need them. That's a lot of rockets for one bird."

"Roger, I'll keep you guys in mind," Hartbarger replied as he took off from MLT2.

Rhodes and his wingman were west of Dong Ha and wanted to know where their Huey slicks were. He called on the VHF radio.

"Gnat Lead, what's your position?"

"I'm about four miles behind you now."

Rhodes informed Gnat Lead of his location and altitude which was 7500 feet.

"Roger, Claw. I'm at 7200 and climbing," Gnat answered.

Heading out of Dong Ha, Rhodes contacted the air force 0-2 observation aircraft, call sign "Covey." Covey had been assigned to work the extraction and to have fixed-wing aircraft available to provide support if needed. The AO, "Fat Capper," a ground officer trained in calling artillery and fixed-wing air support, was the other crewmember. Rhodes checked in with Covey.

"Covey, this is Eagle Claw Lead with a package outbound to your position. We are presently passing the Rockpile heading toward the Anvil. Do you have any plots [enemy anti-aircraft batteries] around that area?"

"That's a negative. Not around the Anvil. I do in the area of Hay Eater. I'll have to bring you in from the west. Keep heading for the Anvil, and I'll pick you up there."

Looking ahead, Rhodes could see the O-2 in the distance, flying an orbit while waiting for the helicopters. "Roger, see you there."

A short time later Covey called again. "Eagle Claw Lead, this is Covey. I have you in sight. I'm at your one o'clock at 5700 feet."

Seeing Covey ahead of and below him, Rhodes called, "Okay, Covey, I have you in sight."

"Good," Covey replied. "Follow me west and stay north of the Anvil. I have several gun plots just southwest of my position so we will need to come into Hay Eater's position from the west. We also have some fast movers working along the trail [Ho Chi Min] so we will have to stay to the east of them."

"Roger, Covey. I'm right behind you. Lead the way," Rhodes answered as he followed the O-2.

0-2 Skymaster reconnaissance aircraft "Covey".

The package passed over the Vietnam/Laotian border. The vegetation turned to lush dark green as the jungle growth grew thicker. Craters caused by constant bombing dotted the rolling hills and the valleys. The crystal clear water of the raging rivers and the waterfalls created a beauty in the jungle that was lacking on the Vietnam side of the border.

The flight followed the O-2 through the valleys, descending as the clouds became darker and lower. Several rain showers had to be circumnavigated, and the wind and turbulence became a concern. They had to get to the team, but the wind and turbulence would make the extraction even more complicated and dangerous.

After holding a westerly heading for about five minutes, the team turned to the south until they were directly west of Hay Eater. Ahead of the helicopters, Covey was coming up to the extraction zone. He attempted to describe the reconnaissance team's location.

"Eagle Claw, we are about three klicks east of the team at this time. If you look straight to the east, you can see that sharp ridge directly ahead. Hay Eater is on the west slope of the ridge. He has been taking fire from the north and west of his position. In close."

Looking ahead of Covey, Rhodes saw the north-south ridge on the top of a long sloping hill. It was about a kilometer long. "Okay, Covey, thanks. I have the ridge in sight."

Wanting to go in ahead and look over the situation without endangering the rest of the flight, Rhodes gave directions. "Gnat flight, hold just to the north of my present position." Without a break, he called the lead Cobra. "Fly flight, come in with me and hold just north of the team. I'll go in and locate Hay Eater."

Covey broke in on the radio, "Claw Lead, we have a prime mover on the trail. Have your Gnats move farther east."

"Gnat copies. Moving east."

Inbound to the ridgeline, Rhodes tried several times to reach Hay Eater. He got no response. Talking on Fox Mike, Covey's flight

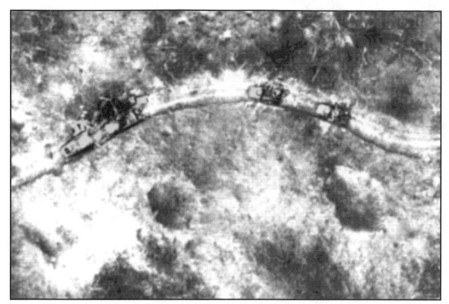

Prime movers along the Ho Chi Minh Trail. Photo by unknown Kingbee pilot.

observer interrupted, "Hay Eater, Hay Eater, this is Fat Capper. I want you to talk to Eagle Claw Lead. He's been trying to reach you. Over."

Because there was no response from Hay Eater, Fat Capper directed Rhodes to the team, "Claw, go straight ahead. I'll be watching and will try to direct you over Hay Eater's position."

"Okay. I understand. At my twelve o'clock I see a white flare parachute."

Fat Capper hesitated. He had lost sight of Claw Lead. Finally, seeing him low against the jungle canopy, he called, "Okay. I have you. It's right about your nine o'clock, right now. Go ahead and make a left turn. Try to talk to him. See if he'll talk to you."

Rhodes, flying his Huey at treetop level, banked his gunship. Making a steep left turn he called, "Hay Eater, Hay Eater. This is Eagle Claw."

"Go ahead, Eagle Claw."

Rhodes, happy to have made contact, replied, "Roger, Hay Eater. I have you Lima Charlie. Let's see if you can talk us into your zone. I'm in a left-hand orbit at this time. I'm a low Huey gunship . . . a low Huey gunship. Do you have me in sight?"

Hay Eater, though unable to see Rhodes, could hear him. He called back, "You are to my west, fly east." The transmission was barely audible.

"Roger, fly north?" Rhodes asked.

Hay Eater quickly called back, "That's a negative. You are to my west. I need you to fly east."

"Okay, I'm turning east at this time," Rhodes replied hearing the transmission better.

Shortly after the turn, Hay Eater called again, "Eagle Claw, I can't tell if it was you or a Dragon Fly that just passed over my position."

Looking up through the jungle canopy, he saw a Cobra go over his position. "A Fly just passed over my position now," he continued.

Swinging his Huey around in sharp right-hand turn toward the Cobra, Rhodes answered.

Already at tree-top level, Rhodes slowed his gunship down to sixty knots while searching for a signal from the team. "Okay, I'm coming in low and slow."

"Keep coming, Eagle Claw. Right on . . . right on. Keep coming."

"Tell me when I pass right over you," Rhodes said as he continued straight ahead, still low and slow, waiting for a call telling him he was over the team.

"Right over us," he heard shortly after his call.

Confirming he was over the team, Rhodes called back, "Okay, I understand a Huey gunship just went right over you."

"That's affirmative. Did you get my shiney [signal mirror]?"

"That's a negative, but I'll be coming right around and I'll be looking for it." After swinging the aircraft around for another pass, Rhodes continued, "Okay, I'm coming back around now."

This time Hay Eater wanted to make sure the Huey crew would see them. "Roger, Claw. There will be eight of us giving you a shiney."

Finding it a bit humorous that the whole team was going to be trying to catch his attention, Rhodes chuckled, "Roger, eight shineys."

As Rhodes came back around, all eyes aboard the gunship were looking down through the jungle canopy, searching for the flash of the mirrors.

"Keep coming, Claw. We're directly on your left. Look on your left, up the hill. Over," Hay Eater called over the radio. Sensing they had been seen, he called again. "You've got us. You've got us, Eagle Claw." Excitement was evident in his voice.

In the Huey, Hartline saw the mirrors. "I've got them. They are just off to my left!"

"Okay, Hay Eater. We have you just off our left wing. My copilot has you in sight. I'm coming around one more time for a quick look. I understand you want us to go ahead and hit . . . hose down the west and north sides?"

"That's affirm, Eagle Claw. Do you have our position?" Hay Eater asked, concerned Rhodes might not have had an exact fix on their position.

"Roger. My copilot and wingman have your position."

Hay Eater wanted to make certain his people were not going to get hit by fire from the gunship's machine guns.

"Okay," he said, "you have our position. I'm going to call all my people to the smoke. Hose down to the northwest. Over."

"Roger. Hose the northwest. Over."

The team popped a smoke grenade. As it filtered up through the jungle canopy, Rhodes got a good mark on the team's position and called, "We've got red smoke."

Hay Eater confirmed it was their smoke.

Rhodes wanted to confirm the whole team was together. "Roger, red smoke. Have you got all your people on the smoke?"

"We will only use 7.62 at this time," he replied after receiving an affirmative.

In his cockpit the pilot of Dragon Fly lead indicated his approval on the choice of weapons.

"Outstanding!"

In preparation for his first gun run, Rhodes gave instructions to his wingman and the flight of Cobras.

"Okay. No rockets. I repeat, no rockets."

"Get it quick. Get it quick. We've got people coming. Make it close! Make it close!" Just then, Hay Eater called, his voice excited and rapid.

Wasting no time, Rhodes started his gun run.

"We're in hot. I will be making a run to your west at this time. Dragon Fly, you can follow us."

After laying down a barrage of machine gun within thirty meters of the team, Rhodes called.

"Hay Eater, this is Claw Lead. Let me know if we are too close. Over."

"Close is not close enough."

Brown set up his gun run by laying down a barrage of gunfire to cover Rhodes's pullout. Byrd fired his two M-60 machine guns from his TAT-101 nose turret. Brown fired his four attached M-60s, and the crew chief and gunner covered the aircraft with their M-60s as it started its pull-up.

As Brown pulled out of his run, Dragon Fly lead made a call, "We are in right behind you."

The lead Cobra set up his gun run. Fly Lead rolled in. Hartbarger gave instructions to his gunner/copilot, "Okay, you take that mini-gun and work out, man."

The sewing machine "rrrrrrrr" of the mini-gun hummed as it spewed out its deadly fire at four thousand rounds per minute walking the tracers to within meters of the smoke.

"Out-fucking-standing!" Hay Eater shouted, elated.

"How was that, Hay Eater?" Rhodes asked, smiling to himself.

"They are weeping and wailing down below us. I'm popping another smoke."

After the team had made their second gun run, Hay Eater asked for rockets.

"Okay, understand you want rockets to the west and north," Rhodes confirmed calling back.

"That's affirmative, Eagle Claw. Put them in close. My people are gaggled up in the smoke. Put them fifty meters west and north."

"That's too close," Hartbarger said to his copilot in the lead Cobra.

"Roger. West to north," Rhodes confirmed as he rolled in on his next run shooting rockets.

Their fire hit just northwest of the smoke. "How's that, Hay Eater?"

"It's right on my position, but it's not hurting anyone. It's outstanding!"

Gusting winds were moving the smoke fast. Once the smoke was popped, the pilots needed to get a good fix on the position because shortly after the first rocket run the smoke would disperse.

Suddenly, the team was in close contact. Hay Eater popped a smoke.

"Smoke is popped. Get it in close . . . in close!" he said, his voice filled with anxiety and concern. "Hit just west of the smoke."

Weapons fire could be heard over the radios.

"I need this run 280 degrees, fifty meters. We are all in the smoke."

Gunfire could still be heard over the radio.

Fat Capper, orbiting high above, interrupted.

"Gnat flight, move to your east. You are getting too close to the trail. We have some fast movers working the area," he said, concerned that anti-aircraft fire might shoot down one of the Hueys while they were close to the Ho Chi Min trail. The danger of a collision with a jet was also a possibility.

Gnat Lead assured Covey he was moving east.

As Rhodes came around for his next run, he searched the jungle for the smoke. There was not any. Again, he called Hay Eater. "Pop a colored smoke. Give me the enemy situation and give me an idea as to when we can get something going," Rhodes said, his concern growing.

The day was growing late, and their time on station was getting shorter by the minute. Just as Rhodes finished telling Hay Eater to pop the smoke, he spotted it.

"Okay, Hay Eater, I've got a yellow smoke."

Sounding desperate, Hay Eater called again.

"I've got movement on my front. Make it quick!" Wanting the fire to stay in close, he shouted. "Get'em close!"

"Okay, Hay Eater. You let me know if we're too close. Get down!"

Again Rhodes made a rocket run firing the rockets as close as he dared. He passed just to the west of the team at tree-top level.

"How was the last?" he asked.

Not getting an answer, with concern clearly evident in his voice, he asked again, "How was the last?"

Worried about shooting so close to the team, Dragon Fly Lead called, "Claw Lead, how was your run?"

Unable to contact Hay Eater since his run, Rhodes responded.

"I can't talk to them. I think they are in contact. They were saying the 'gooners' were on top of them."

Rhodes was now on the bottom of his gun run, just above the trees and taking ground fire. As he was starting his climb, the nose of his aircraft abruptly tucked under and entered an uncontrollable bank to the right putting it in an almost inverted attitude. The aircraft crashed into the jungle canopy, hitting the top of a very large tree which cushioned the crash. The aircraft was swallowed up as it broke through the triple canopy.

Above, Hartbarger, getting set up for his run, had watched Eagle Claw Lead during his gun run low over the trees. What he saw made his heart stop for a second.

"Oh, no! Oh, my God! Claw Lead just bit the dust," he said over the radio.

"What?" an unknown voice asked.

"Eagle Claw just crashed!" Dragon Fly lead answered.

After seeing the aircraft crash, Byrd mentally marked its location. A tree, broken as the helicopter plummeted into the jungle, protruded through the top of the triple canopy. The jungle had literally swallowed up the Huey. Byrd did not take his eyes off the protruding tree.

Back at the scene of the crash, Rhodes was stunned but conscious. Concerned about an aircraft fire, he turned the battery, fuel switch, and fuel boost pumps off. Still not realizing the aircraft was inverted, he unstrapped from his harness and promptly fell hitting his head on the overhead console. He opened his door to get out, but there was no skid to stand on. The aircraft was hanging in the trees five to ten feet off the ground.

At about the same time, he heard movement. He checked with his gunner Cpl L.L. Osborne and crew chief Cpl Henry Bookhardt; they reported hearing him loud and clear. They were not hurt. Looking over at Hartline, Rhodes saw movement. Everyone was alive. They were somewhat banged up, but, considering the circumstances, all appeared to be in pretty good shape.

Once on the ground, Rhodes assessed the situation. Hartline was in the worst condition with a possible punctured lung and injuries in the rib area.

Radio traffic increased immediately. The Cobra pilots were searching the area from above while talking to Brown who was down low searching at tree-top level. Attempting to coordinate, Brown was talking to Dragon Fly lead, but he could not reach Hay Eater.

Brown had to assume the responsibilities of the flight leader. His first task was to make sure he had a good handle on Hay Eater's location and that of the downed aircraft. Time was running short as the fuel gauges on the aircraft dwindled toward a quarter of a tank.

Byrd still had the tree in sight. Because Brown was so busy on the radios, Byrd elected to try to get his attention by pointing in the direction of the tree. It seemed that his efforts went unnoticed.

Still unable to talk to the team, Brown called the O-2 which was circling above. "Covey, this Eagle Claw Two. I can't reach Hay Eater. My Fox Mike is not working. I'll need you to relay for me. See if you can find out what happened to that aircraft."

"Roger. Eagle Claw. This is Fat Capper, I'm the AO. I'll be glad to help out. Give me a position of the downed aircraft from the team."

Brown replied, but was hesitant and sounded a bit uncertain. "Ah . . . I would say 240 degrees 300 meters."

"Roger. 240 at 300 meters."

Fat Capper got right on the FM radio. "Hay Eater, this is Fat Capper. We need to get things moving here. Eagle Claw Lead just went down."

Getting no answer, he tried again. "Hay Eater, this is Fat Capper. Eagle Claw Lead just went in. Did you see or hear him? Claw Two thinks he's about 240 degrees from your position."

This time Hay Eater answered. "That's affirmative. We did hear him crash, but I heard him go in north of my position. Over."

Fat Capper was trying to make a quick decision about what to do next: get the aircraft crew out or get the team out. "Okay, buddy, we need to get this thing moving. How are you doing down there? Do you want them to hose some more? Or do you want us to pull you out?"

Making a quick assessment of his options, Hay Eater decided he had better get over to the downed aircraft. "No, give me a heading to the aircraft and hose down a path to Eagle Claw and we'll go get them. Is it on the other side of the hill?"

"That's affirmative."

Needing to correct the discrepancy between where Brown said the Huey crashed and where the team had heard the crash, Fat Capper made a call. "Eagle Claw Two, this is Fat Capper. Do you have the location of Claw Lead?"

Again, Byrd pointed to the spot. This time Brown saw his signal and started a sharp turn toward it.

"Three hundred meters. My three o'clock."

"Fat Capper, I heard a crash about 100 meters from my position."

"Roger, I understand about ten meters?" Fat Capper responded, not hearing Hay Eater well.

Hay Eater's reply was sudden. "That's a negative. One hundred meters. Over. Do you have my position? I'll pop a smoke. You give me a heading to the aircraft and I will go to him. Over."

"Heading zero-one-zero, 100 meters," Fat Capper replied using Brown's sighting.

Through his window, Brown saw a small trickle of smoke rising through the jungle canopy next to where Byrd was pointing. He broke in on the radio. "This is Claw Two. Do you see where the black smoke is coming up? That's where the aircraft is."

"Hay Eater, this is Fat Capper. We have the aircraft. You had better start heading that way. Pop a smoke right now, and I will give you a heading."

"Roger. Popping smoke."

Knowing Brown had not heard the conversation, Fat Capper called him on his UHF radio. "Hay Eater heard the aircraft go down and they are going to head on over toward the chopper."

About the time Brown found the crash site and started an orbit overhead, Rhodes and his crew had already set up a defensive perimeter near the aircraft. They knew they were not far from the recon team, and they had a lot of ammunition. Bookhardt had been sent to the aircraft to gather weapons. He came back with a couple of M-16s, an M-79 grenade launcher with a good supply of 40mm grenades, and a box filled with at least forty or fifty loaded clips for the M-16s. Bookhardt reported the 90-degree gearbox had definitely been shot off.

The crew heard movement to the west and north in the jungle. They thought it was fairly close. Knowing the team was to the south, they fired in the direction of the movement.

Bookhardt made several more trips to the aircraft returning with a five-gallon can of water and a M-60 machine gun with ammo.

Their defensive perimeter was set up. Some old fallen trees provided excellent cover. The M-60 and M-16 covered one direction and an M-16 and M-79 covered another approach. The crew were all within ten feet of each other in their small fort-like area. They had been on the ground for about fifteen to twenty minutes.

Rhodes planned on staying with the aircraft and was assuming Hay Eater's team would head for their zone, conditions permitting, as per SOP (standard operating procedure).

Overhead, still orbiting the crash site and not being able to talk to anyone with his Fox Mike, Brown called Covey. "Okay, Fat Capper. I still have not heard anything they have said. I'd appreciate if you would continue the relay."

"Okay. No problem," Fat Capper replied. After a quick glance at his fuel gauge, he called again. "We're going to have to hurry! How are you doing on fuel?"

"I've got about 700 pounds right now."

Trying to reestablish contact with Hay Eater, Fat Capper called on his Fox Mike. "Okay, Hay Eater, come on. You need to talk to us. We are getting low on fuel."

Hay Eater's response was immediate. "Roger, we are on the way up to Eagle Claw now."

"Okay, buddy, you're going to have to hustle. We are getting low on fuel. Do you want some ordinance put in?" Not getting an answer, he asked again. "Hay Eater, talk to me. Do you want them to put some fire in there for you?" Still, there was no answer.

Seeing Brown flying low, still circling the area of the crash site, he called Eagle Claw Two. "Okay, Claw, you want to mark the zone for me again?"

"Okay. I saw some parts down there. I'm going to make another low pass. Someone cover me," Brown replied. Turning back toward the downed aircraft and looking down as he passed over the site, Brown saw the aircraft for the first time. He searched for a sign of survivors. The aircraft, almost inverted, was hanging in the trees. The triple canopy had cushioned it, preventing it from hitting the ground.

"Okay. I've got a red flag down in the area. A red flag on the Huey. Fat Capper, do you see the red flag on the Huey there?" Brown asked rapidly.

Fat Capper asked Eagle Claw Two to stand by so he could ascertain how the flag got on the Huey. He then made a call to Hay Eater. "Hay Eater, did you put a red flag on the Huey?"

"Say again," Hay Eater replied, not understanding.

"I said, . . . did you put a red flag on the Huey?"

Still not understanding and thinking maybe he was being called to pop a red smoke, Hay Eater pulled one out of his pack and popped it. As the smoke filtered up through the canopy, Fat Capper saw it and thought the team wanted to be pulled out or needed fire support.

"Okay, Hay Eater, are you ready to be pulled out or do you want some more ground fire down there? We need to get moving. I've got red smoke."

Hay Eater, really confused by all this, was getting frustrated. "Say again," he repeated.

"Are you ready for them to come in and get you? Or do you want some more grunts put in there?" Fat Capper asked.

"Well, we're trying to get to Eagle Claw right now," Hay Eater replied.

Hay Eater was not alone in his frustration. Fat Capper was also frustrated. "Eagle Claw can't read you. I'm relaying to him. Go ahead," he explained.

Hay Eater's voice was calm when he called back. "I'm trying to reach the one on the ground. Over."

"Okay," Fat Capper responded, finally back in the ball game.

Still flying low, Brown got a good look at the crash site and could see people around the aircraft. He called Fat Capper stressing the urgency of the situation. "We've got to get someone in there if at all possible to see how many survivors are down there. I can see people moving around."

The Huey crew on the ground had popped a red smoke. Orbiting high above, Dragon Fly Lead spotted it first and called

Brown, "This is Fly Lead. I've got a red smoke by the aircraft. I have the red panel."

Not having heard the conversation between Fat Capper and Hay Eater, Brown called. "Fat Capper, this is Claw Lead. Is it possible to get the team to join up there by the helicopter?"

"They are moving up that way. I'll talk to them."

Brown was beginning to think the fuel situation might not allow them enough time to get everyone out. He was searching for options. He called Fat Capper again. "Okay. We may have to leave Hay Eater in there with them. We may have to leave them and go back and refuel and get some more assets if that's possible."

Brown circled the crash site. After looking the area over more closely, he decided an extraction was possible. "Fat Capper, it's not as bad as I thought it was. It looks like the canopy cushioned the crash quite a bit. If you make contact with the team, have them set up a perimeter over there, and we'll have to come back to get them. We're running low on fuel."

Concerned about having a good fix on the crash site, Brown called the Cobra making a low pass over the downed aircraft. "Dragon Fly Three, can you see anything? Are you picking up a mirror?"

"They have a red panel out. There are survivors down there. Definitely!"

Elated, Brown called back, "Okay, Dragon Fly, how far away is Hay Eater?"

"Oh, probably only twenty-five to thirty meters from the chopper."

"Okay, give me a heading, and I'll have them get moving, and we can go straight in there."

"Ah . . . tell them to go about . . . straight north," Fly Three responded.

Fly Lead broke in, "Have them go zero-three-zero."

Because of the low fuel situation, Brown determined time was not on their side. If they were going to get anyone out, it would have to be soon. With a little luck, the wounded could be pulled out, but the team would have to re-arm and refuel before extracting the rest. He called, "Fat Capper, would you relay to Hay Eater that as soon as they find out if there are any wounded, seriously or not, let us know so we can get somebody to pull them out."

Acknowledging Brown's request, Fat Capper called, "Hay Eater, what I want you to do is move about twenty meters, heading zero-three-zero. That should put you at the helicopter."

Breathing heavily after fighting his way through the dense jungle, Hay Eater answered, "Fat Capper, I do not know where the helicopter is yet. Is it on the other side of the ridge?"

Before Fat Capper could answer, Hay Eater called back. He sounded excited. "Wait one . . . wait one . . . I've got people coming!" he said, seeing several NVA just outside his perimeter. They were coming toward him.

"Claw, Hay Eater said he has people coming right in to him," Fat Capper relayed to Brown.

Time was critically important. Covey called Brown, "Eagle Claw, what's your fuel state?"

"I've got about twenty minutes on station," he answered.

Covey looked at his fuel gauge. It was also getting low. He called another O-2 in the area.

"Victor Delta, Victor Delta. You had better move on down here. I just looked at my fuel again. I do not know if I can stay here another five minutes," he said sounding concerned.

Hay Eater called again, speaking rapidly. Gunfire could be heard in the background. "Fat Capper, I'm marking my position. I have people in my position. I see the Dragon Flies overhead and will give them a shiney."

Not understanding, Fat Capper replied, "Say again. Say again slower."

"There are people near my position, and I'm breaking fire contact with grenades. I'll mark my position as soon as I see you or Eagle Claw fly over my position. I need some support down here!"

Fat Capper immediately called Brown, "Eagle Claw, the team is in contact. They need some help!"

"Roger, I understand they are in contact. Where do you want the fire? Give me a direction from the team. I have no radio contact."

"They need fire to the northwest . . . close in. They need you to clear an area to their north."

Brown banked his Huey around in a steep turn toward the team. He descended to treetop level, slowing down while looking for a signal mirror from the team.

In Dragon Fly Lead's cockpit, Hartbarger was watching the situation below. From his vantage point, he could see that Brown was setting himself up to get shot down by flying right over enemy fire.

"Look at that, he's going to do the same damn thing if he's not careful."

Rhodes had been moving fast at the bottom of his gun run, but Brown was setting himself up by going low and slow while searching for a signal from Hay Eater.

As Brown's Huey flew over the team, Hay Eater flashed his mirror.

"Claw, do you have the team?" Fat Capper asked.

"That's affirmative, Fat Capper. I understand they are in contact to the northwest. I'm going to make a few runs with the M-60s in close to the northwest. Let me know when Hay Eater is ready to move."

Having confirmed Brown had the team's position in sight, Fat Capper called back, "Hay Eater, Eagle Claw has your position and will be working to your northwest in close. I repeat . . . in close!"

Brown's crew and the Cobras fired their M-60 machine guns and mini-guns within thirty meters northwest of the team's smoke. The jungle was thick, and Hay Eater's smoke was their only reference. After two passes, Brown called the AO, "Fat Capper, this is Claw. Does he need any more ordinance?"

"That's a negative, Eagle Claw. He said the last looked real good. We need to do something real quick!" he added, again looking at his fuel gauge. "My fuel is a lot lower. I'm not going to be able to stay here much longer!"

Just as Brown finished, Hay Eater was back on Fox Mike. "I got people all around my position. We are receiving small arms fire. I need to get off this position soon. I do not want to stay here much longer!"

"Okay, Hay Eater, get moving. What's your heading now?"

"We are heading zero-three-zero."

"Roger, understand. Zero-three-zero."

Realizing he did not have enough time to pull out the team or the crew, Brown called again. "Fat Capper, can you get an observer over here to stay with them while we go back? We are going to have to refuel, reorganize our assets, and come back out here to get them."

"I'm tempted to go ahead and launch my assets out here," Fat Capper responded, knowing that calling a Prairie Fire emergency would give the aerial observer priority access to all aviation assets available in Vietnam.

Surveying the area, Brown saw a clearing about 500 meters from their position. Thinking it would be much easier to extract the team and crew from a cleared landing zone than it would be to lift them out of the jungle on a rope, he flew over to look. Having determined the zone would be suitable, he called Fat Capper, "Tell me something, Fat Capper. Is it possible to get the team to the open area down here? We could get someone in here to pull them."

Feeling the zone was too far through thick jungle, Fat Capper called back, "Okay. I do not know. He's moving up toward the chopper right now and if we can get everyone together, we will have it made."

Gnat Lead, still orbiting off to the west, checked his fuel and decided he had better let Brown know time was running out. "Claw Lead, this is Gnat. If you want to do anything, we had better do it within zero-five."

"I understand that. I don't think we'll be able to do anything right now."

"How long is it going to take to get you refueled and get back here?" Fat Capper asked monitoring the conversation.

"At least an hour and half," Brown replied.

"That's faster than I can get my assets out here."

"Okay. You keep someone overhead and I'm going to run off the rest of my ordinance, and we'll head back."

Covey did not want to waste any more time. He wanted Brown to get going so they could be back before the weather got any worse. Also, since it was late afternoon, he did not want the extraction package pulling them out in the dark. He called Brown, "Claw Two, why don't you head back now? Hay Eater seems to be okay. I'd like to get you guys on the road so we can get this thing finished." After a pause, Covey continued. "Hold on to your fire for a minute. I think the team is just getting up to the chopper."

Fat Capper had just heard from the team. He called Hay Eater, "Hay Eater, we are going to have to leave and come back to get you. Do you understand?"

Not believing what he just heard, Hay Eater replied, "Say again."

Fat Capper repeated himself, "I said we are going to have to leave and then come back. I'm going to leave a Nail over you. He's not familiar with the operation, so you are going to have to explain to him close. Do you understand?"

"Roger, Covey, I will brief him. Hay Eater out."

Another O-2 came upon the scene high above the action. "Covey, this is Nail. I'm overhead. Can you give me a brief?"

"Roger, Nail. We currently have an eight-man team on the ground in contact trying to get to a downed Huey, call sign 'Eagle Claw Lead.' Lead's wingman 'Eagle Claw Two' is currently running the guns. He is a single UH-1 gunship. We also have three Cobras, call sign 'Dragon Fly.' Three UH-1 slicks are holding to the west for the extraction. Their call sign is 'Gnat.' It looks like we are going to have to use McGuire rigs to get everyone out. The team has been in constant contact with the NVA and is now working their way over to the downed Huey. We have had no contact with anyone from the Huey. It appears that there are survivors. We have not had any contact with them. All aircraft are getting low on fuel, so you are going to have to keep things moving. Claw Two's Fox Mike is not working, and he has no contact with Hay Eater. You will need to be a relay between the two. We are just getting ready to send the package back to Quang Tri to re-arm and refuel. I'll need you to stay on station until I get back."

Having received the briefing he needed, Nail replied, "Okay, Covey, I understand. I've got it. Give me a call when you are inbound."

Covey acknowledged Nail as he headed back to Quang Tri for fuel.

After one more fuel status check with Dragon Fly and Gnat flight, Brown decided to head back. "Okay, Fly, get your Dragon Flies together and head out."

"Okay. I've got about 800 pounds. Gnat Lead, did you copy?"

"That's affirm. Heading back."

"Nail, this is Eagle Claw Two, we're heading on out."

As the flight started their departure turn, Rhodes heard noises and shooting off to his left.

"Eagle Claw," someone called.

"Up here," Rhodes responded.

"Hold your fire. We're coming in."

The aircrew heard noise on their left, very close to them. Again the voice said they were getting close. Rhodes heard them, but could not see them because of the thick underbrush. Suddenly, about ten feet in front of Rhodes, someone stood up. It was the RT Mississippi team leader, Staff Sergeant Nicholas "Nick" Manning. Manning made visual and verbal contact before disappearing into the jungle and returning with the rest of his team. Approaching the Eagle Claw perimeter, he saw the cache of ammo and weapons they had. He smiled.

Seeing Hartline was badly injured, Manning called Nail and informed him one aircrew member was badly wounded.

"Eagle Claw, this is Nail. I've just received word from Hay Eater. They have just reached the aircraft and told me that there is one badly wounded crewmember. I think you had better come back and get him. All survived on the chopper!"

"Roger that! Okay, flight, let's do a one-eighty and get this guy out."

Realizing immediate action was needed and that Nail was not in tune with the situation, Fat Capper decided he would stick around a bit longer. He made a call on Fox Mike, "Hay Eater, we are low on fuel and are coming back to get the wounded man out of there. I understand there is one wounded man from the chopper."

"That's affirmative."

Needing to know the Cobra's fuel situation, Brown called. "Alright, Dragon Fly, how much time can you give me?"

Checking his fuel gauge, Hartbarger saw he had about 750 pounds. He had over an hour before burnout. Considering the thirty-five to forty-minute return flight and needing a twenty-minute reserve, he had only ten to fifteen minutes on station. "I have all the time you need," he said, even though his time was limited.

"Okay, Capper, this is Eagle Claw. Are they going to need a sling?"

Fat Capper relayed the question.

"Okay, Hay Eater, this is Fat Capper. What are you going to need to get out of there? Do you need a sling? We are in a hurry." Not getting an answer, he asked again. "Do we need a sling? Come on, Hay Eater, talk to me! We gotta get in there now!" Hay Eater was busy talking to Rhodes on the ground. He did not answer this time either.

Out of nowhere Covey called on VHF. "Okay, Dragon Fly Lead, this is Covey. I'm going to try and form up the Gnats and take them home. Gnat Lead, where are you?"

Gnat Lead wondered where Covey had been for the last fifteen minutes. "I'm at Claw Two's six o'clock. We are going back in and try to get the wounded man out."

Covey acknowledged and got off the air.

Brown called the Huey slick lead.

"Okay, Gnat, it looks like we are going to try and get you in. Stand by." There was a pause. "Gnat, we're going to get a smoke and 'shiney' right now. Let's see if we can get in there and get them right now."

Brown started a low pass heading toward the crash site, leading Gnat in. Approaching the site, he made a call.

"Okay, Gnat, this is Eagle Claw. I'm right over the area now. See where the tree is split and the red flag? It's right off my nose. I'm getting close. Mark . . . mark . . . mark. It's pretty open. The crash cleared most of it down there."

The slick started his approach and spotted the pick-up zone as Brown marked it. "This is Gnat Lead. I'm on about a quarter-mile final at this time."

"Roger that. We'll cover you as best we can," Brown answered. "Dragon Fly Lead, this is Claw Two. We have everyone in a huddle down there. Let's hose down the area with mini-gun. My crew is working their '60s around the zone."

Byrd's two M-60s from his TAT-101 could be heard over the radios as he and the two gunners put a steady stream of fire in a 360-degree circle.

"Gnat, do you have the smoke?" Brown asked.

Before Gnat could answer, Brown took charge. "Dragon Fly, keep the daisy chain going here."

"Roger, I'm hosing down the left side."

Fat Capper was still talking to Hay Eater on Fox Mike. "Okay, Hay Eater, he's almost on your position. He's going to drop it right into you. Gnat Lead, do you have his smoke?"

"Roger, we have the smoke," he replied, as the Huey made its approach before coming to a hover just a few feet above the jungle canopy.

Hay Eater called on Fox Mike and started guiding him in. He could see the Huey high above him. The aircraft was being bounced around by the strong gusty winds. "Come about fifteen meters forward if you can and drop that thing down by the highest tree."

The Cobras were still working over the area. Having expended all his mini-gun, Hartbarger told his copilot to start using the 40 mm grenade launcher. After six shots the launcher was silent. "Did that thing quit?"

"I'm afraid it did."

"Shit," Hartbarger muttered. Dragon Fly Lead was now out of business for close-in air support.

Below, Gnat was fighting the elements. He was trying to get his helicopter into position and then hold it there. Hay Eater guided him over the radio. "Pull up! Pull up! Look out for the tree!" Hay

Eater shouted over the noise of the Huey, his voice tense. "Higher. Higher. Get altitude!" The Huey repositioned. Hay Eater's voice was calmer. "Okay, get it down right there. Do you see me?"

Holding his aircraft in position, Gnat Lead's crew chief lowered the McGuire rig slowly through the trees, watching that the rig did not get hung up.

Seeing the rig being lowered, Hay Eater called again, "Keep coming down! Down! Take up the slack. Take up slack! Hold it right there! Right there! Hold it! Hold it!"

Finally having positioned the aircraft, the remaining three crewmembers strapped Hartline to the McGuire rig. Hay Eater called Gnat, "Haul away! Haul away!"

After hearing the transmission, Fat Capper called Hay Eater. "I understand, . . . he's on?"

Ignoring Fat Capper's question, Hay Eater shouted over the radio, still talking to Gnat Lead, "Lift him up! Lift him up!"

Gnat Lead ascended vertically. Looking below the aircraft, the crew chief and gunner guided the pilot while keeping the rope and Hartline from becoming entangled in the trees. The rig finally cleared the trees.

"Gnat is coming out. I've got the man aboard. I'm coming out to the north."

"Okay," answered Fat Capper.

Then Brown's voice was heard, "Okay, Gnat, can you put him down at Shepherd and get him aboard so we can get him to a hospital today? Or do you think we will need to leave him where he is?"

"He's pretty bad off. I think for now we are going to have to leave him hanging where he is. I do not have the fuel to stop and transfer him. I definitely do not have enough fuel to make Quang Tri right now. I'm going to have to try for Shepherd."

Knowing he needed to make an important decision immediately, Brown searched for a refueling spot or, in the worst case, a secure landing spot.

Shepherd, a firebase located on top of a mountain forty-three kilometers southwest of Quang Tri, had a landing pad but no fuel. It would work as a place for Gnat to land and transfer Hartline to the Huey. He was dangling fifty feet below Gnat Lead.

With Hartline out, Brown called Nail and informed him he was heading for Shepherd. He asked Nail to arrange for a medivac helicopter to pick up Hartline.

Covey and Nail were about out of gas. They needed a replacement to stay with the downed crew and Hay Eater. In an effort to coordinate, Nail called Covey, "Covey, this is Nail. I am going to stay here and mark the position. Get another Nail over here and then head home."

"Okay, I'm out of gas myself. I'm with the choppers at this time. I'm trying to get hold of Sampson to get a Kingbee out here to pick up the other wounded man."

"Okay. Fine. I'll go up. Thank everybody there. I'll see you all over at Quang Tri."

Covey, flying well above the helicopters, was still worried about fuel. He called Brown again, "Claw Two, this is Covey. How's your fuel situation?"

"I've got about four hundred pounds." The pucker factor was rising.

"I'm above you right now, moving to your twelve o'clock. I'm almost out of fuel also. I'll stay with you as long as I can."

Brown, knowing Covey would be leaving the flight shortly, called back, "I want to thank everybody for their cooperation. You did an outstanding job. We are going to try and get everybody else out."

"Roger that, partner."

Wondering how they were going to get the crew and team out after refueling, Brown had real concern about his Fox Mike not working. "Covey, I don't know how we are going to do this. My Fox Mike still is not working right. The only way I could read them is when I was ten feet over them. This has really fucked up my whole day."

Covey acknowledged his concern, "Next time I'll relay everything they say to you over Uniform. You just forget about the Fox Mike. Okay?"

"Yeah. Okay. That will be good enough. Let's go back, reorganize, re-brief, and see what the hell we are going to do after we refuel and come back."

Covey descended and flew adjacent to the gunship. "Okay. Do you have me in sight? I'm off to your left side."

Looking out the left door window, Byrd gave Brown a thumbs up.

"That's affirm," Brown replied.

As Covey moved ahead of the flight, he became concerned about navigation. The helicopters were too far out in the boonies to receive any navigational aid. Also, they were well south of their normal work area and were not familiar with the terrain and enemy anti-aircraft plots. The jungle did not provide many reference points and visibility was only a few kilometers. At best, navigation would be difficult.

Seeing if he could be of any help before leaving, Covey called Claw one last time, "Claw Two, where are you going now? Are you going to hit the river or are you going straight back? Do you know where you are?"

Not hearing the whole transmission, Brown answered, "Say again."

Meanwhile, Byrd was on the maps, scrambling to get a good fix on their location.

Sensing that Brown was having a problem, Covey called again, "Do you know how to get back now?"

"Go ahead and help me if possible, I haven't been here in several months."

"Go north to northwest and pick up the river. You should be okay then."

Brown was having doubts if he could make it back to Quang Tri. "Roger. Can you get in touch with Sampson and see if they can get hold of Phu Bai and get two more Eagle Claws up here?" Hesitantly, he continued. "I may not. I don't know . . . I may have to put my bird down somewhere. I may not be able to make it to Quang Tri. They'll have to get somebody launched up here real quick. We can use all the help we can get."

"Roger. I will as soon as I get in radio range. How many people did Gnat pick up?" Covey asked.

"He only picked up one, the badly wounded man. And the other three are okay. I do not know if the one we have is the pilot, copilot, or who."

"Hey, I got the river at my twelve o'clock. Do you have it?" Covey interrupted.

"Aaah . . . Roger," Brown said as he searched the terrain ahead looking for the river. Byrd had it in sight and gave Brown another thumbs up. Brown did not see his signal.

"I've got it," Byrd said as he pointed to the winding river now coming into sight.

"I've got it in sight, Covey. Thanks for the help," Brown replied.

"Claw Two, I'm going to leave you now. I'm going to climb up and see if I can't get commo with Sampson. Keep moving on up this valley. Get on the river and go north until you can find an area you are familiar with, then head back to Quang Tri. I'll be calling you back in a minute. I'm going to want to know what happened to Gnat Lead."

Dragon Fly Two's pilot had a thought. He vaguely remembered refueling once at Mai Loc, a firebase twenty-five kilometers west of Quang Tri. If it had fuel, it would shorten their flight considerably. After discussing it with his copilot, they decided to give Mai Loc a call and ask if fuel was available.

Scrambling through their unit frequencies, they found a Victor frequency.

"Mai Loc Fox Trot, this is Dragon Fly Two on Victor. Over."

"Go ahead, Dragon Fly. This is Fox Trot. Over."

"Roger. Does Mai Loc still have JP-4?"

"That's affirmative. We sure do."

Without acknowledging Fox Trot, he called on Uniform, "Gnat Lead, this is Dragon Fly Two."

"Two, go ahead."

"Mai Loc has JP-4," Dragon Fly Two answered. Relief was evident in his voice.

Without hesitation, Gnat responded, "Roger, that's where we will go then. We should not have a problem getting there."

The flight coordinated, and all the helicopters elected to refuel at Mai Loc. They could re-brief and re-arm there and coordinate with Covey.

As they approached Mai Loc, the twenty-minute fuel light was flickering on most of the aircraft. Brown had the Fire Base in sight and gave the Cobra a call. "Dragon Fly Lead, I have Mai Loc at my twelve o'clock. I'm not familiar as to where the fuel pits are. Have you been in here before?"

"That's affirmative, Claw. Join up on me. The refueling point is not manned, and we will only take two at a time, so it's going to take us a while."

"Roger," Brown answered. "We'd better hot refuel and shut down off to the side after fueling so we can talk over how we are going to do the next extract. Did you get hold of the extra two Cobras?"

"That's affirm. They are on their way over here and will go out with us."

"Great!" Brown joined the Cobra flight and could see a bare spot ahead. It was Mai Loc. The fire base was the highest peak in the area of rolling hills covered with dense vegetation. The fire base looked like it would barely have room for the flight. It would be tight, but it would have to do.

Gnat Lead was the first to land. As the aircraft came to a high stabilized hover on the tarmac, Hartline, still dangling below on the McGuire rig, was lowered carefully. Medical personnel unstrapped him and carefully moved him off to the side allowing Gnat Lead to land and pick up the McGuire rig.

The rest of the flight landed, refueled and shut down. The extra Cobras arrived and shut down with the flight. Medical personnel on the pad provided assistance to Hartline who had a punctured lung. An RVN Kingbee arrived shortly thereafter and took Hartline to a field hospital at Quang Tri, a twenty-minute flight. As Brown briefed the crews on the extraction of Hay Eater and the rest of the aircrew, the ominous clouds to the west interrupted their concentration. The weather was not getting any better. Their enthusiasm was diminishing as the brief progressed.

The briefing completed, all crews manned their aircraft. Heading west, Brown was the first to lift off. The Gnats followed, with the Cobras being the last to lift off.

Time and weather were not on their side. It was late afternoon. They had to keep moving if they were going to get the team and crew out.

Limited by the ceilings, the flight stayed low. Brown called Nail. "Nail, this is Claw Two. We are back outbound. Our ETE [estimated time enroute] over the zone should be in twenty-five minutes."

"Roger, Eagle Claw. I haven't heard from Covey yet. I still have sixty minutes on station, so we shouldn't have a problem. Hay Eater has not taken fire since your departure. The weather has not improved. The winds are getting stronger, and Gnat may have some problems hovering over the zone."

Not overly excited about the weather report, Brown answered, "Roger. We will see you shortly. Out."

The flight flew a tight formation. Each section kept the other sections in sight. Byrd was on the maps. As the primary navigator, he was responsible to get the flight back to the crash site. The maps were his only navigation tools as they flew through valleys with adjacent dense jungle-covered peaks. The visibility was still only one or two kilometers at best. The jungle was losing its lustrous green coloring, giving way to a darker green coloration with only a sliver of light coming through the thick overcast.

As the flight crossed the Laotian border and headed south, the winds picked up and the clouds grew thicker. The radios were quiet. Each crewmember was deep in thought as they once again headed into bad-man territory. Byrd was doing an excellent job keeping the flight away from the anti-aircraft plots. Once in Laos, their route took them almost exactly over their first one.

Approaching the crash site, Brown called the O-2 on station and informed him they were north to northwest of the crash site. He asked if they were in sight.

Seeing the flight of helicopters, the replacement O-2 answered, "That's affirmative, Eagle Claw. I have you in sight. I'm at your two o'clock, about two klicks. With this low ceiling, I'll move around to the north and hold. That should keep me out of your way. I will relay all Hay Eater transmissions to you."

Brown, who still had no communications on Fox Mike, replied, "Sounds good. Have Hay Eater give me a smoke, and I'll bring Gnat in."

Without pausing, Brown called Gnat, "Gnat, Claw Two, I'm going to go ahead and locate the team. I'll give you a mark on it and then move off to the west to get out of your way."

Nail relayed the information to Hay Eater. "Hay Eater, Eagle Claw is coming in to mark your position for the Gnats. Pop a smoke. If you take any ground fire, let us know right away."

"Roger, I copy."

Brown started making his low pass to what he thought was the crash site. He and Byrd searched for the dead tree but could not find it.

Hay Eater called Nail, "I hear them, but I don't see them."

Nail, confident that Brown had a good heading, called, "Claw, you are looking good. Keep heading up that ridge toward that big field. Hay Eater, give another smoke. Give me another smoke!"

Not seeing one, Nail became extremely frustrated. "Pop another smoke!" he shouted.

"I can give him a flare. How about that? I'm out of smoke."

"Okay."

Because of the triple canopy, everything looked the same. Brown and Byrd were having trouble finding a reference point. Just as Brown was coming up to where he thought the zone was, he called, "Nail, isn't this big brown spot where they blew out of here?"

"He just gave you a flare. Do you see it?"

Looking ahead and a little higher, Brown spotted the small red flare. "Roger, I've got a ground flare."

Nail called back, "That's all he has left. Little smokes and flares."

Brown started a right hand turn to come around again. "Okay, we are going to go into orbit here." As his turn came toward the pick up zone, he called, "Okay, Nail. Have him pop another one."

"Okay."

Brown flew low over the zone searching for a flare or smoke. He saw nothing but jungle.

Nail was talking. "Hay Eater, give a mark . . . mark on Eagle Claw when he passes over." There was no answer. Again, he called. "Hay Eater…did you copy? Give him a mark. Give him a flare."

Brown flew over what he thought was the zone.

"It looks like I'm right over them now. I'm going to swing around again. Don't have them give me a flare until I get around and will be able to see it."

"Too late, Claw. He just fired one," Nail replied.

Nail immediately called Hay Eater. "Hay Eater, this is Nail. Claw just went over your position. Is he over you now?"

"He is to our Sierra."

Nail could see the Huey making a turn to bring it around into a heading for the zone. He was right over the trees searching for the flare.

"Okay, Hay Eater. He's coming back around now. Go ahead and pop another right now."

Orbiting off to the south, Fly Lead could see smoke coming up through the jungle and called, "Claw, this is Fly Lead. You just flew over his position."

"Hmmm . . . wait one," Brown said as he and his crew continued to search for the smoke.

"If you can get to where you can see me, I'll give you a mark."

Brown completed another orbit and was headed back toward what he thought was the zone when he saw the Cobra making a low pass. Before Fly could call a mark, Byrd spotted the smoke and pointed. Seeing it, Brown called Fly, "Okay, I've got the smoke. I've got it. I see the opening."

"Okay, I'm going to move out of your way, Eagle Claw. You've got it!"

Wanting to get the people out as soon as he could, Brown called Gnat. "Okay, Gnat Lead, this is Eagle Claw. The zone is right under the Cobra."

Gnat replied that he had the zone in sight and started his approach.

Brown called back, "Gnat, you are at my eleven o'clock. Follow me in. Fly, you pick up his six, and I'll mark the zone for you. I'm in a left-hand turn here at your nine o'clock."

Wanting to stay out of the way, Nail called and told Brown he was going to stay off to the west and watch the road.

As Brown led Gnat to the zone and was ready to pull out, he called Fly, "Okay, Fly, pick up Gnat. Mark . . . mark . . . mark," he said as he flew over the downed aircraft.

"I think I have it," Fly Lead responded, coming in behind Gnat. His weapons system hot, he was ready to provide gun cover if Gnat took fire.

Low over the zone, Brown began his pull-up. As the aircraft gained altitude, one of the gunners, seeing muzzle flashes below, called, "Taking fire!"

"We have some fire coming out of there," Brown radioed.

Immediately, Nail called Hay Eater, "Hay Eater, you taking fire?"

"That's a negative, Nail."

"Claw, There's negative fire. . . ."

Brown did not answer.

As Gnat Two came to a hover above the triple canopy, Hay Eater could see he was short of his position and called, "Okay, Gnat, do you have us in sight? Slide forward . . . slide forward."

Fighting the gusty winds, Gnat hovered slowly forward. Hay Eater could see he was heading for a collision with a tall tree. "Look out for that tree! Look out for that tree!" he shouted.

The Huey crew had the tree in sight. Maneuvering around it, they positioned the helicopter directly above the team. Hay Eater saw the helicopter above him fighting to maintain a stable hover. "Drop the rope. Let them out slowly so we can get them down here."

In the Huey, the crew chief and gunner began dropping the ropes down through the trees. The winds were still making it extremely difficult for the Huey to maintain a steady hover.

After several minutes of Hay Eater shouting commands, Gnat One, frustrated, but calm, called him, "This is Gnat One. Let me pull the rope. Get over your position and drop it again."

"Move over to your left and slightly to your rear," Hay Eater replied.

Searching for a fix for their problem, Hay Eater activated his strobe light on the ground and told Gnat to drop it on the strobe.

The Huey pilot, guided by his crew chief, positioned the aircraft overhead and again dropped the rope. The rope landed on a branch and got hung up. Hay Eater was really frustrated now. "That fucking thing is stuck in a tree. You are right over a tree. Pull the rope and move to your right. There is a gap in the trees. You just need to drop them right in."

The Huey moved to the right.

"Drop them down. Stay right there. Do not move . . . do not move. Drop them . . . drop them."

About the time the ropes were being dropped, Brown, with no communication, was wondering what was taking so long. "Nail, this is Claw. How's it going down there?"

"They've been having trouble getting the ropes down through the trees."

Nail, hearing on Fox Mike that things were finally working on the ground, called Brown, "Gnat has positioned the ropes right over the zone. It sounds like they have them down now. Eagle Claw, if you can get Gnat Two headed in and closer it might make it quicker. It's starting to get pretty dark."

"Roger, Nail," Brown replied. "Gnat Two, do you want to head on in here and take a look at the area? Gnat Lead seems to have a little trouble getting the ropes down through the trees."

Gnat Two acknowledged and headed toward the zone.

Brown could see that Gnat Two was headed in.

"Nail, Gnat is headed inbound."

"Roger, Eagle Claw."

Gnat Lead finally found a reference point and established a steady hover above the jungle canopy. Three ropes were dropped. The remaining three aircrew were being attached to the McGuire rigs. Once all were attached, Hay Eater called, "Okay, Gnat. They're hooked up. Start picking up."

The Huey started gaining altitude. The pilot carefully held his position as he ascended with the three crew members dangling fifty feet below the aircraft. The last thing he wanted to do was to drift and drag the crew through the trees. Hay Eater was talking to him. "Slowly . . . slowly. Pick them up . . . slowly. Get 'em out of here . . . forward . . . forward."

As the ropes cleared the trees, Hay Eater, exhausted, sighed with relief. "Take 'em away . . . get 'em out of here. Next ship . . . next ship."

Gnat Two, having a good position fix, watched Gnat Lead hover and pull out and set up his approach for the pick-up zone.

Gnat Lead called out when he was clear, "Okay, Eagle Claw, Lead is out with three."

About the time Gnat Two came to a hover, Hay Eater called on radio, "Next ship . . . bring it in."

"Okay, bring it forward . . . forward," Hay Eater said with Gnat Two established in his hover over the zone. "Okay, drop your ropes. Okay, drop your ropes; ease them on down," he continued seeing that the Huey was doing a great job getting into position.

With the ropes clear of the trees, Hay Eater shouted over the radio, "Let 'em go . . . let 'em down. You're perfect, baby. Stay right there."

Gnat Two dropped the ropes. As the three team members got hooked up to the ropes, the Huey maintained a good steady hover. After receiving the signal from Hay Eater, Gnat Two started a vertical climb, maintaining position to get the ropes and three team members clear of the jungle.

As the aircraft cleared the trees and began climbing, Gnat Two called on Victor, "Receiving fire . . . twelve o'clock . . . on the ridgeline!"

Brown swung his Huey to the right rear of Gnat and told Byrd to make him hot. He ordered the door gunners to work over the ridgeline. As soon as Gnat cleared to the left, the Cobras, following Brown, worked it over with mini-guns after Brown pulled out.

Gnat Three had just started his approach to pick up three more of the team when Nail called, "Gnat Three, Hay Eater wants you to pull out of there. He says he will see you tomorrow."

Brown heard only Nail's transmission. "Is the team out?" Brown asked.

"I just got overhead, and they told me to bug off," Gnat Three answered. "They are in heavy contact and said I was getting shot at and told me to get the hell out, so I pulled out. If you want me to go back in, I will. But make sure you give me some good cover. The fire is right in the LZ."

"Roger, just wait one." Unable to hear the whole story, Brown was confused.

Nail had heard the transmissions, but did not understand. He called Eagle Claw, "Claw this is Nail. Do you understand what they want us to do?"

"Okay, the bird went in, and Hay Eater told him to leave." Claw answered. "Do they want him to go back in?"

"Let me check. Hay Eater, this is Nail. Do you want the next bird to come in?" The team, in heavy contact, did not answer. Nail called again, "Hay Eater, talk to me. Do you want another aircraft to come in?"

Finally, Hay Eater answered, "That's a negative, Nail. Things are getting too hot down here. We are on the move. Come back in the morning."

Not questioning Hay Eater's decision, Nail called back, "Roger, Hay Eater. We will be back as soon as the old sun comes up."

"Eagle Claw, Hay Eater wants us to come back in the morning. They are on the move."

Brown agreed with the decision. "Okay, Nail, I understand. I think it's better overall. It's getting too dark out here . . . too dark to make things work right."

"Is there any altitude you want to go back at?" Covey asked.

"I would like to stay out of the clouds if at all possible."

"Okay."

Dragon Fly, looking at his flight of five Cobras, instructed them on what to do if the flight went inadvertent IFR (instrument flight rules).

"Okay, everyone. Hang in together. Tune 1300 on the ADF. If you go IFR, climb to eight thousand feet and follow Nail."

Other than fighting the weather, the flight home was uneventful. The flight landed at Shepherd and put their PAX in the cabin before returning to MLT3 near Dong Ha.

The remainder of RT Mississippi was extracted the following day without incident. I visited with Hartline after he was transferred to the army hospital near Phu Bai. Shortly thereafter, he was medivacked to Japan.

X

Hostage Papa

"HOSTAGE PAPA, HOSTAGE PAPA, this is Beechnut Four. Over," came the call over Fox Mike.

A marine platoon in the southern Que Son Mountains was in trouble. They were under fire and had wounded. A flight of two AH-1 Cobras and two CH-46 Sea Knights was inbound to medivac the wounded marines. The flight leader was Major Howard Henry, the executive officer of VMO-2. His call sign was "Hostage Papa." 1Lt Joseph Lofton was the copilot. Henry's wingman was 1Lt Patrick "Pat" Dumas. 1Lt Deane Swickard was Dumas's copilot.

Henry answered the call from Beechnut Four informing the unit he would be on station in ten minutes. Beechnut Four immediately returned the call. He informed Papa he had one wounded and one Killed in Action. They were pinned down and taking fire from the west.

Needing more information, Henry called back to ask what type of fire was being taken, its location from their position, and how heavy it was. Beechnut Four replied that they were pinned down by a .50 caliber machine gun located to the west. He thought the gun was on a ridge about 300 meters above them. He emphasized the need to get the badly bleeding marine out. As the flight got closer, Henry called again. He gave his location and asked for a zone brief.

Beechnut Four began his brief. They were taking fire from the west. He was sure it was .50 cal. It would have to be taken out before a medivac aircraft could land. Beechnut Four emphasized they could not leave their present position.

Hearing about the .50 cal, Henry needed to come up with a plan. He called Beechnut Four again and told him to stand by. Calling the lead CH-46, Henry told him about the fire and instructed him to orbit his flight at their present location. He would see what they could do. CH-46 Lead called back informing Papa they would be standing by. There was a sense of relief in his voice. He was not in a hurry to go into a hot .50 cal zone.

Wanting to confirm the location of the team and the machine gun, Henry called Beechnut Four again. To confirm the unit's location, he asked him to give him a "mark" as he passed over the unit. Spotting the Cobra, Beechnut Four called and told Henry he had the Cobra in sight. As he passed over his position, Beechnut Four called, "Mark, mark."

Henry had a good fix on them, but still needed a fix on the machine gun. He called again and asked where the fire was coming from. Beechnut Four indicated that it was to the west about 300 meters up the ridge. Henry turned his Cobra westbound and descended. As he approached the ridgeline, Beechnut Four called, "Hostage, you are taking fire!"

Dumas, behind Henry, informed him he had the target in sight. It was located in a cave fifty meters down from the top of the ridge. Henry confirmed the target and fired several rockets. It looked like they were right on the mark, but Henry was not convinced the target had been destroyed. He called Dumas and told him they had better make another run. Dumas rolled in. Swickard was firing 40 mm grenades from the turret grenade launcher. As it too often did, the turret jammed up when it was needed.

"My guns are stuck," Swickard said over the intercom.

Henry rolled in with his second run, firing rockets as he went. "That should do it" he said not seeing any activity from the .50 cal on the pass.

Instructing Dumas to stay were he was, he went in to take a closer look. Putting his Cobra into a steep dive, Henry made a low high speed pass by the cave. He said he still did not see anything, but was going to take another look. This time he slowed down and went even lower.

"God, he's going to fly right over it," Swickard said to Dumas.

Right about the time the words came out of his mouth, Swickard saw flashes from the big gun's muzzle. Small pieces of the Cobra were flying from the airframe.

"I'm hit and going down," Henry called as he pointed his aircraft towards an arca to the east where the slope was not too bad.

The area was on the backside of a ridge clear of the .50 cal fire. As Henry was going down, Swickard could see a red glow emanating from the engine section of the Cobra. Dumas and Swickard watched from above as Henry made his approach. Shortly before the Cobra landed, Swickard heard Henry's voice over the radios. "It's hot."

The Cobra landed upright. With the exception of smoke coming from the fuselage, the aircraft appeared intact. The blades were still turning.

Wanting to get the crew out, Dumas called and told Chatterbox what had just happened. He needed them to get an aircraft there immediately. Still concerned about the .50 cal, the CH-46 lead asked where it was in relation to the downed aircraft. Dumas informed him he would be clear of it as long as he stayed east of the ridge. Lead called that he was inbound.

Dumas was very busy. He needed to get the CH-46 in for a pick up of the Cobra crew. He also needed more assets to deal with the medivac and .50 cal. He called the CH-46 lead and asked his wingman to call Da Nang DASC and inform them of the situation. They needed to ask for another set of Cobras and an OV-10 to take care of the .50 cal.

Dumas made a slow low pass over the landing site. The Cobra was on fire. Smoke billowed from the downed aircraft. Unable to see either of the crew members, he asked Swickard if he could see anything.

"No," Swickard replied. He thought they must have gotten out. Getting closer, the CH-46 called for a briefing on the zone. His concern was the possibility of enemy activity near the aircraft. Dumas answered that it looked clear. He could not see any enemy activity, but the zone was on a pretty good slope. Once overhead, the CH-46 called Dumas and told him he was ready to go in. Dumas informed him that his guns were jammed, and he could only give

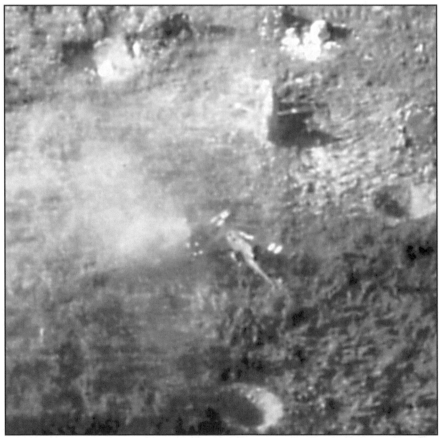

Major Henry's Cobra on the ground burning while a Cobra is passing low overhead. The CH-46 on the ground is the medivac bird retrieving the bodies
Photo by 1Lt Deane Swickard.

him rocket cover. Lead replied that two Cobras were inbound from the east. They had heard about the problem and were coming to assist.

The CH-46 started a spiral into the zone. Once in the zone, he had to hover while searching for a flat spot.

1Lt Michael "Mike" Bartlett, the flight leader of the incoming Cobras, coordinated with Dumas and assumed responsibility of gun cover for the mission.

Lead landed, and a crew chief and medic departed out the back of the '46 and ran over to the burning Cobra. The flight crew was not in the aircraft. After a short search of the area, they found them.

Looking down through the smoke from the burning Cobra, Swickard could see that they had found the pilots. They appeared to be hurt and were being carried to the medivac aircraft. Once aboard, the CH-46 lifted out of the zone.

En route Dumas received word that both Henry and Lofton were dead. Apparently Lofton had been hurt and Henry was helping him get away from the burning aircraft when a blade, still turning, struck both men on the head, killing them instantly. The flight back to Marble Mountain was quiet. The CH-46 dropped off the bodies at the field hospital near Marble Mountain.

XI
Going South

IN LATE SEPTEMBER, I was scheduled with Major Hornsby for medivac standby supporting the 1st Marine Division at An Hoa combat base about thirty-five kilometers southwest of Da Nang. Our squadron's primary working area was north, and we did not get south often. This was going to be my second trip south and Hornsby's first. I sensed he was somewhat uptight about the mission. I was hoping it was not because he still was in the mood to do me bodily harm for my wake-up escapade the previous week. More than likely, though, it was because he was not familiar with the area or the contacts for required artillery clearances.

Our launch had an 0600 takeoff. We were the lead gunship for a flight of two. Our mission was to go to Marble Mountain, refuel, and join up with two CH-46s from HMM-364. Known as the Purple Foxes, their squadron call-sign was "Swift."

After refueling at Marble Mountain, we joined up with our two CH-46 Sea Knight medivac helicopters and proceeded to An Hoa, about a twenty-five minute flight. The terrain just south of Da Nang along the coast and inland for about thirty kilometers was flat. Rice paddies covered most of the flatland. Mountainous terrain lay to the west. South of An Hoa, the Que Son Mountains which served as a major supply route for the North Vietnamese extended cast-west. They were the site of many fierce battles between the U.S. Marines and the NVA.

At An Hoa we "topped off" and repositioned to the stand-by shack on the end of the tarmac. After settling in, we sat back and relaxed. By noon the stand-by excitement had turned into sheer boredom. Around 1400 hours, after playing what seemed like our fifteenth game of Acey-Deucy, a call came over our FM radio, "Medivac, medivac, this is Da Nang DASC. I have an emergency medivac. Are you ready to copy? Over."

Repositioning next to the radio with his kneeboard and pencil, Hornsby answered, "Roger, DASC. I'm ready to copy. Over."

We received a mission to evacuate a marine who had been severely injured by a booby trap in the Que Sons. Hornsby copied the coordinates and other pertinent information before heading for the aircraft. I had already strapped in and was going through the starting checklist. By the time the Swift lead pilot got to his aircraft, his copilot had started it and was ready to go. Hornsby passed the coordinates to the rest of the flight and called for a priority taxi and take-off. The weather was cloudy. The top half of the mountains was in the clouds. Ceilings were low. This mission was going to be interesting.

Enroute Hornsby called the unit, "Whiskey Lima Three Four. This is Scarface Lead. We are inbound. How about a zone brief? Over."

Lima Three Four had been waiting for the call. He answered immediately, "Roger, Scarface. We have an emergency medivac. He stepped on a land mine, and his legs are in bad shape. He is bleeding real bad, and we need to get him to a field hospital ASAP. Over."

"Roger, Whiskey Lima. What's your situation? I need a zone brief. Over."

"Roger, Scarface. We have a small zone. There are no obstructions in the zone, but we have trees on all sides. There is rising terrain to the south. We have not taken any fire today. If you were to take fire, it would probably be from the rising terrain to the south. Over."

Concerned, Hornsby said, "It looks like you are in the clouds. What does the weather look like where you are? Over."

"It's foggy here, but you gotta get in here. If you do not, this guy is going to die. Over." His voice indicated the need for immediate action.

From the map we could see the LZ was in the mountains on the side of a hill near the end of a long narrow valley. Maneuvering would be tricky. Looking toward the LZ as we approached the valley, we could see that visibility was down significantly in the mountains.

Hornsby called Swift Lead, "Swift Lead, this is Scarface Lead. The visibility is looking sort of skosh. You had better leave your playmate [wingman] out here and follow us in. Over."

"Roger, Scarface. Will do. It sure does not look good in there," Swift Lead responded.

We entered the valley with Swift Lead following. The visibility went down to less than one-half kilometer almost immediately. The pucker factor was increasing. Hornsby slowed down and followed the side of valley. I worked the maps trying to see enough terrain to navigate and to get to the landing zone. About five minutes into the valley, the visibility went down even more.

"Swift Lead, I can't see anything. Let's go back out and regroup," Hornsby said.

Listening from the landing zone, Whiskey Lima called, "Scarface, this is Whiskey Lima. How are you doing? I don't hear you yet. Over. We need to get this guy out of here soon. Over."

"Roger, Whiskey Lima. We are having a problem getting to your poz. The weather is really down between us, so stand by while we try to find a better route in. Over."

"Roger, Scarface," Whiskey Lima replied.

"We'll give it another try in a bit. Over."

Deciding we had a real need to get this marine out, Hornsby made the decision to try again. He called Swift Lead, "Let's give it another try. Over."

"Roger, Scarface, but it does not look any better to me. Over." Swift Lead replied.

Our flight headed into the valley for the second time. When we were about as far as we had gotten the first time, we were forced out of the valley because of low visibility. Hoping the weather would give us a break, we orbited the valley for about twenty minutes.

"Swift Lead, this is Scarface. You wait here. I'm going in alone to see if I can find the LZ," Hornsby told the flight.

"Roger, Scarface, I've got about fifty minutes to bingo fuel. Over."

Hornsby told our wingman to stay with the Swift flight, and we headed into the valley. Going low and slow, we were an easy target for any gooner with a sling shot. Hornsby told the crew chief and gunner to be "on their toes."

As we crept up the valley, I recognized terrain I could follow on the map.

Establishing contact again, Hornsby called, "Whiskey Lima, this is Scarface. I'm going to try again to see if I can find a route for the Medivac. Over."

"Roger, Scarface. Our man is really in bad shape. I hope you make it here soon."

"Roger, Whiskey Lima. Let me know if you can hear me coming. Over."

"Roger, Scarface. I do not hear you yet. Over." It seemed like forever before we heard him come up on the radio. "Scarface, I hear you coming. You are at my twelve o'clock. Over."

"Roger, Whiskey Lima. That doesn't help us much as I don't know which way you are facing. What direction are we from you?"

"You are to the west of me. Over," he responded after a short hesitation.

Hornsby perked up. "Is the sound getting any louder? Over."

"That's affirmative, Scarface. I think you are almost here . . . you're getting real loud now. I have you in sight! I am at your one o'clock. Over."

As we moved ahead, I spotted the platoon on the edge of a small clearing.

"I've got them, sir. They're right at two o'clock. We are almost on top of them."

"Okay, Whiskey Lima. We got you. I'm going back out to get the medivac bird, I'll be back in about fifteen minutes. Over."

"Roger, Scarface."

Hornsby made another call. "Swift Lead, this is Scarface, I'm coming back out. Be ready to head on in when I get to you. You'd better plan on leaving your wingman out on the flats. There just is not enough room for all of us in there. The zone looks tight but you should be able to get in. We didn't take any fire on the way in or out. Keep your eyes open as the terrain is high on both sides."

As our Huey neared the valley entrance, Hornsby called, "Okay, Swift, I'm just coming out of the valley. Have you got me in sight?"

Seeing our Huey, Swift Lead replied, "That's affirm, Scarface. I've got you."

"Roger. Join up on me, we are going for a ride," Hornsby said. "Tell our wingman to stay out there," he continued.

"Roger, Five."

As we headed got closer to the pick-up zone, Hornsby made a call, "Whiskey Lima, this is Scarface Five. We're on our way. Pop a smoke. Over."

"Roger, Scarface. Smoke popped."

Hornsby spotted the smoke. "Okay, I have a green smoke. Over."

Hearing that we had identified the smoke, Whiskey Lima verified the color for us. "Roger, Scarface. Green smoke."

The wind was relatively calm. The CH-46 had no trouble getting into the zone. The wounded marine was hustled aboard, the CH-46 joined up on us, and we headed out.

"Thanks, Scarface. I don't think our man would have made it much longer. Thank Swift for us."

"I sure will. Talk to you later. Out."

We came out of the valley, and our wingman and Swift Two joined up. We had just enough fuel to get back to An Hoa. After escorting the medivac birds to the evac hospital, we refueled and settled in at the medivac shack.

The rest of the day was uneventful. Our replacement crew showed up shortly after shut-down at An Hoa.

Returning to our aircraft, we strapped in. Hornsby ran through a quick check list and started the aircraft. As he reached up and hit the inverter switch, the two M-60 machine guns in our TAT-101 fired about twenty rounds into a berm in front of the aircraft. I looked around. Everywhere, marines were jumping for cover.

"What did you just do?" Hornsby asked looking at me.

"I didn't do it," I said, shrugging my shoulders.

We checked the systems. The turret control was in place. Everything looked normal. The armament control system showed all guns and rockets were cold. We figured we had better get the hell out of there before some "heavy" decided to be a prick about things.

Approaching Marble Mountain we decided we might as well stop and eat. Marble Mountain had an Officers' Club with the Officers' Mess attached. The food was great. We could not pass up the chance. Phu Bai Officers' Mess had the worst chow in the Marine Corps. Usually the "mystery food" was so bad I wished I had c-rations.

By the time we finished pigging out, the weather had really turned bad with low ceilings, rain, and restricted visibility. To make matters worse, it was pitch black outside. The weather report indicated we would break out into the clear just past the Hai Van Pass north of Da Nang. Hornsby decided it would safer to go north over the water until we broke out. Going over the water would keep us clear of the mountain. Hornsby passed the lead to our wingman. He told him he would fly a tight formation on him if we went IFR. Taking off from Marble Mountain, we turned left putting us over the water. We were in total darkness. I could not see anything. Our lead informed us he was on instruments. We went up departure control to see if we could get on radar.

Hornsby was not kidding when he said he would fly a tight formation. I was thankful I was with a former jet jockey who had experience flying formation at night. Flying formation can be tricky business. Depth perception at night was difficult for me. Hornsby tucked our UH-1 in so close to our lead I thought our blades were overlapping. In the total darkness with absolutely no visibility, Hornsby flew on our lead's position lights.

We got up Da Nang departure and got on their radar. We received clearance and radar vectors out of the area. As predicted, sweaty hands and all, we popped out of the soup about twenty kilometers north. Hornsby did a great job that day. Bone tired, we all slept well that night knowing we had played a part in saving a marine's life.

XII

Collateral Duties

THE NAVAL AVIATOR HAS ONE THING IN MIND when he goes to work. Flying! If he cannot fly he would just as soon not go to work, but squadrons do not operate on flying alone. Someone has to perform collateral duties such as administration (S-1), supply (S-4), intelligence (S-2), operations (S-3) and aviation maintenance. Some areas had specialists who performed these duties, but most were run by aviators. Collateral duties were accomplished after the flying day was finished.

The commanding officer of a squadron was a lieutenant colonel; the executive officer, operations officer, and maintenance officers were usually majors. Along with the Skipper, the squadron had four to six majors and one or two captains. The remaining officers were lieutenants with the exception of one or two non-flying warrant officers. All but a couple of these officers were aviators who preferred to be flying rather than doing squadron duties. In the military, as with most large organizations, the stinky stuff "falls down hill." Guess who's at the bottom of the hill. The lieutenants!

One day, John O'Meara was walking out of the XO's office when he spotted me.

"Robby, the XO just informed me that you are my helper. I'm the Awards Officer."

"What? Just what is an awards officer?" I asked.

"Piece of cake," he replied. "We take the award write-ups, rewrite them, throw in a few fancy words ensuring everyone is a hero, and then send them to headquarters for the awards board for approval."

127

When the first few awards came in, I tackled the job with the enthusiasm of a young marine literary whiz, but I lacked the imagination required to conjure up phrases such as "He attacked the enemy phalanges with total disregard for his own safety." It did not take the S-1 long to make the decision that I might be more comfortable in some other arena. I was assigned as the Special Services Officer. Now, this was more up my alley. My special services job was to take care of the entertainment and welfare of the troops. To fulfill that role I had to see that they had equipment for sports, games to play, and something to do during their time off.

After about a month I found it was a great job. After my day job, I would go to the Group Special Services office to learn what was new and available in games and sporting equipment. I would then take them back to the squadron and spread them around. It made the troops happy, and it certainly was easier than trying to create war heroes on paper.

Apparently I did a good job. Shortly after negotiating the trade of a piano for a squadron sailboat, I found myself the new Group Special Services Officer. Group was short for Marine Air Group which was typically the headquarters for about seven squadrons.

I belonged to the squadron full time, and my role in special services was part time. I had a full time NCO who took care of the day to day operations. As before, I would normally go to my office after flying. The biggest problem my NCO had was in finding new movies. Both the NCO club and Officers' club showed movies every night. The movies procured were also issued to navy units such as the Seabees and facilities in the area such as the navy hospital.

I had a few run-ins with senior officers while there. The first was with a marine major. Somehow I finagled a car, a Ford Bronco, for myself. I really do not remember where I got it, but I was the only lieutenant at Phu Bai with his own car. Well, one night, shortly after getting my prized vehicle, I was confronted by a major from another marine squadron.

"You have my car. I want it back," He said looking me in the eye.

I bravely looked up at all six feet six inches of him. "Sorry, sir, you must be mistaken. That's my car." I had been assured by the Wing Special Services Officer in Da Nang that I owned the car. I was not about to give it up without a fight. I was especially brave that night, as I had had two Bloody Marys with about four beer chasers.

We argued back and forth.

"No, it's not," he said.

"Yes, it is," I said, not about to give up.

After about five minutes of heated discussion between the major and myself, the conversation turned to something like, "Lieutenant, that is my car and I had better get it back soon or your ass is going to be sent to Recon." After considering the consequences, I gave in and handed him the keys.

About two days later, I was sitting in the "O" Club having had a couple of beers when I heard the bartender holler for me. I had a phone call. *Who in the hell would be calling me?* I wondered. "Lt Robinson, sir," I said, picking up the phone.

"This is Lt Anderson, navy-type [letting me know that he really was a captain and out-ranked me]. I'm from the naval hospital. My NCO club manager just informed me that you would not give him a movie for tonight because we did not rewind the movie we turned in yesterday."

I had not been informed this had happened, but I did know my NCO had a problem with movies that had been returned. Many had not been rewound and an inordinate amount of time was spent rewinding them. I figured my NCO must have gotten fed up. He must have figured that if he penalized the offenders by not giving them a movie it might teach them a lesson.

"I'm sorry, Lieutenant, but if my sergeant felt you were not living up to your end of the bargain and that you should do without a movie tonight, I will have to support him," I replied not knowing the whole story.

"Lieutenant," he responded, "I realize that we may have been at fault, but I really feel your sergeant got a little carried away here, and we have a whole unit that is going to suffer because of what one guy did."

"I'm sorry Lieutenant," I replied, "but that's the way it has to be."

Now he was angry. "Lieutenant, is your superior officer there?" he asked, barking with authority. I looked around and saw our new commanding officer, LtCol Cretney, standing about twenty feet away.

"Sure, my commanding officer is right here," I said. I was confident my CO would back me up. I gave the colonel a quick brief, and he took the phone.

After hanging up, Cretney told me he had backed me up, but felt I had made a bad decision. Oh well, you win some and lose some. I gave myself an "oops." We did not have any more problems with rewinding.

There was a nice "perk" with this job. I was rewarded with a three day "huss" trip to Hong Kong. That sounded like a pretty good deal to me. My only duty while in Hong Kong was to deliver a letter requesting some goods.

I showed up at the Da Nang airport for the flight on the C-130 and was manifested. A few other passengers and I climbed aboard and strapped into the troop seat, a row of canvas seating along each wall of the C-130. The cargo was tied down in the center. We got our briefing from the crew chief, and the aircraft taxied for takeoff. I do not know if there was a maintenance problem or the if pilot could not get his IFR clearance, but, whatever it was, I know we sat on the end of the runway for at least an hour before take-off.

Finally we were airborne. After a couple of hours in the loudest airplane I had ever been in, we landed in Hong Kong. We received our instructions regarding show-time for the flight back and procurement of communist-produced goods before being turned loose.

I had been told that the Hong Kong Holiday Inn was a good place to stay and that was my plan. Another guy and I fought our way out of the airport to find a cab. Little Chinese guys, all trying to take care of anything we needed, literally surrounded us the whole way. Finally, we made it to the front of the terminal and found a cab. We jumped in and told the driver to take us to the Star Ferry.

Somewhere in the translation he must have missed something, for along the way he decided to stop at his favorite tailor shop. The tailor cordially invited us in and offered us a cold beer. We accepted without hesitation. The beer was followed by a sales pitch promoting the benefits and savings that could be had by purchasing a complete wardrobe from him. Obviously the pitch had been developed for rich Americans.

We thanked him for the beer, but graciously declined his offer before continuing on our trip to the ferry. When buying tickets, we discovered that there were three or four classes of tickets for the ferry. We bought the cheapest tickets.

On board, we found ourselves sitting in a very crowded area with Chinese peasants and laborers. We were a bit apprehensive, but we need not have been. They ignored us.

I spent the days eating and drinking. For two and one half days, I gorged on steak and lobster. Prices in Hong Kong were fantastic. Everything was dirt cheap, but it was important to be aware of imitations. The Chinese were great at copying brand name merchandise. Eagerly I set out to find a great deal.

My best buy would have been from Red Chinese store located near the Star Ferry. We were authorized to buy from them, but the total value of all purchases could not exceed $90.00 U.S. money. The store had a lot of hand-crafted Oriental furniture and figurines which would have cost a fortune in the states, but the best buy was a full Bengal tiger rug, head and all. The price was $500.00 Hong Kong which was equal to $100.00 American. I really wanted it, but knew I would never get it past customs.

At the same store were two long tables covered with red Chinese propaganda on the Vietnam war. Most had pictures of downed U.S aircraft and POWs in the north. I was very uncomfortable while there.

Once back at the C-130, I could see where special services got their stuff. The plane was full from front to back with goodies and games for the troops.

I stayed on as Group Special Services Officer until we moved to Marble Mountain in December.

XIII
<u>Right Seat</u>

IN MID NOVEMBER it was time for me to start thinking about becoming a HAC. One afternoon as I walked into the ready room after a mission, the Operations Officer called me over.

"Robinson," he said, "I have you flying with Hanavan tomorrow. I want you to start getting some right seat time. I've talked with Hanavan already so he knows about it. You've been down south a bit lately. We just received a request to support a recon mission tomorrow for the 1ˢᵗ Marines. Briefing is 0600."

"Yes, sir." I replied. I was tickled pink. I had about 300 hours in the Huey and was happy to hear I was going to transition to the other seat and be an aircraft commander.

Lt Ed Watson, call sign, Scarface Four Three, was going to be the flight leader. I would be flying with Lt L.M. Hanavan on Watson's wing. We flew to Da Nang and landed at Camp Reasoner, the 1ˢᵗ Marine reconnaissance compound located on the west edge of Da Nang. We shut down beside two CH-46s from HMM-262. Their squadron call sign was "Chatterbox." The CH-46s would be the transports for the team, and we would provide gunship cover.

Inside a small operations room, the reconnaissance battalion's S-3 operations officer gave us our briefing. We were to insert three reconnaissance teams from the 1ˢᵗ Marine Division out of Da Nang in an area west of An Hoa. The LZs were in an area about fifty kilometers southwest of Da Nang and west of any known marine units. Each CH-46 would have a team on board.

We headed south out of Da Nang toward An Hoa where we would refuel. We really did not need fuel, but the extra twenty-five minutes of fuel we picked up on the way would come in handy if things got hot.

After refueling, our flight departed An Hoa and headed west. Watson called the lead transport as we approached the area of the first LZ. "Chatterbox Lead, this is Scarface Four Three. I have the first LZ in sight. I'm going in and take a look. Over."

"Roger."

As we approached the first LZ, Watson started his run for a low pass over the zone. A small clearing was located on a flat area on top of a hill. Jungle terrain covered the slopes on all sides. I slowed down so I would be set up to make a gun run to cover Watson if he started taking fire. Passing seventy-five feet over the zone at high speed and not seeing anything unusual, Watson called.

"I do not see any problems here. Chatterbox, you are cleared in. The wind is out of the north. It looks pretty light."

As the CH-46 started a spiral down to the zone, I set myself up 180 degrees from Watson on the opposite side of his orbit.

Chatterbox Lead touched down in the zone, and six marines ran out the back and disappeared in the foliage.

The unit, needing to establish communications with their operations at Camp Reasoner, called on their Fox Mike.

"Aroma, Aroma. This is Spillway. Commo check. Over."

"Roger, Spillway. This is Aroma. I read you, Lima Charlie. Over."

The recon team had just checked with the command post at Camp Reasoner through a radio relay site that would remain in continuous contact with the team. If the team failed to make initial contact with Aroma, we would have to go back in and pull them out.

"Spillway, Spillway, this is Scarface. How's everything down there? Over."

"Situation's a go. Over."

"Roger, Spillway. We'll see you later. Scarface, out."

With the first team in, the four helicopters proceeded to the next zone which was another six-digit grid coordinate on the map.

The copilot on the lead gunship had the awesome job of finding a landing zone that was such a small hole in the jungle that a CH-46 could barely make it in. Then, after finding the zone, the flight lead had to make the decision as to whether or not he wanted to put a team in.

The second zone was easy to find as it was a rather large clearing on a hill overlooking a small valley. Though it was big enough for several helicopters, it had a lot of tree stumps that would get in the way of the '46s.

Watson did a low high-speed pass again and called "clear." Chatterbox Dash Two followed, and the six-man team made a hasty retreat out the back of the CH-46. Chatterbox Dash Two wasted no time getting out of the zone.

As we orbited while waiting for the team to check in with Aroma, Team Blackjack's radioman called, "Scarface! Scarface! This is Blackjack. We are in contact! We are taking fire! We are headed south. Fire is coming from the north edge of the zone. Over."

The team had just reached the edge of the foliage when they started taking small arms fire. Watson made an immediate decision to go back in to get them out. "Four Three in hot."

He was already in a gun run, and I could see the rockets headed for the tree line on the north side. I brought the nose of my Huey up and did a pedal turn and started my gun run covering Watson on his pull up. As Watson pulled out of his run, I started my first right seat rocket run.

Rolling in, I thought, *Okay, Robinson, center the ball and squeeeeze the button.* As I did, two rockets headed right for where I wanted them

Huey gunner's view. Photo by George Curtis at *Pop a Smoke*.

to go. I fired several salvos, and Hanavan started working out with the TAT-101 machine guns. Both door gunners blazed away as we pulled out of our run 150 feet above the zone.

After we each had made two gun runs, Watson came up, "Blackjack, Blackjack, this is Scarface. What's your situation? Are you still in contact?"

"Negative, Scarface. We are no longer in contact."

"Roger that, Blackjack. Stand by and let me see what we can do about getting you out of there. Over." After a slight pause, he continued, "Chatterbox, what do you think? Are you ready to go back in there?"

"Roger, Scarface. I guess we're going to sooner or later. I'm coming in."

Watson called back, "Okay, I'll lead you in and lay down some Willy Pete. If I take fire, break it off and I'll see if we can get some fast movers in here. Over."

"Roger, Scarface. I'm right behind you."

Huey gunship pilot's view. Photo by George Curtis at *Pop a Smoke*.

Watson started his run. Except for his Willy Pete, he was about out of rockets. Rolling in, he laid down a smoke screen along the north edge of the landing zone in hopes of providing a wall of smoke to cover the CH-46.

Dash Two followed Watson right down to the zone and touched down. The recon team was all "assholes and elbows" as they headed toward the noisy helicopter. As the last marine was climbing on board, tracers started coming from the CH-46's .50 caliber machine gun located on its right side.

Over the radio we heard voice of the CH-46 pilot, "We are taking fire! Three o'clock!"

The instant the last team member got aboard, the CH-46 was airborne with both of its .50 cals chopping up real estate as they departed.

I had started my gun run when I heard they were taking fire and came in shooting the remainder of our rockets. After they were expended, I looked over to Hanavan. He was either out of ammo on his TAT-101 or it was jammed. In back our crew chief, Sgt J.D.

Huey gunship working out. Photo by George Curtis at *Pop a Smoke*.

Boyd, had a jammed M-60 and was working on getting it cleared. On the other side the gunner was firing. I still had ammo left in the four fixed machine guns. I fired them, moving the rudder pedals in and out to move the nose of the Huey left and right, spreading the bullets along the tree line.

"Did you see that .50 cal?" one of the gunners called out. "There's a gooner on the south side of the zone with what looked like dual .50 cals. It looked like it was jammed up, and he was trying to get the chamber open."

We've been set up! I thought.

The NVA had let the recon team in, holding their fire hoping to ambush us and get a helicopter or two when we came back in. We had just flown over the .50s at no more than two hundred feet. Had the gooner's guns not jammed, we would have been a turkey shoot.

When everyone was clear of the landing zone, Watson came up on Fox Mike, "Okay, flight, let's get the hell out of here."

Watson, pissed at being set up, called Chatterbox Lead and told him to head back to An Hoa. "Let's go over the valley to the west and call in some arty. I have good coordinates," he said calling us.

"Roger that."

Watson called in the artillery mission and after directing fire for a few minutes, told them to fire for effect. The ground around the zone exploded.

As we watched the impact from the explosions, Watson briefed an OV-10 Bronco on the situation and coordinates of the zone so they could either bring in fixed-wing or call in more artillery.

We headed back to Da Nang to drop off the team and debrief the mission. *Not bad for the first time in the right seat,* I thought. Hanavan was probably happy to have survived with a "rookie" in the right seat.

XIV
<u>Orphanage</u>

ON A COLD RAINY DAY IN NOVEMBER when the weather was too bad to fly, Frank "Sac" Sacharanski, Dennis "Denny" Grace, and I decided to take a few things to an orphanage in Hue City. Sacaranski had been there before. He had told a nun there that he would return and bring some things for the children. It was my first day off in over a month. I had not driven off the base, but I had flown over Hue city. From the air, it appeared to be a beautiful city, and I was eager to go.

We borrowed the Skipper's jeep and headed out. We drove up Highway 1, the only north-south highway running the entire length of the country. Though only a two-lane highway, it hosted quite an array of machines ranging from bicycles to tanks. There were very few cars, but the ones I saw were usually black and looked like they were probably left over from the days when France had a large presence in the area. Using my Super 8 movie camera, I recorded our trip.

As we drove up the highway, a Vietnamese civilian was hitch-hiking.

"Let's give that dude a ride," Grace said. We stopped. He climbed in and sat next to me in the back seat. Unable to speak English, he smiled and responded "Yeah, yeah," to everything we said.

"I wonder if this guy is really a civilian," I said to myself as we traveled up the highway. "More than likely he's Viet Cong." Suspicious, I kept one eye on him as we motored up the road. I was wearing my .38, but I was not sure if there were any bullets or flares in it.

We dropped off our passenger at the turn-off to the orphanage. He appeared to be very grateful. Sounding happy, he continued speaking in Vietnamese as he climbed out of the back seat. About the time his foot hit the ground, his shirt slid up his back exposing an army .45 cal pistol. I thought about grabbing it but did not. Standing next to the jeep, he smiled. Nodding, he jabbered what sounded like "Thank you." As we drove away, I told Sacaranski and Grace about the pistol.

After arriving at the orphanage, we drove into a fenced-in compound. Immediately little people, all talking at once, surrounded us grabbing everything that was not tied down.

Sacaranski met with the nun he had talked to previously. He handed her a bag of goodies before going inside a building with her. Grace and I remained in the courtyard and amused the children. As it turned out, these little guys and gals were professional thieves who stole everything they could get their hands on, including a few parts off our jeep. I had to hang on to my camera with a good grip as they pawed at it.

I felt sorry for these children; they were the real victims of this crazy war. All had lost their parents, some had lost limbs, and some had American fathers. The mixed-blood children were looked down upon and treated poorly by the Vietnamese. I could not blame the children for grabbing everything they could. It was simply a matter of survival. I have often wondered about the fate of these innocent victims of war.

We departed the compound and turned toward Phu Bai. There he was again, hitchhiking.

"Let's pick him and turn him over to the MPs on our way back," I said.

"Okay," both Sacaranski and Grace responded.

We stopped and picked him up again. Just as friendly as he had been earlier, he seemed to agree with everything we said, even though I'm sure he did not understand a word of it. We stopped where an MP was directing traffic. We told him about our passenger and the gun he had stuffed under his shirt. The MP did not seem to think the situation was unusual and did not want to bother with him. Nonetheless, we motioned to him that it was time to leave. He climbed out of the back seat and went on his way. We continued back to Phu Bai.

XV
The Lighter Side

IN EVERY WAR there are incidents that are out of the ordinary. Our squadron had its share of interesting and unusual incidents. Sometimes these incidents were a result of our own stupidity, at other times strange things just happened. Although there were more, I recall three.

The first could be classified under "probably not too smart."

Life is good. SgtMaj Valentine receiving a kiss. Cruise Book photo.

Early one morning I was flying a V.I.P. slick with 1Lt Perry Unruh. After launching, we checked in with DASC. We were not happy to learn that our mission had been postponed until 1400 hours. Rather than returning to Phu Bai, we elected to continue to Quang Tri. We were low-leveling along Highway 1, not much higher than the little people riding their bicycles down the highway when, suddenly, things changed.

Rrrrrr-rrrrr-rrrrr. The high pitch of an emergency beacon came over our headsets. A strong, loud signal, it must have been close.

All aircrew carried survival radios which transmitted on the emergency "guard" frequency. The radios also had an emergency locator beacon or "beeper" enabling aircraft to home in on the signal's location. All marine aircraft had homing capabilities on their UHF radios. After switching from the transmit mode to the home mode, the number one needle on the pilot's RMI (heading indicator) would point to the signal's location.

"Let's check this out. Maybe someone just punched out," Perry said as he switched the radio to "home."

Unruh turned the aircraft to a northwesterly heading until the head of our number one needle on the RMI pointed straight ahead. We continued on the heading for no more than a few minutes when the needle swung around and pointed behind us. We swung the aircraft around looking for a downed pilot. On the ground below there was nothing but one lone bush.

"I think we've been had," said Unruh. "I'll bet some 'gooner' has a hole under that brush and would just love it if we landed next to him."

The beacon signal continued as we circled overhead.

After circling the bush several times and seeing nothing, Unruh and I both agreed that further pursuit would not be healthy. The situation smelled of ambush. A single slick Huey would be an easy target.

Meanwhile, I heard 1Lt Kent Ellison talking over the DASC frequency we were monitoring. Ellison and I had gone through flight school together. He was with VMO-2 flying OV-10s out of Marble Mountain. I gave him a call and told him about our findings with the beeper.

After discussing what to do next, we thought that maybe we should do some deer hunting. Some guys in the squadron reported having good luck in finding a small species of deer living in the area. We asked Ellison to monitor our Fox Mike because we would be working in the area as a single slick. He came back saying that there was not much happening and would be glad to keep track of us. It was good to know we could get hold of someone who could bring help if we had to go down for any reason.

Along with my .38 caliber pistol, I carried a .45 caliber burp gun. The burp gun was relatively small and easy to carry in the helicopter. It fit right next to the seat. The gun's only detriment was that the ammo was heavy. I carried a bandoleer of ammo with about six clips. After adding the ammo to the rest of my flight gear, which included a fifteen-pound "bullet bouncer," I felt like I needed a mule to help me carry all of it out to the aircraft in the morning.

We began our hunt for the wily deer in an area south and west of Quang Tri. Suddenly, out of nowhere, a herd of wild boar ran out of the brush. The chase was on!

Spotting the pigs, Unruh swung the Huey around to the left-hand turn. Pointing the burp gun out of the left window as Unruh made a slow, low approach from behind the running herd, I let loose with the sub-machine gun. The deadly bullets made their way out of the barrel toward the swine below. I had not fired a burp gun before. The recoil lifted the barrel, and my fire went up right through the rotor blades. Not one bullet hit a blade! How I managed not to hit any is beyond me. At least two or three rounds had to have gone right between the spinning blades!

"Okay, hang on to this thing," I said to myself blasting away again.

Author and LCpl Delgado with hog and Montagnyards. Photo by Perry Unruh.

I could see the rounds hitting the ground. I was just to the right of the herd. Unfazed, they stayed tight. I continued firing. The rounds walked right up to the lead pig and hit him in the head. He went down. The rest of the herd scattered, disappearing in the surrounding brush.

Now what the hell should we do? Here we were, a lone Huey with a trophy pig on the ground in or near an area where we had seen a fire fight a few nights earlier. After discussing the situation, we decided to land and use a rope we had in back to tie up the boar and external it out under the helicopter.

As we made our approach to the clearing, the hog was still kicking.

"Okay, Delgado," Unruh said to our crew chief, "when we get on the ground, take your M-16 and shoot the pig in the head with one bullet. Okay?"

"Yes, sir," he replied.

Coming to a three-foot hover, we were just ready to descend for touchdown when Delgado let loose with the whole damn clip. His M-16 was on full automatic. I looked to see if there was anything left of the pig. It was still kicking! In the excitement of it all, Delgato had missed with all thirty-odd rounds.

"Okay, Corporal, take your knife . . . go over and cut his throat. Then take the rope and tie the pig up. Tie the other end of the rope to the skid. Okay?"

"Yes, sir," he replied as he jumped out and ran over to the pig.

Meanwhile, Unruh and I were nervously keeping a close eye out for any bad guys who might have seen us land. I was beginning to think this was not such a good idea. With all the shooting and landing the aircraft, I am certain every gooner within a klick knew we were there. They just did not know why.

I looked to see how Delgado was doing. On top of the hog, he had his machete out and was proceeding to chop away at the neck of the pig like it was a log. The pig finally died and was tied to the skid of our helicopter. At least he did a nice job on tying him to the skid. We took off vertically out of our LZ with the hog dangling under the Huey. All eyes searched the area for gooners as we climbed. With the barrel of my burp gun pointed out the left window, I was ready to fire.

Reaching altitude, we flew over to the Montagnyard compound near Quang Tri, our staging area for Mission 72, Prairie Fire. We attracted a good crowd as we lowered the hog to the ground. After taking some pictures of our trophy and chuckling with SOG members, we gave the pig to the Montagnyards. They were happy to take it. We heard they had a ritual they performed with the jawbone. I'm sure the meat did not go to waste!

1Lt Roland Scott amusing himself with a rubber duck. Cruise Book photo.

The second incident provided some very real pain and a chuckle or two.

Landing on a ship in a helicopter proved to be considerably different from my first carrier landing in a fixed-wing. My landing was on the hospital ship Hope located offshore from the northern I Corps. It was not nearly as exciting as landing with a T-28, but it was interesting. The ship, essentially a moving helipad, moved along at about twenty knots, pretty much into the wind. The approach was not difficult, but the fun started when coming to a hover over the landing pad. The pad moved up and down and I had to move the helicopter with it. Once the helicopter was on the deck, it began to rock and sway with the boat. Helicopters were not supposed to move like that! It was a strange sensation.

After the tricky landing a good-looking round-eyed nurse brought out cold Cokes for the flight crews.

Medical personnel aboard the ship worked hard giving medical attention and performing combat surgery. However, not all their work was combat related, at least not in the following instance.

Many men who have not been circumcised have experienced the pain resulting from a zipper being pulled up before retraction. *Ouch!* When the foreskin and zipper meet, it makes for a bad day. This happened to one of our lieutenants who shall remain nameless. In fact, the zipper did the job so well in connecting, that there was a tear. *Ouch again!*

The medivac went something like this: "Hope, this is Scarface, a single Huey, five klicks west, inbound with a medivac for an emergency circumcision."

"Roger, Scarface. You're inbound for an emergency what?" After an embarrassing explanation met by groans and laughter, arrangements were made for landing and medical treatment. The operation was successful, but our nameless friend had a new call sign, "Scarface Shorthorn."

The third incident was just plain strange.

LtCol "Bobby" Wilkinson (center) Commanding Officer, 20 February 1969 to
14 October 1969 with SSgt C.A. McSwain (R) and enlisted personnel
enjoying Boss's Night.

Shortly after Third Force Reconnaissance Company A's arrival in Phu Bai, I was scheduled to insert a team southwest of Quang Tri. The briefing was routine. We were going to handle the mission much like we did during our "Prairie Fire" missions. I was flying with 1Lt Richard Crawford. Crawford was the flight leader of two gunships. We would cover two CH-46 Sea Knight helicopters. Their lead would carry the team and the chase would be available to pull the team and aircrew out in the event they were shot down. Major Lee, the 3rd Force recon commander normally rode on the chase aircraft and was available for command and control if the team got into trouble.

The plan was to make two fake insertions as deceptions before the team was actually inserted. Because the North Vietnamese usually investigated any aircraft landings, the deceptions would keep them busy and give the team more time to get out of the actual LZ.

The area we were going into had rolling hills rather than the usual mountainous terrain. The vegetation was thick but did not provide good enemy concealment.

We came to the first LZ for a deception maneuver. The plan was to make a low fast pass over the zone to give us a good look for possible obstacles and to draw fire if the gooners were waiting.

Our guns went hot, and we started our pass. The LZ looked relatively open. There were no big trees and the brush was fairly short. Feeling quite relaxed, I sat back in my seat with the TAT-101 machine guns in the ready position.

This is going to be a piece of cake, I thought.

We passed over the zone at 100 knots and fifty feet when a Vietnamese voice came over the Fox Mike.

"SCARFACE, YOU NUMBA TEN BULL SHIT!"

I damn near jumped out of my seat.

"SCARFACE, YOU DIE!" the voice followed.

Expecting to take fire I went on alert. Nothing happened.

I should have called the gooner back and told him Scarface had some re-supply for him.

XVI

Moving

IN OCTOBER OF 1969, rumors about the marines pulling out of Vietnam started flying. I had some mixed feelings about the marines being shipped out. For the past eighteen months, I had been mentally preparing myself for combat. Now, with only two months in country, there was talk of shipping us out to Okinawa. I knew anyone with an iota of common sense would have been ecstatic about getting out, but I was not.

When word finally came down, the 3rd Marine Division was going to be the first to go. Their area of responsibility was ground operations in the northern third of I Corps, our primary area of operation. The helicopter units in Quang Tri were also going to Okinawa. Nothing was said about what was going to happen to us.

Because of our uncertain future and, since I had been in country for only two months, I was not eligible for R&R. I decided that before I was pulled out of country, I might as well submit the paperwork and see if I could go in December. One never did know what would happen if he did not try.

The timing was not the best for my wife who was teaching in Crookston, Minnesota. Christmas vacation would still be a week or two away, but through phone calls patched through the MARS network (ham radio operators), we worked out a plan to meet in Hawaii on a specific day. I put in and received word that my request had been approved.

Shortly after that, LtCol Cretney called the squadron to the hangar for a meeting. *Here we go*, I thought. *I bet they are thinking we are probably going to be the next unit pulled out.*

Sensing the tension all of us were feeling, the Skipper came right to the point. "Men, we are moving out to Marble Mountain. We are going to join up with VMO-2. They are moving their OV-10s over to Da Nang, and Scarface is going to take the Cobras." His audience was silent. This was not what we had expected. "What I need to know from you is what you want to fly. Officers, coordinate with Major Lively. If you want to keep flying Hueys, you will be transferred to HML-167. Enlisted, you will also need to select what you want to do. Coordinate with SgtMaj Valentine on which squadron you want. I need to have your decision by tomorrow. Any questions?"

There were many questions, mostly concerns from the HACs as to what their status would be at HML-167. They certainly did not want to have to play second fiddle to anyone. After Cretney

LtCol Cretney addressing the squadron. Cruise Book photo.

answered all the questions, mostly with, "I do not know at this time, but will let you know if I hear anything else," the meeting was over.

I did not know what to think. I was just getting ready for a check ride as a HAC and going to Cobras would mean more copilot time. On the other hand, the Cobras I had seen in Vietnam were impressive. I had not worked with many marine Cobras because we had only one squadron, but I had worked with army Cobras on Prairie Fire missions. I was impressed with the way their Cobras flew and by the ordinance they carried.

The plus options in Cobras for me to consider included flying in an air-conditioned aircraft versus one with open windows, having the capability to carry seventy-two rockets versus fourteen, and having a SCAS (stabilization system) which made for a more stable shooting platform. There were many other differences as well. The Cobra's weapons system included a turret with an eight-barrel Gatling mini-gun that fired 4000 rounds of 7.62 mm per minute. An onboard device compensated for the aircraft's airspeed while firing. The Huey had eight M-60 machine-guns. A Huey gunner could fire 40 mm grenades one at a time with his 40 mm single-shot grenade launcher. The Cobra turret also had a 40 mm grenade launcher located next to the mini-gun. The Cobra carried 350 rounds of the 40 mm grenades. When loaded as a gun ship, the Huey cruised at an air speed of sixty to eighty knots. Fully loaded the Cobra cruised at 140 knots and had a red line (maximum airspeed) of 180 knots with rocket pods and 190 knots when the pods were off.

Needless to say, my decision was not difficult. I decided to go Cobras. Many of the pilots, especially helicopter commanders, flight leaders and flight/strike leaders were not about to revert back to copilot status and elected to stay with Hueys. I accepted the fact that I would have to fly copilot for a while longer. I did not like it, but I was getting comfortable flying in a combat environment. I had built up about 300 hours of combat time and figured my time in the front seat would be short. A few of the senior pilots elected to take a ground job with the Air Wing or with the Air Group. I guess they had had enough excitement and did not want to go through the hassle of joining a new squadron.

Somehow, I did not get the word that anyone going on R&R had to stop flying three days prior to leaving. The day before I departed for Da Nang to catch my flight to Hawaii, I was on a Prairie Fire mission in Laos rolling in on gun runs wondering how smart that was. The reasoning behind the three-day no-fly policy was that more than one woman had shown up at an R&R location only to learn her husband or boyfriend had been killed since she had left home.

The day after completing my mission, I climbed aboard the DC-8 along with a plane load of soldiers and marines looking for five days of bliss in the "world." We refueled at Guam where I bought four bottles of liquor, one of Chevas Regal Scotch whiskey, one of Crown Royal, and two of champagne. At that time Chevas and Crown Royal cost about $4.00 a bottle. Arriving in Hawaii and following a short briefing on where and when to show for the return flight, I met my wife. We proceeded to have a very good time for five days. I did find it difficult to adjust because I had been in a combat zone one day and in Hawaii romping with my wife the next. I literally had been in combat two days before.

The only problem my wife and I had was jet lag. When it was three o'clock in the afternoon for her, it was three o'clock in the morning for me. We managed to overcome the jet lag problem and the end of our five days came far too quickly.

With five days of fun in the sun over, I headed back. When I got off the plane at Da Nang, I began looking for a ride north to Phu Bai only to discover the squadron had already made the move to Marble Mountain.

Luckily, I had packed my gear before leaving Phu Bai just in case this would happen.

After hitching a ride, I arrived at Marble Mountain and wandered into the squadron ready room. There, along with the guys from our squadron at Phu Bai, I also found quite a few guys I had last seen at Camp Pendleton.

I was assigned quarters. They were not as nice as those at Phu Bai. The rooms were built in a row like a motel. Rather than glass, the windows had wire mesh. There was no air-conditioning. Luckily, I had a fan. Placing it at the foot of the bed not only kept me cool, it kept the bugs off as well. Our quarters had one perk: we were about 300 meters from the beach and had a nice sea breeze.

During my first night at Marble Mountain, I was initiated to rocket attacks. After the first attack, I found myself airborne and under my bed all in one motion. The blast had to be the loudest I had ever heard. It was followed by three more, then silence. I hollered to 1Lt Richard "Rich" Bennett in the room next to me, "Rich, are you all right?"

"Yeah," he replied.

"You have a weapon over there?" I asked, concerned the base was going to be under attack.

AH-1 Cobra, the new squadron helicopter. Cruise Book photo.

"No, I left mine down at my locker."

"Me, too" I replied, thinking that I had not been very smart.

As it turned out, there was no ground attack. The rockets had hit the flight line and caused some damage to a few CH-46s.

Because it was such a pain in the neck to check in our weapons everywhere we went, we usually did not carry our weapons back to our quarters. Marble Mountain was considered a relatively secure area, but I wondered about an attack from the sea. The company of marines assigned to protect the perimeter must not have considered that side a threat because the only security along the ocean was concertina wire.

In December HML-167 got into the Christmas spirit. They added a little color to the war business by painting a Huey red with white stripes around the tail boom. Scrounging up a Santa Claus outfit, they made trips to local villages. Christmas music blared through a speaker as Santa threw candy from the helicopter to the kids below. Also, children from a nearby orphanage were brought to

Christmas Huey. Author, 1Lt Rich Bennett, and 1Lt Denny Grace. Author's photo.

the Officers' Club where Santa came to visit via the helicopter. I thought the idea was pretty neat and so did the children.

Because we had a cease-fire during the Christmas holidays not much happened in our area. We continued to fly missions but could only fire when fired upon.

We later heard that a small church filled with worshippers for a Christmas service in a village southwest of Marble Mountain had been blown up by the VC. Apparently, they had placed some explosives under the floor of the church. It was said the explosion killed everyone. News of this event certainly did not improve our opinion of the VC.

XVII

Cobra Medivac

ON DECEMBER 28, Capt Roger Henry launched as flight leader on a medivac mission; priority, routine. Their mission was gunship escort for two CH-46s for pick-up at LZ Baldy. With the low priority of the mission, the weather appeared to be the only real danger. Monsoon rains were still drenching the area and the ceilings were low, making even routine missions a work-out. 1Lt David "Dave" Cummings was flying back seat. Henry was giving Cummings a HAC evaluation.

While sitting at LZ Baldy, waiting for the CH-46s to be loaded, the flight received another mission. This one was an emergency evacuation. A marine had tripped a booby trap. He was bleeding badly and going into shock. He needed to be picked up as soon as possible. The flight of four launched immediately and headed for the Que Son mountains.

Enroute the weather was deteriorating. The LZ in the mountains appeared to be socked in. Henry contacted the pilot of an OV-10 from VMO-2 who was in radio contact with the recon team and received the situation brief from him. It did not look good.

Rain and the low ceiling were causing a real predicament. The package maneuvered through the weather trying to find a suitable approach to the LZ. Henry made a decision. Calling the rest of his flight, he told them to orbit outside the weather mass. He was going in alone. Hopefully, he would find the LZ.

Henry and Cummings worked their way up the mountainside in visibility nearly zero-zero. Precariously, they hugged the side of the mountain as they climbed. The wind, swirling over the jagged mountainous terrain and peaks, created turbulence, at times causing the Cobra to bounce around like an out of control yo-yo.

With the weather deteriorating, they had to descend back to the valley floor to search for another route. After three failed attempts to find the LZ, the flight was in a bingo fuel situation and departed the area to refuel at An Hoa.

After returning, Henry held the rest of his flight on orbit and again tried to find the LZ. After searching for an hour and failing, he received a radio report that the injured marine's condition was worsening. He would die if the medivac did not arrive soon.

Henry decided he had to make another attempt. Thirty minutes later he found the team hunkered down by small clearing surrounded by trees. It was decision time. The flight was again getting low on fuel. Henry was not confident he could find the zone again if he went back to lead the medivac bird in. Making a decision, he hovered the Cobra over the opening in the trees then descended and

1Lt Toby Gritz. Cruise Book photo.

Capt Roger Henry. Cruise Book photo.

1Lt Dave Cummings. Cruise Book photo.

landed in the small LZ. Henry told Cummings to get out and see what they could do.

The wounded marine was badly injured. He needed immediate medical assistance. Cummings had two team members carry the marine to the Cobra. They strapped him into the pilot's seat in the rear cockpit. Once he was securely strapped in, Cummings jumped onto the rocket pod and gave Henry the signal to go.

Because the weather was still bad, Henry decided to climb through the clouds to get to clear skies above. As the Cobra gained altitude and airspeed, Cummings learned riding on a rocket pod was not all that he thought it would be. He was freezing his ass off, his helmet was being pushed forward over his face by the 140 knot wind, and his chin strap was trying to take his head off. Fortunately, the wind was holding him tightly against the stubby rocket pod wing.

After descending through the clouds near Da Nang, Henry landed at a medical facility. The news about a crazy guy riding a rocket pod had already reached them and a crowd was waiting to see the Cobra land. After tending to the wounded marine, they helped pry Cummings, now very cold, from the wing.

The word of the event spread fast. The "heavies" questioned whether riding home on the wing was stupid or heroic. There was even talk of the possibility of a court-martial.

The following day the two aviators were invited to have dinner and spirits with the Commanding General of the 1st Marine Air Wing. A great time was had by all. The question of court-martial was never brought up again.

A few days later Henry found himself in an identical situation. He and 1Lt Tobias "Toby" Gritz did what they had to do to save another wounded marine. This time it was at night and Gritz rode the pod home. Regrettably, this mission did not get much attention, probably because it was night and riding the pod had already been done. Far more important than the recognition they did not receive was the fact that two marines were alive because of these three aviators.

XVIII

Kingfisher

AFTER FLYING ROUTINE MISSIONS for a couple of weeks in the Cobra, I was scheduled for a flight/strike mission. The briefing was at 0600. Looking at the schedule board, I saw that eight pilots had been scheduled for the mission, and I wondered what was up. It was unusual to have four Cobras on the same mission.

We all showed up in the ready room just prior to 0600 and got settled in. LtCol Warren C. Cretney briefed the mission. He would be the flight/strike commander, and Col Hayward R. Smith, the Marine Air Group Commander, would be his copilot. I thought it was a bit out of the ordinary to have a full colonel fly with us, but as the briefing continued, I learned this mission was not the normal run-of-the-mill mission; instead, it was going to be an experiment in helicopter assault tactics similar to those being used very successfully by the army.

In this operation, called Kingfisher, we were to provide gunship cover for four CH-46s and close air gunship support to the ground troops. Two platoons of marines would be inserted to engage any enemy found. If contact was made and additional troops were needed, a company of marines, call sign "Bald Eagle," were to be standing by near Da Nang.

Cummings and I would be on Cretney's wing as number two in the flight. Major Stroman, our operations officer, would be lead on the second flight with 1Lt Mark Byrd as his copilot. Capt Ronald Fix would be number four with 1Lt J.T. Lewis as his copilot. The

Cobra copilots, with the exception of Smith, were from the Phu Bai squadron. All were looking forward to a good shoot-em-up.

Departing at dawn, the OV-10 Bronco, call sign "Hostage Duke," would be the first aircraft airborne. His mission was to complete a reconnaissance looking for any unusual movements or enemy activity. Hopefully, he would find something suspicious. The rest of the strike force would depart at 0730 and orbit north of the OV-10's search area. Hostage was assigned six areas to check. All locations were south of and within twenty miles of Da Nang. Because he had worked it daily, he was very familiar with the area.

The ceiling was 400 feet with visibility less than three miles. Our takeoff, scheduled for 0730, was delayed. Finally, at 0800, Cretney walked into the ready room.

"Hostage Duke found a target. The weather is marginal, but looks good enough to go. Radio check at 0830, button three."

Hostage Duke had been airborne over the working area southwest of Marble Mountain. Finding no unusual activity in the first two areas, he later found what looked like a recently traveled trail leading into a patch of woods. Smoke from a campfire was coming up through the trees.

We all jumped up, headed to the flight line, and cranked up our aircraft. At 0830 Cretney came up on Fox Mike for his radio check.

"Scarface Six . . . up."

The rest of the flight checked in.

"One Seven . . . up."

"Three . . . up."

"Two . . . up."

With all flights up and running and radio checks completed, Cretney called the control tower for taxi clearance.

As we taxied toward the runway, Scotch Flight, the four CH-46s, were just ahead of us. Also ahead of us was the UH-1E Huey

CAC (Command and Control) bird, call sign "Whiskey Three." He would be in charge of the strike and would make the decision whether or not to make the strike. After take-off, we joined up with Whiskey Three. Cretney told his second flight of Cobras to stay with Scotch Flight while we went ahead to take a look at the situation.

Whiskey Three called the OV-10, "Hostage Duke, this is Whiskey Three, airborne, Marble Mountain. What have you got for us? Over."

Hostage Duke called back immediately, "Roger, Whiskey Three, this is Duke. I've got a possible target at coordinates Alpha Tango 951560. Looks like a group of VC may be hanging out in a clump of woods. I've got an LZ just to the west of the target. The weather is marginal, but we should be able to get in. The bases of the clouds are running about 600 feet. Over."

"Roger, Duke," Whiskey Three replied. "We should be with you in about one five minutes. Over."

As he moved his OV-10 westbound, Hostage Duke answered, "Roger, Whiskey. I'm going to move out of the area for a few minutes. No sense in letting the bad guys know something is up."

Seeing the two Cobras and the Huey inbound, Hostage Duke called, "Whiskey Three, this is Hostage Duke. I've got you in sight. I'm at your eleven o'clock, one mile. I'll lead you in. The ceiling is still running about 600 feet over the zone so we'll have to scoot in low. Sorry, but unless the weather breaks I won't be able to use the fast movers. I've got two Fox 4s [F-4 Phantom jets] on the hot pad if the weather breaks. I'm coming up on the zone now. I'll give you a mark when I'm over it."

As the OV-10 headed toward the zone, he called again, "It's just off my twelve o'clock. I'm coming up on it now. Mark . . . mark. The area where I suspect activity is the clump of trees just to the east of the zone. Over."

"Okay, Hostage. I've got the zone in sight," replied Whiskey Three. "Scarface, I'll mark it. Give it a one-pass prep. We'll have Scotch Flight sneak right in."

"Roger, Whiskey Three," Scarface Six replied.

Whiskey Three rolled in, made a high-speed low pass over the LZ, and dropped a smoke grenade.

"I've got the zone in sight. Going hot," Scarface Six said as he rolled in and shot four 2.75-inch rockets into the landing zone.

We followed, spraying the zone with mini-gun in hopes of triggering any booby traps that might have been planted to destroy unwanted helicopters. Suddenly, out of the corner of my eye, I caught a glimpse of a CH-46. My heart stopped. He ran right through my mini-gun pattern before I could do anything. Fortunately, the Lord was with me. Every ten seconds the mini-gun paused for one second to cool down the five Gatling gun barrels. Fortunately, the mini-gun had paused just long enough for the CH-46 to clear. The CH-46 had not been cleared into the zone. If it had flown through my fire, the result would have been the wounding or killing of friendly troops. My career as a marine aviator could have ended that day.

Scotch One landed in the zone and the troops jumped out the rear of the helicopter the second it touched the ground. Scotch Two touched down about a second after the first and was followed by Scotch Three.

Almost immediately after landing, Scotch Three called, "I'm taking fire! Taking fire! Nine o'clock!"

I could see the tracers from his gunner's .50 cal machine gun as it blasted away at the tree line on its left.

Stroman and his wingman, in position covering Scotch Three, called, "Scarface Three rolling in."

Byrd's mini-gun was placing a solid stream of tracers into the tree line. I could see VC bullets splashing in the water around the marines as they lay in the rice paddy firing back.

When all three Sea Knights were clear of the zone, Scotch Lead called on UHF, "Whiskey Three, this is Scotch Lead. Scotch

Three has one wounded crew member and has taken several hits on his aircraft. He should be able to make it home. Over."

"Roger, Scotch," Whiskey Three answered.

Cretney, feeling the need for a gun escort in the event they had to make an emergency landing, called, "Scarface Three, take your flight and escort the '46s to Hill 55. Over."

"Roger, Three."

Whiskey Three, thinking he needed to get out of the way and let our Cobras go to work, called, "Scarface Six, I'm going to move to the south so you can work out. Over."

"Roger, Three."

Looking down, Cretney saw gooners on the run. "Scarface One Seven, I've got movement on the south side of the trees. Looks like a lot of confusion going on down there. I'm in hot."

Putting his Cobra into a steep dive, Cretney started his gun run.

Cummings acknowledged and set our Cobra up to be rolling in so we could cover the Skipper as he finished his run. We were set up for a rocket run just as the Skipper rolled out.

Cummings set the armament on rockets, four at a time. We started our run. Rockets came out of the pods in multiples of four, one after another, all into the edge of the tree line where the automatic weapons fire was coming from.

Looking at the tree line, I could see movement. "I have gooners grouped in that little clearing," I said as I began pumping 40 mm grenades into the clearing.

"We've got what looks like thirty to forty of them on the run on the south side of the trees," the Skipper said excitedly.

"Roger, we have them too," replied Cummings. "We'll swing around and follow you in. Over."

Cobra shooting mini-gun. Photo by Barry Pencek.

"Roger."

The VC were caught totally by surprise. In confusion, they were on the run under mini-gun fire.

Shooting mini-gun and pumping out 40mm grenades, we were taking control of the situation.

Within fifteen minutes we were out of ammo and rockets. Our second flight of Cobras had not returned from escorting the CH-46s. The Skipper was directing the troops to an area where he had seen the VC run. Packs, rifles, and helmets lay here and there on the ground where they had dropped them as they ran.

All eyes were watching the activity on the ground. I glanced up. *Holy shit*, I thought. All I could see was the nose of the Skipper's aircraft directly in front of us. We were three seconds away from a mid-air collision. Instinctively, I grabbed the controls from Cummings and did a sharp sixty-degree banked turn to the right.

The Skipper, not amused by the situation, barked, "One Seven, go orbit high and dry."

We climbed as high as the weather allowed and watched from above. We had no sooner established an orbit, when a VC broke out of a clump of elephant grass. As we watched, he fell right into a bomb crater full of water and started swimming for the other side. Cummings called the Skipper on the uniform, "Scarface Six, this is One Seven, I have a gooner swimming across a bomb crater down here. Over."

Cretney, busy working with the ground troops on the other side of the area called back, "Roger, One Seven. Keep an eye on him and I'll direct some troops over there as soon as we finish up over here."

We watched him as he swam across the crater. After crawling out on the far side, he sat on the edge trying to regain some strength. He looked exhausted.

"That gooner's bleeding pretty bad. See the blood running down his left arm?" I said to Cummings.

"Yup, too bad," he replied. "Look. It looks like he's giving up!"

Looking at him, I could not believe my eyes. He stood up and raised his arms in the air.

"I'll be damned, we just got us a 'captured by air'!"

Just as I was telling the Skipper about the guy with his arms up, Hostage Duke came up on the radio.

"I got 'em . . . rolling in hot."

His OV-10 rolled in firing two 20 mm cannons strapped to the belly of the aircraft, an experimental weapons system for the OV-10. The VC disappeared in a cloud of dust.

The dust settled and there he was . . . still standing with his hands up. This guy had to be the luckiest VC in Vietnam.

A few minutes passed and, with no one coming to get him, he must have decided that standing there with his hands up probably was not the healthiest. He walked over to a clump of elephant grass, went in, and sat down. Later, Cummings directed some troops over to the spot and the VC gave up without incident. We had just gotten ourselves a prisoner.

While waiting for Scarface Three flight to return, we saw another VC running down a trail. As we flew directly over him looking straight down, we saw him pull a piece of camouflage over himself and literally disappear. I had never seen anything like it! That had to be the best camouflage I had ever seen. No wonder we had so much trouble finding VC when we were looking for them.

We slowed down and were orbiting over him when he broke and started running down a trail.

"Let's get this guy with our skid," Cummings said, not having any ordinance.

"Are you crazy?" I replied. "That guy has an AK-47 and I think he might just enjoy shooting the shit out of us trying to do something dumb like that."

"I suppose you're right," Cummings replied. That was a relief. I really could not see the benefits of looking down the barrel of a gooner's AK-47 as we were trying to take his head off with the skid, especially when I would be the first guy he would see.

Scarface Three flight checked in with the Skipper, and our flight headed back to Marble Mountain to re-arm and refuel. By the time we returned, the operation was winding down. The grunts were rounding up prisoners. The shooting appeared to be finished.

Stroman's flight still had ordinance and action in the area remained a possibility. We refueled and re-armed at Marble Mountain. The enlisted crews had heard that we had been in a "shoot-em-up" and were hungry for information. We filled them in as they re-armed the aircraft.

When we returned, the situation had not changed much. Cretney told Stroman to orbit off to the west, and we resumed overhead cover.

Watching from above, I spotted a VC pack, helmet, and rifle the grunts had missed next to a trail. We tried to talk them to it, but they could not quite get the instructions. Frustrated, Cummings and I decided we might just as well land by it and show them. We touched down about twenty-five meters from the find and spotted a grunt in the area. He was headed toward us. He seemed to be more scared of the Cobra than the gooners who may have been lurking in the bushes. I pointed to the pack, and he walked over. Bending over, he brought a pith helmet up and showed it to us. Not thinking, I gave him a thumbs-up, and he picked up the rest of the stuff. After lift-off, I kicked myself in the butt for not telling the grunt to bring the helmet to us in the Cobra. It would have made a nice souvenir.

When it was all over, twenty-three VC were killed, seven by ground troops, the rest by air. We received credit for two "captured by air."

It was a good party that night.

Two days later at 0630, another Kingfisher launched heading toward an area twenty miles south of Marble Mountain near an area controlled by the ROK Marines (Republic of Korea).

The OV-10 had spotted some unusual activity in an area just north of the ROK's area of responsibility. I was flying with Cummings again, and Major Womack was the flight lead.

Enroute Womack gave the OV-10 a call to get his position, "Hostage, this is Scarface Five, with a flight of four guns and four '46s. Have you made contact with Comprise Six yet?"

Before he could answer, LtCol Weber, commander of HML-167, interrupted his call, "Hostage, this is Comprise Six. What have you got for us today? Over." Comprise Six was the CAC bird for the mission. It sounded like he wanted assurance everyone knew he was in charge.

"Comprise Six, I've got unidentified gooners all over the place out here. It looks like they are starting to get nervous with me hanging around. I'm going to move out a bit until you get in closer. Over."

"Roger, Hostage. I'll give you a call when I have you in sight."

Ten minutes later Weber called again, "Hostage, this is Comprise Six. I have you in sight. What's up? Over."

"Okay, Comprise. The gooners are really starting to split up. I'm going to take you in. Have the '46s follow you and maybe we can get a few of these guys and see what they are up to. I can't tell if they are armed. They could be civilians . . . although, I do not think civilians would be out here at this time of day. Over."

"Roger," Comprise replied. "Scarface and Chatterbox flights, did you copy? Over."

"Scarface flight copies."

"Chatterbox flight copies."

As the flight arrived in the area, it was beginning to get light enough for the terrain to be seen easily. Nearing our target area, we could see people dispersing in all directions in small groups. Not running, just dispersing. They were dressed in what looked like white gowns with hoods very much like what the KKK used to wear. Most of them were carrying baskets on each end of a stick balanced over their shoulders. They did not seem to be in a big hurry; it looked like church was over and everyone was heading home.

The OV-10 briefed the C&C Huey and showed him what he thought would be the best area in which to land. When the Huey was in position, the CH-46 flight followed the OV-10 in and marked the zone. The Cobras did not prep the zone. The flat area was mostly rice paddies. The '46s had the option of picking their spot. It looked like the OV-10 was going to lead the '46s near a group of five standing in a huddle on a paddy dike.

Chatterbox Lead touched down, and the marines charged out of the back toward the group. Four of the white-clad gooners froze. The fifth took off like a bat out of hell. The group of marines ran over to the four gooners who had stopped . . . that is, all but one marine who took off after the runner. The race was on. Orbiting above the scene was like sitting in the balcony at the race track.

"Scarface, I want this guy alive," called Comprise Six. "Do not shoot him. Use your mini-gun and shoot ahead of him. See if you can get him to stop."

We were right in position to lay down some fire. I fired the mini-gun, laying down a hail of bullets just five feet in front of him. He just kept on going.

"Comprise Six, how about if I just shoot him in the leg?"

"Negative, Scarface. I do not want to risk killing him. We need a prisoner."

This guy was hauling ass. He could really run, and the grunt chasing him was just as fast, if not faster. He was catching up. I was still shooting up the ground in front of the running gooner. The scene was comical. A grunt was in hot pursuit of a gooner, the C&C Huey was behind him, hovering fifty feet above him, and bullets were flying five feet in front of him. Yet, this guy was not about to give up.

We played this game for about a kilometer before the marine got close enough to the gooner and tackled him in a manner that would have made any football coach proud. After the tackle, the Huey landed, and the marine and prisoner climbed aboard. It turned out the prisoner was a North Vietnamese officer. The baskets he was carrying contained some very good intelligence information and a North Vietnamese pistol. Later, the story came out that a lieutenant colonel in the back of C&C Huey scarfed up the pistol and put it in a pocket of his uniform. I guess he thought he deserved it more than the grunt who had just run a kilometer chasing the gooner. I hope the marine who gave chase was given an award for his efforts because he certainly earned his pay that day.

By the time the big chase was over and the four other prisoners had been loaded, the rest of the white-clad "churchgoers" had disappeared. We all went home. The Kingfisher mission continued to be extremely successful for another month or two. The marines worked the area south of Da Nang several times a week. It did not take very long for the VC to get wise to our tactics. They soon realized if they looked toward Marble Mountain in the early morning hours and saw an OV-10 snooping around, they had better get their asses under a bush.

XIX
<u>LZ Ryder</u>

"HOLY SHIT! Did you see that?" I asked, having witnessed an F-4 Phantom explode.

I was flying with 1Lt C.D. Baker, the flight leader of a flight of two aircraft. 1Lt Lynn McCall was HAC of the aircraft on our wing. We were about twenty kilometers south of Marble Mountain along the coast and had just turned west on our way to LZ Ryder.

Our mission was Bald Eagle Standby, Mission 80. Our flight had launched from Marble Mountain at 2400 hours. The night was stellar. Visibility was unlimited, the stars were bright, and the half-moon's light reflected off the calm South China Sea as we flew along the beach. We got our clearance through the area. LZ Baldy indicated no fire missions in progress. The AO was calm.

Our mission was to link up with "Hostage Six," an OV-10 air-borne controller piloted by LtCol J.M. Moriarty. He would be our controller as we worked out in the area around LZ Ryder, a fire base located on a ridgeline on the western edge of the Que Son Mountains. The mission's purpose was to provide a night familiarization of the LZ perimeter in the event the area should come under attack during Tet.

As we made our turn to the west, Baker brought the flight up the tactical frequency. Immediately, I recognized Moriarty's voice. He was talking to "Crossbill One Two Two," a Marine Corps C-117 flare ship. The C-117 was dropping flares over the LZ Area and two F-4 Phantoms were making their final run. The napalm they were dropping could be seen clearly from our vantage point ten kilometers away as the bombs of fire exploded.

We continued inbound. Hostage Six briefed the next two Phantoms, "Lovebug Two Two Eight." "Dash One" was flown by 1Lt D. Van Horne, 1Lt W.M. Meyer was his RIO (Radar Intercept Officer). "Dash Two" was on his wing. Hostage marked the target with a Willy Pete. Lovebug Dash One was cleared hot on the target and began his first run.

The Phantom had his position lights on. We watched as he made his dive, dropping napalm close to the bottom of his run. The napalm exploded below, but he was too low. The ball of fire continued moving toward the aircraft. It exploded and became a ball of flame. The event was over in a matter of seconds.

Wanting to help, Baker immediately called the OV-10, "Hostage Six, this is Scarface Two Two with a flight of two. We are about ten klicks east. Can we be of assistance? Over."

"Scarface, continue inbound and stand by," Moriarty answered. "Crossbill did you see any chutes?"

"Negative, Hostage. I can't imagine that they got out."

Moriarty called Baker, "Scarface, this is Hostage Six. When you get here, I'm going to have you do a low-level search on the north side of the ridge for parachutes. The explosion happened so fast I doubt that they got out. The ground unit at Ryder is up primary Fox Mike and call sign is 'Moose Beak One Four'."

After checking his fuel state, the C-117 flare ship called Baker, "Scarface, this is Crossbill One Two Two. When you get here I should be able to give you lighting for at least another hour. I have requested a replacement ship."

We passed over the ridgeline next to LZ Ryder from the south and descended down the ridge. Baker needed our wingman to stay high while we went down for a look.

Baker told McCall to stay at 1500 feet. We were going down low level to take a look. We had no sooner started our low-level search, when we heard one of the Lovebug crew on Guard frequency.

"Hostage Six, this is Lovebug Two Two Eight Dash One Alpha. Over."

Jubilantly, Moriarty called back, "My God! Lovebug, I can't believe you got out. Are you okay? Over."

"That's affirmative, Hostage. I have no clue as to where I am . . . other than in a jungle and that a helicopter just went over my poz."

"Have you heard from Bravo? Over," Moriarty asked concerned about the RIO.

"That's a negative. Not yet."

Hearing the conversation, Bravo interrupted, "Hostage Six, this is Bravo. I copied your last conversation. I am okay. How about getting us out of here? Over."

"Okay, Bravo," Moriarty responded. "Here's the plan. I am requesting a Jolly Green to come in and pick you up. I'm bingo fuel, so I'm going back. I should be back by the time the Jolly Green gets here. We have not had any enemy activity in the area lately so we should not have any problems getting you guys out of here. Scarface Two Two will be the on-scene commander until I get back. He will coordinate to get you and Bravo together if possible. I also have a team of infantry available if we need them. Okay?"

"Sounds good, Hostage. The sooner the Jolly Green gets here the better." Not happy crashing around in the bush, he added, "This sucks!"

Baker decided it was time to take charge, "Okay, Alpha, this is Scarface Two Two. I'm the low-level Cobra. Can you see me? Over."

"That's a negative, Scarface. The grass is too tall. I can hear you. You are directly east of my position. Over."

"Roger, Alpha. I am going to slow down and head toward you. Let me know when I am getting close. Bravo, I'm going to ask that you sit tight until I find Alpha, then I'll try to get you two together for the pick up."

Baker slowed the Cobra down to the speed of a fast walk and headed west. It did not take long for radio contact. "Scarface, I see you now. You are headed my way. I'm about 75 meters from you."

Baker turned on his spotlight and began pivoting it back and forth ahead of the Cobra. Down below and just in front of us, Baker and I could see the pilot standing in tall elephant grass waving both arms. Baker came to a hover and moved the spotlight off to his right so he would not be exposed to any enemy in the area.

"Okay, Alpha. I've got you in sight."

"Roger, Scarface."

Bravo, watching from the west, called us, "This is Bravo. You are about 100 meters to the east of me. Over."

"What luck!" I said to myself. It was fortunate these guys ended up relatively close to each other.

Baker spotted Bravo. "Okay, Alpha Bravo. It looks like you two are about 200 meters from each other. Alpha, I want you to start moving to the west. Bravo, start moving east. I will keep my light on midway between you and will stay above you guys until you get married up. Over."

"Roger, Scarface. We're moving out."

As we hovered at 100 feet, I got a bit nervous. Our guns were hot, and I was ready with mini-gun if we took fire. The tall elephant grass and vegetation made for slow movement. It seemed to take forever to get them together.

About the time they found each other, Hostage Six returned on station and checked in. "Scarface, this is Hostage Six. I'm back overhead. DASC is not helping one damn bit. There is not any transport to be had anywhere and they won't release the medivac standby. I thought I had a Jolly Green, but they could not get clearance to come until daylight. I think we need to have the troops from Ryder come down and take them back up the hill."

The marines on LZ Ryder called immediately, "Hostage, this is Moose Beak One Four. I've been monitoring your traffic. I can have my team on their way in fiver mikes [five minutes]. Over."

"Roger, Moose Beak. Send them on their way. I will have the Cobra stay over them until your team gets there. Over."

A short time later, Moose Beak called again. "We are on our way, sir. Moose Beak out."

The marines headed down the rough terrain. We continued our hover over the downed aviators until Moose Beak's team arrived. Because we had been hovering for an hour and a half, we could not hang around until they got back to the firebase. Moriarty stayed with them. The team and their two new members headed back up the steep terrain to the relative safety of the firebase where a CH-46 picked them up shortly after daylight.

XX

1st Recon

By January, the 3rd Force Reconnaissance Company had been sent to Okinawa. Members wishing to remain in country had been transferred to the 1st Marine Division.

1st Marine Reconnaissance worked out of Camp Reasoner. Located on Hill 327 on the southwestern edge of Da Nang, the compound had been named in honor of 1Lt Frank Reasoner, the first marine in the Vietnam war to be awarded the Medal of Honor. 1st Marine Air Wing was their only air support for helicopters.

1st Recon's usual area of operation in the north was in an area beginning at the Hai Van Pass then going west to the Laotian border. The southern edge started approximately forty kilometers south of Da Nang then again went west to the Laotian border. Occasionally, 1st Recon would operate in the A Shau valley, a very scary place. Supporting helicopters flew to Camp Reasoner for briefings and team pick-ups. The landing pad was large enough to support three or four CH-46s and a couple of gunships.

Normal procedure was to have aircrews depart Marble Mountain for Camp Reasoner for mission briefings. The twelve-by-fourteen-foot briefing room was normally packed with as many as twenty aircrew and grunts. The thorough briefings covered known aspects of the mission including the six-digit coordinates for insertions or extractions and expected enemy activity. Frequencies would be assigned and call signs of all the teams and participating aviation assets would be distributed.

185

After all inserts, teams were required to make radio contact through a relay site with Operations at Camp Reasoner, call sign "Stone Pit." If contact could not be made, the team would be pulled out.

"Okay, guys, it looks like we have another day out in the woods," 1Lt Robert "Skip" Massey, call sign "Scarface Four Five," said as he briefed his copilot, wingman, "Curveball" (not his real call sign) and me. In country for five months, Massey was a cool, level-headed aviator.

We would fly in the number two aircraft with Massey as the flight leader. Our flight would work with two CH-46s from HMM-364. Their squadron call sign was "Swift." Recon, with many teams in the field at any one time, was an outstanding source of information about enemy activity. Their mission was not to engage the enemy, but to observe them without being detected. If detected, they were to call for extraction.

Our day began with repositioning to the compound at Camp Reasoner and getting our brief. We arrived on time, but could see the '46s had already arrived. Their crew was headed for the operations shack.

A skinhead grunt major gave us our brief. "Sniffer" had come up "hot" over a large area west of Da Nang. Division HQ wanted three teams inserted into the area to find out what the hell was going on. Two teams south of the insertion area were to be pulled out. We were going to have a busy day.

After the brief, the teams were loaded onto the CH-46s. Each CH-46 had an eight-man team to insert. The first insertions were to be west of Da Nang in Elephant Valley. They would be followed by extractions of two teams in the bush south of the insertions. Massey led the gaggle northwest to the entrance of Elephant Valley and we headed west into "bad man" country.

Ten minutes into the valley, Massey called the flight, "I've got the zone at my twelve o'clock, about three klicks. Right next to that knob on the right. Stay back while I take a look at the zone. Over."

Photo of Elephant Valley, looking west. Photo by John Stevens II.

The zone was an open area of tall elephant grass on the valley floor. The valley was encompassed by high terrain on both sides.

Massey made a low pass over the zone, and we stayed in position providing cover. Pulling out of his pass, he made a call, "Swift Lead, the zone is plenty big. I did not see any stumps. There is vegetation on all sides. The wind looks like it's out of the west. It looks light."

"Roger, Scarface," replied Swift beginning his approach.

Once high over the zone, the CH-46 leaned over on its right side and started a spiral descent. The Cobras began an orbit over the zone 180 degrees out from the other in position to roll in on a covering gun run at any sign of trouble or enemy fire.

The Sea Knight, just coming to a hover in a landing zone, was now the most vulnerable to enemy fire. Surrounded by heavy vegetation, the VC might be set up for an ambush. When the helicopter landed, the team ran out down the rear ramp and headed for cover in the jungle. The CH-46 took off the moment the last man on the team hit the ground.

No sooner had the helicopter cleared the zone, when a call came over Fox Mike. "Scarface! We're taking fire! We're taking fire!"

The team was "leapfrogging" along the southern edge of the landing zone. One or two team members stopped every few yards to fire toward the north side with intent of making the VC keep their heads down.

The VC had used one of their favorite tricks. They had held back until the team was on the ground. We would have to go back in and get the team giving the VC a good opportunity to shoot down a helicopter.

Massey, wanting to get a firm confirmation on direction of the enemy fire, called, "Team X-ray, where is the fire coming from? Over."

A call came back from the team. X-ray was breathing heavily as he ran for cover. "We are taking fire from the north edge of the zone. It appears to be a small force. Small arms fire only. You going to get us out?"

"That's affirmative, X-ray. Keep your heads down. We're going to give Charlie some re-supply first." Continuing, he said, "Six Two, I'm in hot!" Massey rolled in firing rockets. They hit the north edge of the zone right where the tracers were coming from.

Curveball started his roll-in covering Massey's pullout. I thought we were a little high, but did not say anything. He started firing his rockets two at a time. All the rockets swung hard to the left and hit in the middle of the zone. I followed with 40 mm grenades along the north edge.

"What the hell are you shooting at?" I asked as we were pulling out.

He did not answer. He knew what the problem was. The Cobra was not in balanced flight. When firing rockets from any air platform, the air stream needs to be smooth. That is, the aircraft has to be in balanced flight. In the Cobra balanced flight is controlled with the rudder pedals. If the "ball" on the instrument panel is not centered rockets hook or slice like a golf ball.

Having a good fix on the team, Massey called Swift. "Swift, this is Four Five. I'm going to make one more run. I'll lay down some Willy Pete on the north side. You follow Six Two in. Over."

"Roger, Scarface," Swift acknowledged.

Massey rolled in firing his white phosphorus rockets into the north tree line. White smoke billowed up as the rockets hit. Curveball followed with his Willy Pete. This time they went into the jungle north of the zone, a good fifty meters away from being useful. After they hit, I followed shooting the 40 mm grenade launcher, this time into the smoke made by Massey's rockets.

The smoke obscuring the VC's vision of the zone allowed the CH-46 to make his approach and land close to the team on the south side of the zone. We continued fire on the north side as the helicopter landed. The recon team made a hasty dash and jumped into the helicopter. The CH-46's .50 cal. machine gun fired into the north side of the zone as the team boarded and departed.

"Six Two, what's your fuel state?" Massey asked.

"Ah, it looks like I've got about 950 pounds. Over."

Wanting to know the '46's situation, Massey asked, "How about you, Swift?"

"I've still got one plus thirty [1-1/2 hours]. Over."

"Good. We have more than enough fuel to make the next insertion. Feel up to go to number two?" Massey asked.

"Sure." Swift's wingman had the other team in his helicopter. The second team's assigned zone was another ten kilometers west. The team had been assigned both primary and secondary zones. During our briefing at Camp Reasoner it had been stressed that it was important to get this team in. "Sniffer" had been receiving signals of heavy enemy movement in the area.

As we approached the next zone, the terrain changed to rolling hills and the vegetation became forest-like. The LZ was a clear area with stumps throughout. There was plenty of room for a CH-46, but he would need to watch for the stumps.

The procedure remained the same. Massey made another low recon of the zone and called in Swift Dash Two.

The CH-46 entered another right spiral to the zone with the two Cobras orbiting above. Swift Dash Two made his approach into the zone. He was coming to a hover when suddenly both .50 cal machine guns started shooting into the heavy forest on each side of the aircraft. Tree branches fell and the helicopter waved off his approach.

"Taking fire! All over the place. Dash Two waving off," he said, relatively calm considering the situation. The sound of his .50 cal machine guns could be heard in the background.

By this time Massey had begun his gun run. Curveball was just bringing up the nose of our Cobra and getting ready for our run. We rolled in shooting rockets. Once again, they hooked and hit in the middle of the zone. The CH-46 would have been smoked if he had not waved off. I was getting scared!

"This guy is going to get someone killed the way he is shooting," I said to myself.

As the CH-46 gained altitude, he reported that he had received hits but no damage.

"Are you in good enough shape to go to the alternate? "Over," Massey asked.

"That's affirmative."

These guys have more guts than brains, I thought. After getting shot up, the '46 was willing to go back into another zone. He was one cool S.O.B.

The secondary zone, about two kilometers east of the zone we had just departed, was about the same size as the first.

After Massey made his low recon, the CH-46 again spiraled into the landing zone.

The team was out the back and headed for the closest cover on the east side of the zone.

"We are taking fire! Taking fire! Twelve o'clock!" came the call from Dash Two as he departed the zone.

"Scarface, this is Team Zulu. We're taking fire from the west side of the zone! I have one wounded. Over," the recon team radio man's voice shouted over the sounds of fire. The team was in the jungle on the east side of the zone.

We had ourselves another situation. This force was larger than the one that had ambushed us in the first zone, and we had expended some of our ordinance on the two previous extractions. To add to that, we had only about an hour and ten minutes of fuel left and it was a 30-minute ride to the refueling point.

Massey had called in "hot" and was pumping rockets into the area of fire. We followed. Curveball's rockets were going into the general area.

As we pulled out of the run, I fired the last of my 40 mm grenades into the edge of the jungle. Massey was on the radio.

"Da Nang DASC. Da Nang DASC. This is Scarface Four Five. Over."

Not waiting for a response, he rolled in on his next rocket run. Climbing out of his run, he came up again on Victor. "DASC, this is Scarface Four Three. I am in contact. I have a shot-up '46, one wounded on the ground, and I'm getting low on fuel and ordinance. I need an OV-10 on station as soon as possible. I also need another set of guns to relieve us for refueling along with a pair of '46s. Do you copy? Over."

"Roger, Four Five. I have been monitoring your situation and have a Hostage OV-10 enroute to your position. He has some fast movers on station. Scarface Two One flight has been scrambled from the medivac pad along with the medivac CH-46s."

"Roger, I have a copy."

Wanting to know how the team was doing, Massey called, "Zulu. This is Scarface. What's your situation? How's your wounded doing? Over."

"He's bleeding bad. He's hit in the back. We need to get him out of here now!" he responded, his voice full of stress. I could hear the sounds of the firefight on his radio.

Massey knew it was decision time. We had just enough ordinance to make one good rocket run with Willy Petes to give the '46 a good smoke screen.

"Swift Lead, where's your wingman? Looks like we may have to go back in now."

"Scarface, this is Swift Lead. My wingman is starting to lose oil pressure on his number one engine. He must have taken a hit in the engine area during the last insertion. I am sending him home. I still have a team on board. I should be light enough to handle picking them up. Give me some smoke. We can't wait for the cavalry. Let's get this over with. I'm going in."

"Roger," Massey replied. "Six Two, we are going to pull them out. I'm going to put my Willy Pete right into the west side where the fire is coming from. You cover Swift with your mini-gun along the edge of the zone. You copy?"

"That's a Roger."

Massey again came up on the radio to DASC. He requested the OV-10 be assigned to meet Swift Dash Two and escort him back to Da Nang.

DASC complied. I was glad Massey wanted mini-gun. The way Curveball was shooting rockets, the CH-46 would have been in more danger from him than the VC.

Swift "corkscrewed" down to the zone. The smoke Massey put down covered the whole western side of the LZ. It looked like the Sea Knight might even be in it.

Watching not to get too close to the foliage and have a blade strike, Swift landed as close as he could to the team. His crew chief was shooting his .50 cal into the smoke.

The team darted out of their cover carrying their wounded comrade. They climbed aboard just as we were at the bottom of our run. My mini-gun was firing into the area west of the Sea Knight. The smoke had started to drift over the zone.

Swift Lead was nearly engulfed in smoke when he called. "Coming out."

We headed for Da Nang, our two Cobras on Swift's wing. Massey made contact with DASC and canceled the medivac package. The Hostage OV-10 arrived on station after escorting Swift Two. His A-4s were on station ready to drop their ordinance.

By the time we had re-armed and refueled at Marble Mountain, Swift Lead had returned from dropping off the wounded and the rest of the recon teams at Camp Reasoner. Coordinating, we agreed on meeting back at Reasoner. Swift needed to refuel and find his wingman. He was back in the squadron area getting another aircraft. We also needed to re-arm and refuel.

It was 1000 hours. We had already pulled two teams out after inserting them. We had taken fire in three zones and had one shot up CH-46 and a wounded marine. It was beginning to look like it was going to be a long day.

1100 hours. Swift Lead landed at Reasoner and joined us in the operations shack. We needed to take another look at what was happening.

Division HQ knew something was going on out there. A team was needed in the area of the last zone. Another zone was picked with a secondary. By 1145 hours we were airborne. Again, we headed west into Elephant Valley.

When we got back into the area, the sky was hazy from smoke. The A-4s had left their mark. Their napalm and our Willy Pete had started several fires in the area. The smoke from the fires brought the visibility down to about two kilometers. This was not unusual. Any time there was a good "shoot-em-up," fires were started, and the air filled with smoke as the battle progressed.

The new primary LZ was only one kilometer from the last, but on higher ground toward the top of the valley ridges. This would give the team a good observation point. None of us were excited about going back into the area.

Swift Lead would make the insertion. Massey went through his brief about the zone and made a low pass. This time he called on UHF radio as he passed over the zone.

"I see flashes. I'm taking fire! Two o'clock!" It is almost impossible to hear small arms fire in a Cobra with a closed cockpit. Normally the only way one can tell where the fire is coming from is by seeing the tracers coming by or by seeing the muzzle flashes of the weapons being fired. If flashers or tracers could be seen while making a high-speed pass, the fire had to be intense. There was reason for concern.

Covering Massey's pullout, Curveball called, "Six Two is in hot."

After he finished firing three salvos of two, I hosed down the area with our grenade launcher to cover our pull out.

This was getting strange. First of all, Cobras seldom, if ever, got shot at during the low recon pass of a zone.

"Okay, Swift," Massey said over UHF. "I do not know what's going on today, but let's give the alternate a try."

"Roger, Scarface," was Swift's less than enthusiastic reply.

We could see the secondary zone off to the west and headed for it.

The '46 made another circling approach from above. As he came to a hover in zone, he called, "Taking fire! Twelve to three o'clock." This time there was concern in Swift's voice.

"Going in hot!" Curveball said to me.

Oh, shit! Here we go again, I thought as we pulled out of the covering gun run. Tracers were whizzing by our cockpit. The CH-46 cleared the zone and was scrambling for altitude.

"Swift, this is Four Six. I think I've had enough of this area for a while. What do you say we take your PAX home?"

"You won't get any argument out of me."

We headed toward Reasoner to regroup and hold a pow-wow with the 1st Marines. We had been shot out of five zones without getting a team in, and we had not even had lunch.

We had another brief with Recon Operations. They were determined to get a couple of teams in. I imagine the "heavies" wanted to know what the hell was causing us so much trouble out there. "Sniffer" must have been right.

The next zone was straight west of Da Nang, about five kilometers south of where we had been working. The zone looked good when we arrived. Massey's recon did not show anything unusual. Swift made his spiral descent and came to what looked like a hover in the zone. As the helicopter came to a slow hover for touch down, tracers started spitting out the right side of the Sea Knight as it waved off.

"We got one!" he called, his voice full of excitement. "There was a gooner standing next to the zone. The dumb shit was just standing there watching us land. Chalk up one confirmed! I did not see anyone else."

After covering his wave-off, we decided enough was enough and headed back to Reasoner. Once back at the compound, the "heavies" decided the next day had to be a better one for insertions. I'm guessing, but I suspected the NVA in the area were about to find out what a B-52 Arc Light was all about.

We finished the day by extracting the two teams we had scheduled. The day had to be a record for taking fire . . . six zones in a row. Anyway, it was a record for me.

After debrief back at squadron operations, I saw Lts. Gallo and Silva in the next room. They were making up the schedule for the next day. Pissed off, I stomped into the room.

"Don't ever schedule me with Curveball again. That son-of-a-bitch damn near smoked friendlies today. He can't shoot a rocket to save his ass." I had never flown with anyone who shot rockets so badly. We were lucky marines on the ground did not get hurt because of his incompetence. I swore to myself that I would never fly with him again. And I did not!

A few days later I was again scheduled for recon. Finally, I was scheduled for back seat time in preparation for a HAC ride. I was scheduled with Captain D.W. Kane, call sign "Scarface Four," a second-tour pilot. Experienced back-seaters did not like giving up their seats and Kane was true to form. We had not flown together, and he was apprehensive. I am sure he had given up his seat reluctantly. The look on his face was less than encouraging. Captain "Ron" Fix, call sign "Scarface Two," would be on our wing.

We had an 0630 brief at the Recon compound at Camp Reasoner. It was dark when we launched from MMAF and joined to CH-46 crew on the pad at Reasoner.

After walking up the hill to the briefing shack, the eight pilots and four CH-46 crewmembers squeezed into the small briefing room along with three more grunt recon team leaders. We would be inserting three six-man reconnaissance teams into the Elephant Valley. The briefing was routine with the usual warning: "Enemy activity and movements are known to be in the area of the insertions." A few excerpts on the events of a few days earlier were included.

It was daylight as we walked to the aircraft. We loaded two teams on the Sea Knights and launched for Elephant Valley. We were only twenty minutes into the flight when Kane who was on the maps had the first insertion point in sight. The LZ was right on the floor of the valley, pretty much dead center with tall elephant grass.

"Scarface Two, this is Four . . . I've got the zone in sight. I'm going to go in for a low pass." Unable to use my call sign because Kane was the HAC, I had used his.

"Roger, I'll cover your six," replied Fix.

The '46s were about three to four minutes behind us and would arrive about the time I completed the low recon of the zone.

With the LZ straight ahead, I nosed the Cobra over and made a dive for the zone. I was doing 160 knots by the time I reached it and made a pass at about 75 feet.

"I got the controls," barked Kane as I pulled up. "What the hell are you doing?"

"Just making a low pass, sir. That's the way we did it in Phu Bai."

"Well that's not the way we do it here," he said, irritation evident in his voice. "We do it at about two to three hundred feet. You can get a better feel for the zone plus you can see the edges of the zone better."

"Yes, sir." That sounded okay to me. Who was I to argue with this guy? It was his second or third tour. He gave the controls back to me and I called the transports.

"Cattle Call Lead, this is Scarface Four. The zone looks okay to me. You've got some heavy brush to the north. Wind is right out of the west. Over."

"Roger, Scarface. We are coming in right."

Cattle Call Lead started a right-hand spiral descent to the landing zone. This told us the HAC was making the approach because he normally sat in the right seat and would make his approach turning on his side so he could see where he was going.

The CH-46 did not waste any time getting down, nor did he waste any time sitting in the zone. As soon as he touched down and the rear gate of the helicopter touched the ground, the team was out the rear and the CH-46 was airborne.

The first thing I needed to do was establish communications.

"Tiger Seven, Tiger Seven. This is Scarface Four. How do you read? Over."

"Scarface Four. This is Tiger Seven. I read you loud and clear. Stand by. Let me make contact with Stone Pit. Over." His reply on Fox Mike was in the usual whisper.

"Roger." The team made contact with Stone Pit at Reasoner, and we headed on down the valley for the next insertion.

We heard a call on Victor. "Scarface Four, Scarface Four. This is Da Nang DASC. Over."

"I've got the radios," said Kane over the intercom. "Da Nang DASC, this is Scarface Four. Go ahead. Over."

"Roger, Scarface Four. We have a mission change. Are you ready to copy? Over."

"Go ahead, DASC."

"We have a recon team in contact. We request immediate extraction. Coordinates are . . . I shackle, Romeo over Alpha, November Bravo 239865. Hostage Sam is on station, primary Victor plus point two. How do you copy? Over."

The coordinates had just been given to us in code. Each pilot carried a card with two wheels, one slightly smaller that the other. Each wheel had the alphabet along with the numbers from zero to nine.

When they gave us "Shackle Romeo over Alpha," Kane placed the "A" on the larger wheel over the "R" on the smaller wheel. Then he read the letter on the smaller wheel opposite the number giving him the correct number. After matching them up, he had the proper coordinates.

Our primary UHF frequency was 255.0. When DASC told us Hostage was up primary plus point two they were telling us to go up to the frequency 255.2.

Shuffling his kneeboard, Kane wrote down the instructions and called back, "I have a good copy. Scarface Four and flight are outbound at this time. Over."

"Roger, Scarface. Good luck. DASC out."

Checking to see if Fix was hearing all this, Kane called. "Scarface Two, did you copy? Over."

"That's affirmative, Four."

Kane took out his "whiz wheel" and decoded the coordinates.

"Okay, flight. It looks like the team is south of here about twenty klicks. Do you concur, One?"

"How about you Cattle Call?"

"Yup."

I still had the flight controls and was flying. Kane was busy looking at his map. "Okay, Robby, hang a left up here just past the next ridge."

"Yes, sir," I responded, and we headed to our new mission.

Inbound, I gave the Hostage Sam a call. He informed us the team's call sign was "Razor." On the run, they had one wounded who was being carried in a make-shift stretcher made out of a poncho and a couple of tree limbs.

Seeing the OV-10 ahead, I called again, "Hostage, this is Scarface Two and flight. We are about three klicks to your north, Anything new? Over."

"Okay, Scarface, the situation is still the same. I have the team on the move and they are headed for a LZ located about another klick west of their position. They are being pursued and are taking fire. I've expended everything I have, and the bad guys are too close for me to move in the fixed wing. I've got a flight of A-4s on station with two Fox Fours on the alert pad. Over."

"Roger, Hostage. I'm going Fox Mike."

Needing our flight to be on the team's primary Fox Mike frequency, I called, "Flight, go primary Fox Mike."

"Roger," replied all three aircraft.

I was surprised Kane was letting me lead the flight. With the situation as it was, I thought he would pass the lead to Fix, who was also a qualified flight/strike leader.

"Team Razor, Team Razor. This is Scarface Four. Over."

A reply came immediately. The voice was one of a man on the move. He was breathing heavily as they moved through the thick vegetation. "Scarface, this is Razor. I'm moving west taking fire from my six. I have one wounded. He cannot move on his own and we are having trouble . . . he is a big man." The voice sounded exhausted.

Having the OV-10 in sight, I came up on UHF. "Hostage, give me a mark on their position. Over."

"Roger, Scarface. They are right on my nose. I'm coming up now. Mark . . . mark," he said as he made a low pass over the team.

When I came over the area he had marked, I looked straight down and could see three or four marines moving west along a narrow path. About half a kilometer ahead of them was an open spot that would work as a pick-up zone. It was closer than I had thought it would be.

"Razor, this is Scarface. I'm overhead and have you in sight. Have the last man in your team pop a smoke."

"Roger."

Below I could see a red smoke. "Have a red smoke, Razor. I understand you have no friendlies east of it. Over."

"Roger, the red smoke and affirmative on the friendlies."

I called Fix, "Two, I'm in hot. Let's work out to the east of the smoke."

I started a gun run. Kane wasted no time putting down a deadly stream of mini-gun along the small trail followed by the 40 mm grenade launcher. I did not fire any rockets. Not being a HAC, I did not have much experience firing rockets. The team was too close. Fix's copilot laid a volley of mini-gun right on target just east of the smoke.

Making two passes, I looked for the team. I needed to know their exact location. They had just moved through a thin patch of woods and stopped.

"Razor, how are you doing?"

"Scarface, this is Razor. We had to stop. Our wounded is just too big. He must be 240 pounds."

"Where's he hit?"

"Half of his ass is gone. His right cheek is in bad shape. He's not bleeding bad, but he can't walk."

Confirming that Kane and Fix both had the team in sight, I continued "I can see where you are, and do not see any VC headed your way. Take a break. We are not going anywhere. We can see what's happening around you."

After a short break, the team headed out and made it to the pick-up zone.

Looking over the zone, Kane and I thought it would make a good LZ. The VC would not be able to get very close to the zone without being seen.

"Cattle Call Lead, it looks like the wind is still out of the west. If you receive any fire I think it will come from the east. Are you ready to go in?"

Cattle Call Lead had made the insertion in Elephant Valley and did not have any troops onboard. He would make the extraction.

"That's affirmative, Scarface. I'm going in right." As he made his circling descent to the right, we kept a close eye on the trail to the east. The pick-up was uneventful. The team ran aboard as soon as the '46 landed, and they were airborne in a matter of seconds. We escorted them back to Da Nang where the medivac bird landed at the hospital pad.

"Well, how did I do?" I asked Kane during debrief. He looked at me with a funny look.

"You need work."

I left mumbling to myself.

A few weeks later, I was a new HAC assigned to fly wing on Massey. Our mission was recon. Our brief was not unusual. We were to make three insertions and two extractions in an area north of Antenna Valley.

The two insertions went well. The teams had been put into their primary zone, and we had not taken any fire. Good communication had been established with the recon radio relay site by both teams.

The first extraction also went well. The team had a good zone, and the CH-46 did not have any problems getting in.

The second team was not near a zone that would work and was going to have to be pulled out by dropping an 80-foot ladder into the jungle. The team would have to hook on with a D-ring. They would then ride home on the ladder under the helicopter.

As we headed for the second extraction, Massey gave the team a call on the Fox Mike, "Jackknife" this is Scarface Four Five. Over."

"Scarface Four Five, this is Jackknife. I have you in sight. We are at your twelve o'clock along the stream bed." I looked ahead. A stream was flowing in a wide gully about two kilometers off our nose. The clearing the stream made was not wide enough for the CH-46 to land but it was wide enough to make the ladder extraction easier.

"Jackknife, this is Scarface. I think I have the stream in sight. How about a zone brief? Over."

Jackknife gave the brief. They had not had any contact, and it looked like it would be a routine pick up. The team popped a smoke. We identified it and the CH-46 made his approach. Massey and I entered an orbit over the pick-up spot and watched as the long ladder was dropped from the helicopter.

Ladder extract. United States Marine Corps file photo.

The team started climbing on the ladder and attaching their D-rings. As each marine attached himself the ladder, the pilot would increase the helicopter's hover slightly higher and the next grunt would jump onto an open step.

With the sixth team member hooked to the ladder but still on the ground, the team leader gave the "okay" signal. The CH-46 was just getting ready to start his ascent when the marine highest on the ladder jumped off!

Looking down from above and seeing him jump, Massey called immediately, "Peachbush, hold your position. You have a man on the ground." As he was speaking, two more marines jumped off the ladder. Reaching the ground, they knelt over the team member who had been the first to jump. It looked like he was hurt. They picked him up and attached him to the ladder and followed suit. I had no idea what was happening or why the guy had jumped.

The CH-46 pilot also had no idea. We took them back to Camp Reasoner. After we landed and shut down we looked over to where the team had been dropped. We could see a lot of activity. Several marines were kneeling next a marine lying on the ground. Medical personnel were attending the injured marine.

We learned the last man to attach his D-ring to the ladder had gotten his foot stuck between two rocks and could not get it out. As the helicopter was getting ready to depart, the team leader who was the highest on the ladder jumped to give him assistance. After falling about ten or fifteen feet to the rocky stream, his head struck one of the rocks. The blow killed him. He died trying to assist a fellow team member.

XXI
F-4 Phantom

"LOVEBUG FLIGHT, you are cleared for take-off. Turn left, heading zero-niner-zero after takeoff. Left down-wind departure approved."

"Roger, tower." Lovebug Lead replied. He asked, "Two, are you ready?"

"Two's ready."

Loaded with napalm, both F-4B Phantoms went full afterburner and headed down the Chu Lai runway. My heart was pounding as I sat in the back seat of the number two Phantom pretending to be a RIO. This was not only my first ride in a fighter, but it was going to be a real-life combat mission dropping napalm on suspected NVA positions in the DMZ north of the Rockpile.

Marine F-4 Phantom jet. Photo by Doug Orahood.

205

A week before, as luck would have it, Skip Massey, Bob McKiernan, and I happened to be standing in the ready room when Major Womack, our executive officer entered.

"Anyone want to go for a ride in a Phantom?" he asked.

All of us jumped up and answered with a resounding "Yes!"

Womack went on to explain that our squadron was going to start an exchange program with an F-4 Phantom squadron at Chu Lai. They were going to send their pilots and WISOs (weapons information systems officers) to fly with us for a day, and we were going to send a few of our people to Chu Lai to fly with them. We would be giving them familiarization rides in the front seat of the Cobra. They would be checked out on working the turret and then would fly with us for a day. In turn they would check us out in the ejection seat and give us familiarization rides in the back seat of the F-4.

The following week we jumped on a CH-53 heading for Chu Lai, an airbase eighty-eight kilometers south of Marble Mountain. The flight took about twenty-five to thirty minutes.

We scrambled off the Sea Stallion to a flight line of Marine Corps jets and army helicopters. The marines, who had fixed-wing, shared the base with the army. After landing, we noticed several buildings with big red crosses on their roofs. I assumed a medical unit and hospital must also be located at the facility.

After checking in with the Squadron Operations Officer and throwing our gear into our assigned hootches, we headed for the club. We were a little early and did not have anything else to do. We were not going on our flights until the next day, so we indulged in drinking some nice cold beer. By the time we had our third Hamm's, others started drifting in to grab a beer or two before chow.

As they drifted in, we noticed a big difference about Chu Lai . . . there were round-eyed women on base. The army had a major medical unit on the field. Nurses were everywhere. That night they were even going to have a dance. This was definitely going be something different!

The evening festivities had been scheduled to begin early and quit early. We chowed down, had a few more beers and lively conversations with the jet jocks. We were getting a feel of how these boys were fighting the war.

North Vietnam was not being bombed at this point in the war, but fixed-wing support were sneaking into Laos and Cambodia bombing the Ho Chi Min Trail. On television reports back home politicians were declaring that we were not doing anything like that. But, then again, they were 8,000 miles away.

In our discussions with the jet jocks, one thing that kept coming up baffled me. It sounded like they came home with big holes in their airplanes on a regular basis. Even so, that did not bother us any. After all, we were just going for familiarization rides.

Watching all the good looking, round-eyed women dance later that evening, we agreed that these guys lived quite well. The evening ended at about 2200 hours. The three of us, having consumed enough beer to cause major problems in finding the right hootch, finally made it to our racks.

0600 came much too early. I do not know about Massey and McKiernan, but I had a terrible hangover. After breakfast the first item on the agenda was to get an ejection seat check-out, a task that took about an hour. We learned what to yank and what not to yank. We also learned that we probably would not hear the pilot say "eject" more than once. By the time you asked "What?" the guy in the front seat would be gone.

Each seat had two ejection handles, one above the crewmember's helmet and the other between his legs. Pulling either one would send the crew member on a rocket ride never to be forgotten. The chances of ejecting at a high speed and not injuring one's back or hurting some other part of the body were slim.

The pilot had the option of setting the switch so each seat would eject independently or he could select the second option, in which case both the front and back scat would eject in sequence if either crewmember engaged the ejection handle. We were told that more than likely the pilot would select the second option for us greenhorns.

After being introduced to my pilot, the flight lead, and the WISO, I wondered why we needed to be a flight of two. After all, I was just going for a ride. Our briefing was at 1000 hours. We went to the briefing room where a first lieutenant was standing at a podium. A big map covered the wall behind him. To my surprise, I learned we were not just going for a ride. Instead, we were going to drop napalm on some little people in black pajamas up at the DMZ.

The whole crew was made up of first lieutenants. My pilot had been in country for about three months, and the flight lead for seven.

Having been briefed of my duties as a back-seater and having been shown what all the gizmos and gadgets were for, I was instructed to turn them on but not to do anything with them. My primary mission once we had a target would be to call off the altitudes to the pilots as we made our bombing run. I would be told what the MSL altitude of the target would be. This information was necessary so we knew at what altitude to make our drop. My job upon being given the MSL altitude was to add 1000 feet to it. As we made our bombing run and hit 1000 feet above our pre-determined drop altitude, I was to call off "one thousand feet." Then I was to begin calling hundreds when we were 500 feet above the drop site. On my mark, the pilot would drop the load.

Shortly after the briefing, we walked out to the flight line where I was introduced to the crew chief. My pilot did his preflight. It did not appear that he had to do any more than a cursory "look-see." When he finished, we climbed in, and the crew chief helped us strap in and pulled the safety pins out of the ejection handles. I was told the pilot had set the control for both seats to eject if he did. The possibility of having to eject was heavy on my mind. I had no desire to punch out.

I checked out my oxygen mask. I tried to talk through it and discovered it was like talking through a hollow tube. My intercom was set on "hot mike" so I did not have to push anything to talk with the pilot. After both of us were properly strapped in, the canopy was closed.

The radio check procedures between the two aircraft were very similar to our squadron's procedures. After the check, Flight Lead called the tower for taxi instructions. We were cleared to runway one eight.

At the end of the taxiway, the before-takeoff checks were completed. The tower cleared us for takeoff. We taxied out to the runway and lined up.

Throttles were advanced. The familiar "bang" followed the lighting of the afterburners. Brakes were released, and we accelerated down the runway in formation. I was surprised by the noise level in the cockpit. The flight instructors at Pensacola were always talking about how quiet jets were. I determined they must not have flown in the F-4 because there definitely was a loud roar as we sped down the runway. The flight rotated, the landing gear came up, and we were off on an unforgettable experience.

After take-off the flight was cleared to a heading of 090 and reported "feet wet" over the South China Sea. We leveled at 2,000 feet and turned north and started our climb to altitude. We leveled off at our assigned altitude of 20,000 feet. Wow! Vietnam looked a lot different up here. Within ten minutes we could see Marble Mountain.

We were flying a tight formation. Doing so required constant power adjustments. The drag of the F-4 was unbelievable. When power adjustments were made by reducing power in order to stay in position, the drag slowed the aircraft down so fast my head would snap forward; then, when power was increased, the thrust would slap my head back against the rear of the seat. My head was bouncing back and forth continuously. The bouncing certainly was not helping my hang-over.

Our mission was to head north to the DMZ and be on station

for an army 0-1 birddog with the call sign "Danny Three." He would be our forward air controller.

As we passed north of Phu Bai, Flight Lead gave him a call and checked in. Danny Three replied that we had arrived just in time. He had a recon team in contact. They were taking only small arms fire. The team was on the move headed for a pick-up zone. The helicopters were on their way. I could tell Danny Three had been in country for a while. His slow, deliberate southern drawl was confident. He knew what needed to be done. It seemed he had done this many times before.

Shortly after our first contact, he called back, "Lovebug, I'm going to lay down a Willy Pete where I think the VC are. The team will be to the south of my mark. I'll let you know how far after I mark the target. It appears that there is only a small unit in pursuit. If you take fire it will be from the north of my mark. Do have you have me in sight? Over."

"That's an affirmative, Three."

Looking down from 20,000 feet, I strained yet could barely see the ground. I certainly could not see the birddog down there. The front canopy of the Phantom provided excellent visibility; however, the same was not true of the back canopy. The back seat sat low in the cockpit and, because the canopy started at about shoulder height, upward visibility was good, but downward visibility was poor.

The birddog rolled in and marked the area with two Willy Petes. Looking down, Flight Lead spotted the smoke and called, "I've got your mark. Where are the friendlies?" He had no sooner finished his sentence before he went inverted and started descending. We followed suit.

"Roger, Lovebug. Friendlies are 200 meters south of the mark. Targets are fifty meters north of the mark. Over."

This is fantastic, I thought.

Both Phantoms were descending out of 20,000 feet, inverted. Straining my head back I could see down through the top of my canopy. The belly of Lovebug Lead was below as we descended. It would have been a great picture, but, as usual, I did not have my camera.

The two Phantoms did a "split S" recovery at about 5,000 feet, and Flight Lead rolled in for his first pass. We were right behind them covering his pull out.

We had determined our release altitude would be 1200 feet MSL which we figured would be about 400 feet AGL. The altimeter was spinning as we made our descent. I was trying to keep track of our altitude and getting ready to start my call.

Reaching 2,200 feet I started my call, "One thousand feet."

With my peripheral vision I could see the ground screaming at us. At 1,700 feet I started my countdown. "Five, four, three, two, one. Mark."

The F-4 dropped two canisters of deadly napalm. The pilot pulled back on the stick with vengeance. The Phantom pulled out screaming for altitude. I thought I had just left my ass back in the DMZ.

Fighting G-forces, I looked through the mirror. I was searching to see where the napalm had hit behind us. The instrument panel in front of me became a blur and my field of vision narrowed until I "grayed out." I certainly was not ready for the seven to eight Gs on my body.

We were wearing G-suits designed to retard the flow of blood from the upper body to the lower extremities. Decreased blood flow to the brain would cause blackout. Up to this point, I was impressed as to how many G-forces we had been pulling, but I was not prepared for what had just happened. I lost vision only momentarily before the Gs decreased, and I recovered. In the mirror located on the right side and top of the instrument panel, I could see the blast and fire from the exploding napalm.

We screamed upward to about 4,000 feet and set up for our second run. This time we came in from the opposite direction and I prepared myself for the pull out. Following the fast moving altimeter was easier during this run as my mind was catching up with the airplane. Giving my pilot the mark was much easier, and I managed without difficulty. We dropped four canisters of napalm. Looking through the mirror, I saw the devastating blast.

Pulling out, Danny Three called Flight Lead, "Lovebug, I've got gooners on the run! Forty meters north of your last hit. It looks like about fifty or more running to the west. What have you got left? Over."

"We can give you a couple of runs of twenty mike-mike."

"Great! You are cleared in!" The lead Phantom rolled its 20 mm Gatling gun tearing up a path of destruction.

We followed. Inside the cockpit, the sound of cannon fire was awesome. It was similar to our mini-gun, only much louder and deeper. The Phantom shuddered. I wondered what kind of terror the NVA troops on the ground must be feeling. We made two passes with the 20 mm and headed home.

"Robby, shut off all your radios . . . now!" The pilot said as we were climbing to altitude after our second cannon run. I knew better than ask why.

I was "assholes and elbows" shutting them down. I did not notice anything flashing or making noises. Something had locked onto us. *Oh, shit! I'm going to have to punch out of this thing* was my first thought.

A few minutes later the pilot said that everything was alright. A radar-controlled weapon had just locked in on us, but their lock-on had been lost. That made my day!

"Is this as fast as this crate will go?" I jokingly asked as we got back to 20,000 feet and were heading home.

Boys being boys, the F-4 jocks had to do a little showing off for the "rotor head." I heard a slight boom behind us as the afterburner kicked in. I looked at the airspeed. It had just jumped fifty knots and were starting to haul ass. This older "B" model F-4 was not as fast as the newer models the air force flew, but it managed to get me faster than the speed of sound, mach 1.2, before entering another inverted descent that culminated fifty feet above the beach at 500 knots. The world was moving by . . . fast! Sampans were small black dots whizzing by my eyes as we passed. We went back to altitude after about ten minutes of the F-4 crew showing their "helicopter jock" a thing or two and scaring the hell out of me in the process.

As we approached Chu Lai from the north, Lovebug Lead called Chu Lai tower and got our clearance for the break. The flight came in directly over the landing runway at 800 feet. Midway down the runway, Lovebug Lead kissed off and broke left with a ninety-degree bank entering down wind. Three seconds later we did our break.

To my amazement, the aircraft pulled about four Gs in the break.

"No wonder you jet jocks have hemorrhoids," I said to my pilot as I fought the pressure of being four times heavier than normal.

The landing was uneventful. We taxied to the squadron area where the crew chief was waiting for us by the revetments. After we shut down, he helped us out of the aircraft, and we walked into the squadron briefing room for de-brief. I thanked the pilots and started looking for my squadron mates.

I compared notes with Massey and McKiernan. All three of us had wild experiences. Their rides were similar to mine, except they were over Cambodia. Massey's jet had taken some anti-aircraft fire. He said the tracers coming at them were as big as softballs.

We were glad to be back from an experience none of us would ever forget. We were looking forward to having our day with these guys when they came up and flew in our front seats. Thanking our pilots again, we jumped on an army CH-47 headed for Marble Mountain. The Chinook rained hydraulic fluid the whole trip. The crew chiefs must have had to have a Ph.D. in hydraulics to keep it flying.

Landing at Marble Mountain, all three of us jumped out of the monster, kissed the ground, and swore we would never fly in a CH-47 again.

XXII
March

MARCH ROLLED IN. The weather was hot with midday temperatures running over 100 degrees. In the heat, a loaded Cobra would struggle to get airborne, bouncing and sliding its way to the runway. The pilot would nose into the wind, hoping for a breeze to give the overloaded machine some help. True to its name, the Cobra would start its takeoff slithering down the runway while struggling for airspeed in order to develop enough speed to enter translational lift. Once obtained, cleaner airflow through the rotor system gave the helicopter enough lift to defy gravity and begin flight. During his feat of clever maneuvering, the pilot would carefully watch his power while delicately adjusting collective to maximize available engine torque without adding too much and consequently losing valuable rotor RPM. Many a pilot had to clean his pants after watching a fence or some other obstacle at the end of the runway get bigger and bigger.

Too many times the aircraft, especially the under-powered Hueys, would have minds of their own and head for terra firma. These short-lived flights would culminate in clouds of dust as a red-faced HAC sat in the dirt burning off fuel.

I had been getting back seat time in preparation for my scheduled HAC ride. I'd had my fill of flying in the front seat. Shooting the turret guns was exciting, but I needed to get pilot-in-command time. My buddy Paul Williams was my mentor. Paul had been in the front seat the first time I had a chance to shoot the 2.75 mm rockets. I had smooth-talked him into letting me fly the back seat. The day had been relatively uneventful and we were headed back to Marble Mountain when we heard an OV-10 talking to Da Nang DASC. He was looking for some guns. He had seen several VC run into a bunker and wanted to roust them out. He was about six kilometers south of Marble Mountain, and we were about ten minutes away.

Williams called him, "Hostage, this is Scarface. We are a flight of two about ten minutes south, headed your way. Can we be of assistance? Over."

"Roger, Scarface. I've just run about ten gooners into a bunker complex. How about working it? Over."

Happy to get some shooting, Williams called back, "We would be glad to be of service. I have your position. I'll give you a call when I have you in sight. Over."

As we approached the area, the Bronco was in an orbit at 3000 feet.

"Hostage, this is Scarface flight. I have you in sight. We are about four klicks south, two thousand five hundred. Over."

"Okay, Scarface. I have you in sight. The bunker is just north of the river, west of a lone clump of trees. I will mark it with Willy Pete. The bunker entrance is on the east side."

Williams instructed me to line myself up behind the OV-10 as he rolled in so we would have a good vantage point to spot the target and would be set up for an immediate rocket run.

As the Bronco rolled in with his marking run, I could see the bunker. His Willy Pete had flown just over the top of the mound.

Pulling out, Hostage called, "Scarface, your target is fifty meters east of the mark."

"Roger, Hostage. I have it."

"All right, Robby. Start your run about 1500 feet, bring the nose up, do a pedal turn to target, and start your run." After I made the pedal turn and rolled in, he continued, "Set the selector switch for 'two' and roll in. Make sure the ball is in the center and when your target is set up on your sight . . . squeeeeze. Squeeeeze that button. Squeeze it just like you squeeze the trigger on a rifle. The better you get set up, the better the rockets will run. When the first set is on the way, adjust your cross hairs on the rockets as they hit."

I lowered the nose to a diving attitude, much steeper than a Huey gun run and steeper than my comfort level. My run had started. Everything Williams had said was running through my mind. I had the target in my sights. I looked down, and the aircraft was in trim with the ball centered. Everything seemed to be right.

"Squeeze. Easy now, do not jerk this thing," I said to myself.

I did not want to make the "snake" jerk just when everything was ready. The opening in the bunker was in my sights. As I slowly squeezed the button on the cyclic, the Cobra jerked slightly as the two rockets were launched from their tubes. Straight as an arrow, the rockets sped toward the bunker. I must have done everything right. I adjusted the cross hairs on my sight. The impact area was just above the target.

I fired the next set of rockets. To my amazement, one of the rockets went right through the small hole the VC had used to get into the bunker!

The ground was coming up fast.

"Pull up, do not get target fixation," said Williams.

I pulled the cyclic back and started my climb, straining to see what damage had been done. A beautiful orange mushroom secondary explosion erupted from the bunker.

"All right! Did you see that?"

I was ecstatic. Back in the states we had seen films of the jet jocks bombing the north. When they got a secondary explosion, they almost creamed their pants. Now I could understand why.

We emptied our ordinance and headed home. Williams complemented me. "Nice shooting," he said, not nearly as enthusiastically as I thought he should have.

From that day on, I considered myself a master at shooting rockets. It took probably another five hundred rockets to really be good consistently, but I did become a master. I could put the rocket right where I wanted. I took pride in my skill. The secret was make everything right and then squeeeeze.

March 6 looked like a pretty routine day for Recon. They had a mission to insert three teams in a mountainous area northwest of Da Nang and just southeast of the A Shau Valley. 1Lt "Ted" Soliday was leading a flight of four, two Cobras and two CH-46s. Flight Lead normally carried the first insertion team and number two flew empty as back-up in the event number one got shot up.

Upon reaching the first LZ, the Cobras checked out the landing . The insertion went as briefed. As the '46s departed back to Da Nang to pick up the second team, the Cobras elected to loiter in the area and make themselves available if the first team should run into trouble.

The ceiling was about 600 to 700 feet. Loitering below the clouds made them a good target for NVA anti-aircraft and small arms fire. There were plenty of holes or breaks in the ceiling showing clear blue sky above. Soliday decided it would be a whole lot safer above the clouds than down low. He elected to climb through them knowing he would not have any trouble finding a hole to get back down. He climbed to about 5000 feet and began cutting circles in the sky. It was a beautiful day. The mountaintops in the distance were sticking through the clouds. The warm morning sunlight poking through the clear canopy, and the smooth air made conditions perfect for just sitting back and enjoying the day. Everything was peaceful.

Cawoomp!! Suddenly the nose of the aircraft pitched to the right and tucked. Horns blew. Red warning lights flashed on the instrument panel.

Soliday had taken a hit! His first reaction to enter autorotation was automatic. He looked down at his trim ball. It was pegged to the left. The aircraft was beginning a spiral to the right in almost uncontrollable flight.

"Two Nine, your tail is gone!" his wingman said over UHF.

Soliday had lost everything from the forty-two-degree gearbox on up. The vertical stabilizer on the aircraft was completely gone. The change of the CG (center of gravity) caused a loss of weight in the rear of the aircraft. The aircraft was now in an unusual attitude with the nose tucked severely. The Cobra was in 60-degree bank. Soliday, reacting with full aft and left cyclic, decreased the steep angle of bank and abruptly brought the aircraft's nose up. The airspeed diminished to a dangerously slow level. The aircraft was close to getting into a negative G-force situation where rotor blades have been known to bend down and come through the front cockpit, putting an end to any chance of controlled flight. The situation was deteriorating!

After correcting his airspeed, Soliday regained some similitude of control. His mind searched for the emergency procedure for losing a vertical stabilizer.

There was not one! Loss of tail rotor procedures were vague. An autorotation was normally thought of as being the best solution.

The aircraft needed airspeed to maintain control. If it got below forty-five knots, uncontrollable spinning would result.

Knowing death was a high probability in his near future, Soliday's thoughts turned to his son Ted, Jr. who was only one month old. A sudden sense of sadness overcame him as he realized he might never have the chance to hold him.

Descending in a right spiral while continually working cyclic, he was able to maintain enough airspeed to keep the Cobra in a controlled flight. The airflow over the Cobra was sufficient to keep it from entering an uncontrollable spin. He experimented by adding power to slow his rate of descent, but that did not work. It resulted in an increase in the rate of spin which made it even harder to control.

The top of the clouds appeared to rise up to meet Soliday as he made his descent. The base of the clouds was still about 600 to

700 feet above the ground. The Cobra popped out, and Soliday could see the valley floor below. He was off to the side of the valley and it looked as if he was going to hit the side of a hill. It was coming at him!

Rapidly approaching the hill, Soliday feared they would not clear the top. Thanks to pure luck, the Cobra cleared the hill through an opening in the foliage where prior air force bombing had blown away the trees. The aircraft continued its spiral. Soliday could see where he would meet the ground. It was on the side of another hill no better than the previous one.

Slowly rolling on power in hopes of getting some cushioning to soften the impact, Soliday inadvertently diminished the airspeed. The aircraft went into an uncontrollable spin. He pulled full collective as they crashed into the hillside, hitting with such G-force that some of the rockets from the rocket pods fired.

The hill was steep and the Cobra tumbled down with the rotor blades and pieces flying in all directions before finally coming to rest against a burned-out tree stump. It was the only stump on the side of the hill. The aircraft was on its right side, nearly inverted.

Soliday regained consciousness smelling JP-4 jet fuel. Realizing he was not dead, he wondered how he had gotten upside down. He had no memory of going down the hill. He could see his copilot in the front shaking his head, trying to get back to reality.

Strapped in, Soliday was inverted. The pilot's door was on the right side, resting against the tree. Strapped upside down, with no way to open the door, he contemplated his options. Releasing his seatbelt, he promptly found himself sitting on his head. Training had taught him this could happen. All crewmembers carried survival knives. The end of the handle was metal and worked well for breaking Plexiglas. Soliday reached for his survival knife and found it had come out of its sheath and was gone. He reached into his survival vest and grabbed the smaller pocket switchblade pilots also carried. He soon learned how difficult it is to cut yourself out while sitting on your head.

When he made the first whack at the canopy, the blade deflected, narrowly missing his arm. The second went through easily. Soon there was a hole big enough to get through. Soliday began crawling out of the aircraft. He about halfway out when he realized his head was still locked inside the aircraft. He had forgotten to unplug his mike cord! Disconnecting, he looked around and found his survival knife lying in the canopy. Grabbing it, he climbed out onto the tree, ready to fight the bad guys! He pulled out his revolver and cocked it. With his knife in his other hand, he stepped off the tree stump and proceeded to roll down the hill nearly sticking himself with his knife and almost shooting himself with his own gun. Once at the bottom, he immediately put both weapons back where they were safe.

Looking up at the Cobra, he spotted his copilot, 1Lt S.B. Nielson, climbing out of the front seat. Because the copilot's door was on the opposite side of the pilot's, he was having no trouble getting out. He was shaken, but not hurt.

After joining up, they saw their wingman overhead. The gunner's turret was moving back and forth, ready to deter any hostilities. Grabbing the survival radio from his vest, Soliday called his wingman and told him they were all right. He could not get an answer from him, so he told him to rock his wings if he could hear him. Dash Two promptly rocked his wings.

Looking over the area and searching the terrain for a suitable LZ for the CH-46 to pick them up, Soliday spotted an area that looked suitable about one-half kilometer away. The only problem would be the jungle in between.

After a three-hour trip through heavy foliage, a CH-46 picked them up and gave them a welcome ride home.

Neither pilot sustained any measurable injury. That was remarkable as the aircraft was a complete pile of junk. Soliday had done a great job controlling an aircraft in an emergency situation for which there were not any defined emergency procedures. His professionalism, along with help from God and a lot of luck, allowed them to fly another day.

On the same day Major H.F. Stroman, our Operations Officer, decided to give Lt Joe Gallo a little back seat time. He made this decision not when in a secure zone, but when he was out in the boonies. To the east of An Hoa was an area called the Arizona Territory. The vegetation, banana trees and other smaller trees and brush, hid the VC very well. Stroman found a flat, clear area to land so he and Gallo could switch seats.

With the controls tightened down, the two pilots quickly switched seats and strapped in. One of the two did the takeoff. Once airborne, there was a mix-up as to just who was on the controls. Both pilots thought the other had the controls. The aircraft nosed into the ground and did a somersault. Gallo was not hurt in the accident, but Stroman, who had a compound fracture on one leg, had to be medivaced out of country.

All marine pilots were trained in positive transfer of the controls. The pilot making the transfer would say, "You've got it," or "You've got the controls." The other pilot would respond with "I've got it," or "I've got the controls." Somehow, the communication

Major H.F. Stroman. Cruise Book photo.

between them had been misunderstood or not heard. I learned a valuable lesson from that accident, but it is sad to learn from the misfortune of another.

March 7. I called my wife through the MARS system to give her the good news that I had just made HAC. I was excited about making aircraft commander. I was ready. Actually, I thought I was overdue. It was not until I hung up that I realized that it was the 6th of March back home, and I had not even wished her a happy anniversary. I had totally forgotten that it was our 6th. I survived it without getting any nasty letters from my bride. I think she had forgotten as well. She usually did.

On March 11, a flight of two Cobras departed MMAF on a recovery mission. This mission was a culmination of events which had begun on March 2. Captain "Ron" Fix was the flight leader. His copilot was Major "Jim" Rider. Rider had just come back to the squadron after a tour at Hill 55 as the Air Liaison Officer. The extraction was in an area west of An Hoa called the Tennis Courts. The team had a wounded lieutenant, David W. Skibbe. Because the terrain was mid-level vegetation, the CH-46's hoist was used. Skibbe was attached to the hoist and as he was being brought up, the team moved out to the new LZ. Shortly afterwards as Skibbe was being brought up to the helicopter the hoist cable broke.

In the confusion, the communication between the team and the air crew was interpreted incorrectly. The team did not realize the medivac cable had broken and Skibbe had fallen to his death. They continued moving to a better area where they were extracted and transported to An Hoa. After landing, it was discovered Skibbe was missing. It was late in the day and, after checking with Da Nang DASC, the mission was postponed until the next day rather than going back after dark to retrieve Skibbe. The crews returned to their hootches at Marble Mountain.

The flight was called back the next morning and they flew to Camp Reasoner. They were briefed on going back in. Captain Lavoy McVey, the company commander, insisted that he be taken out to the scene so he could look for Skibbe.

The flight departed. When they arrived at the area, Capt McVey was lowered from the CH-46 on its hoist. While he was being lowered, the hoist malfunctioned. The aircrew brought the captain back up manually. When he reached the hole on the bottom of the helicopter [Hell hole] and was attempting to climb in, he reached in, placed his rifle on the floor of the aircraft just as the cable broke. He fell to his death from over 100 feet.

The following day was filled with the insertion of a Recon Company along with a company of ARVN.

On March 11, Rider was scheduled to fly on the Skipper's wing. Lt Dennis Grace would be his copilot. They were going back to the Tennis Courts to mop up and extract the remaining marines and ARVN.

Prior to the briefing, Rider noticed reports of air bursts on the operations board. Apparently, the VC had developed a timed fuse for their hand-held B-40 rockets and were firing them at passing aircraft.

The briefing, preflight, and takeoff went as scheduled. During the zone brief, they were informed there was hostile fire in the area.

On the second sortie, after refueling and rearming at An Hoa, the flight begun the final extraction. The Cobras were firing rockets into a suspected enemy position. As Rider pulled out of a firing run, he felt the aircraft lurch. In his peripheral vision he saw a reddish pink cloud. The nose of the aircraft swung to the right and tucked. All tail rotor control was lost. Because of the slow airspeed during his climb, the aircraft went into an uncontrollable spin.

Rider entered autorotation and increased the airspeed enough to stop the uncontrollable spin. He recovered from the unusual attitude but could not stop the descending spiral. As the Cobra approached the top of the trees, Rider slowed his descent. Reaching about forty knots, he pulled full pitch just about the time the aircraft started an uncontrolled spin to the right. The aircraft descended through the trees and crashed to the ground.

1Lt Dennis F. Grace. Killed in Action.
14 March 1943-11 March 1970.

Rider passed in and out of consciousness. In a moment of consciousness, he saw a couple of North Vietnamese troops around the aircraft. After the remaining Cobras cleared the area around the crash site with fire, a crew chief and his gunner were lowered from a CH-46 and dragged Rider out of the aircraft, Rider regained consciousness. The crew assisted him and carried Grace to the hovering CH-46 and attached them to a jungle penetrater before hoisting them up through the hell hole.

Rider had sustained serious injuries and was later medivacked out of country. Grace had died instantly from the injuries sustained when the rotor blade flexed down upon impact and penetrated the front canopy and struck his helmet.

"Denny" and I had been very good friends. We had spent a lot of time together at Camp Pendleton and in Vietnam. When we got back to the ready room, the XO asked me if I would go to Da Nang Airbase to identify the body.

"You should be able to recognize him though his head may be banged up pretty bad," he said.

I was in no mood for that shit. I had to hold back my emotions as I thought about seeing my friend lying in the morgue in a body bag. I told the XO he had better find someone else. I wanted my memory of Dennis to be as he had been, not lying in a body bag all banged up. I did tell the XO I would pack up his personal belongings for shipment home.

The next day Bob McKiernan and I went about going through Denny's belongings, inventorying them, and packing them for ship-

LtCol Warren G. Cretney, Commanding Officer, October 1969 to March 1970.

ment back to his family. Included in our duties was the task going through all his mail to make certain there was nothing that would be embarrassing to his family.

LtCol H.E. Sexton, Commanding Officer, 15 March 1970 to 15 October 1970.

As we packed, McKiernan, who had come across the pond with Grace on the same aircraft, said to me, "You know, Robby, when Denny and I went 'feet wet' on the way over here Denny looked over at me and had tears in his eyes. He said he'd never see these shores again. I guess he had a premonition."

I had a bit of trouble figuring out what to say to the hooch maid. When she came in and saw us packing she asked where Grace was and what had happened. I did not want to tell her he had been shot down. I was convinced that every civilian on base was a direct hook-up to the NVA or VC.

"Dennis is gone." She understood. I could also see that she had liked him and was visibly upset. We finished the packing and separated the letters from home and the ones from his girl friend back in California. We felt she would like to have them. I knew the CO would be sending a letter to Grace's parents but, I felt it was something I had to do as well. That evening I sat down and wrote a letter to a mother in Buffalo, New York, who had just lost a son. It was a very difficult thing to do.

I spent the next ten days learning to be a helicopter commander and getting more comfortable flying in the back seat. I liked it.

March 25 was a sweltering hot day in An Hoa. A CH-46 driver, sitting under a rocket pod on a Cobra, was trying to find a cool spot. Seeing us walk by, he spoke, "Did you guys hear about the mid-air?"

1Lt Roger A. Lakin 27 July 1944 to 25 March 1970
No picture available.

"What mid-air?" we asked. He had our attention.

"I heard two of your Cobras just had a mid-air coming in for the break at Marble. Killed all four of them. I don't know any names."

My heart sank. Questions raced through my mind. *Who?* I tried to remember the mission schedule on the board in the ready room. *Who was flying with whom?* I could not remember a thing, nor could the three pilots with me. The schedule had come out at 0400. The duty NCO had awakened the early

1Lt Michael Justus
15 November 1944-25 March 1970.

1Lt Toby R. Gritz(l.) 09 December 1944-25 March 1970.
1Lt Frank E. Sacharanski(r.) 24 September 1945-25 March 1970.

flight crews at about 0530, and we were not too concerned about what everyone else was scheduled to do. Our concentration was on the our own missions. Going through the list of pilots in my mind, I hoped it would not be any of the guys I was close to. I felt guilty thinking it would not be quite as bad if it were so and so or this other guy.

The afternoon was long. After being relieved from standby at about 1600 hours, we headed back to Marble Mountain. Not looking for a target to unload our ordinance on, we did a straight shot home.

After landing and taxiing back to the revetments, we shut down. Major H.P. Miller met us on the ramp and gave us the grim details of the mid-air. 1Lt Roger Lakin had been the flight leader with 1Lt Michael Justus as his copilot. His wingman was 1Lt Frank "Sac" Sacharanski. 1Lt Toby Gritz was his copilot. Lakin had brought his flight of two into the "break." The two aircraft had come over the runway in formation with "Sac" on Lakin's left wing. Their altitude was about 800 feet. Near mid-field, Lakin had broken to the right at about a 45-degree bank. Sacharanski had been flying a tight formation . . . too tight. So tight that the blades overlapped. When Lakin broke off, his rotor came up and the rotors hit. Both rotor systems flew off sending both helicopters to the ground inverted, killing all four pilots instantly.

I cannot describe how I felt. Toby, the "Sac," and Mike were all from the old squadron at Phu Bai. Toby had just returned to the squadron after a three-month tour as a forward-air controller. The "Sac" and I had gone through flight school together, and he checked into the squadron the day after I did. Mike checked in shortly after that. I had liked all three men. Lakin had been in VMO-2. I did not know him as well, but I did know he was a good officer, an efficient pilot, and a nice guy.

Later in the day I talked with McKiernan. He said he was walking back to the flight line when he heard the flight coming in. He had stopped to watch the break. He said that when the rotors hit, everything seemed to be in slow motion. He could see the pilots in the plummeting inverted aircraft. Their heads were bent back; they were looking at the ground as they came down.

I think it was on that day I started to subconsciously build an internal defense mechanism for death. From that day on, death seemed to become an accepted fact of life. I became cold to the deaths of people I had known. That mentality stayed with me for many years.

Again, McKiernan and I were packing personal effects for close friends. I did not fly for about four days after the accident. I do not know if it was coincidence or not.

March had been quite a month, the Marine Corps lost nine helicopters and fifteen crewmen.

XXIII

LZ Ross

McKIERNAN WAS ONE OF MY FAVORITE WINGMEN. We had a mutual trust and friendship. We knew we could count on each other to cover our six o'clock, and, if we ever got shot down, we would do whatever it took to get the other crew out.

In June McKiernan got the word he would be doing a tour as a forward air controller (FAC). I shuddered at the thought. Doing three months with grunts, humping over the Que Son Mountains, worrying about snipers, booby traps, ambushes, and whatever else was not my cup of tea.

The FAC's mission was to accompany ground troops in the field. He was trained to determine the correct method of support and had the knowledge to call in and direct fire if the ground troops came under fire or had a lucrative target and needed naval gunfire, artillery support, or aviation assets.

McKiernan took it in stride. In fact, he seemed to look forward to it. He had gone to FAC school just prior to his departure from the States. He had also completed the six-month Officer Basic School. He knew how to survive in the world of a ground pounder.

McKiernan's assignment took him to LZ Ross, a.k.a. Hill 51. The compound and firebase were located in the Que Son Valley approximately 42 kilometers south of Da Nang.

I began to take a special interest in activities of the units at Ross. Every time I worked with a unit on the ground in that area I checked to see how their token aviator was holding out. Reports indicated he was adapting well. I got him up on the radio once in a while to give him a whole barrel of shit for turning grunt on us.

During June and July there seemed to be more activity in the Antenna and Happy Valley areas. Sightings of NVA and of patrols making contact were becoming more frequent.

Shortly after McKiernan's move, I was leading a re-supply flight. When passing through Antenna Valley for LZ Ryder, I looked down at the valley floor and saw a column of NVA troops. I could not believe my eyes. Wearing packs and helmets and toting AK-47s, they were walking down a rice paddy dike in broad daylight. I continued south for a kilometer or two before beginning an orbit. I still had them in sight.

"Da Nang DASC, this is Scarface Four Two. I have gooners in the open with packs and helmets. Positive ID as NVA. Request clearance to fire. Over."

"Stand by, Scarface."

After what seemed like forever with no response, I called again.

"Scarface Four Two, stand-by," said an impatient voice. "We have friendly troops in the valley and are trying to get a positive location on them."

By this time I was getting damn mad. There was no doubt in my mind that these AK-47-toting pith-helmeted troops were North Vietnamese regulars. I could see they were getting nervous and was surprised they had not scattered.

"Scarface Four Two. Da Nang DASC. Sorry, but we can't get a positive location on the friendlies. You are not cleared to fire."

"Roger, DASC."

"The hell with it," I told myself. "I'm not going to pass up an opportunity to work out on fifty gooners in the open." I called my wing man and asked him what he thought of the situation. His confirmation the troops were NVA was all I needed to hear.

"DASC, Scarface Four Two. I've just taken fire. I'm rolling in."

The nose of the Cobra came up as we went into a 45-degree bank, the NVA scattered. They knew what was going to happen. After expending 8000 rounds of mini gun, 700 rounds of 40 mm grenades and 110 rockets, we really had their attention along with that of everyone else in the valley. An OV-10 showed up as we were finishing. This time I could honestly say we had taken fire. He had a couple of fixed-wing standing by that he wanted to work out. I briefed him on the situation, and we departed the area. I never did hear anything else about that day, but the NVA paid dearly for being cocky.

Two days later we were covering re-supply at LZ Ross. A CH-46 had just landed in the LZ. My flight was in a left-hand orbit at about 700 feet. I looked down into the foliage just outside the perimeter of the fire base and saw another column of AK-47-toting, pith-helmeted NVA troops walking along a path no more than 100 meters from the fire base.

"Jackal Seven, this is Scarface Four Two. Do you have any friendlies just outside the perimeter?"

"That's a negative Sir."

"Stand by. I just saw a column of NVA no more than 100 meters from your perimeter. I'm going to take another look."

With a nose up 60-degree bank, the Cobra did a 180-degree turn. As we came over the spot where I had seen them, there was nothing. The path was empty. The NVA must have done a disappearing act off to the sides of the path.

"Jackal, this is Scarface. I can't see them anymore, but you had better tell your 'six' and get someone out there and find out what's going on."

"Roger, Scarface."

I watched for them for the rest of the re-supply but did not see them again. "Something is not right," I kept telling myself.

That night I was on the schedule as standby guns in the event a recon team needed extraction or a unit needed gun support. The next morning at 0500 the duty NCO woke me up and informed me that LZ Ross was under attack, and we needed to launch as soon as possible.

As we were getting ready, we were briefed. The weather was marginal. The fire base had been under mortar attack most of the night and the medivac aircraft had barely been able to get in. Not much was known about the current situation.

We arrived at the firebase at daybreak. Making radio contact with Jackal, we were informed they were no longer taking fire. At daylight the NVA had disappeared. The attack was over. Jackal wanted us to take a look around the area to see if we could find any targets. Apparently there were not too many wounded or killed, and the medivac aircraft already had them out.

Maybe I've been here too long, I thought. I felt somewhat left out. I was all pumped up for a good fight and when I got there it was over.

Approaching the firebase, I descended to 600 feet and began circling the base. Looking down, I saw a tube sticking up. I wondered what it was. Then it dawned on me; it was a mortar. I swung around to go back and take another look. When I got to where I thought it was, it was gone. I definitely was not having a good week. We searched the area for about an hour, found nothing and headed back to An Hoa for fuel.

Two miles to the east of LZ Ross was a village which had caused no problems and no doubt was frequently visited by marines from Ross. Low level clouds were still lingering and we were forced to descend to about 150 to 200 feet above the ground. Passing the village, something caught my eye, and I looked down over my left shoulder. Just outside a house we were passing, a VC wearing black PJs and a straw hat was shooting his AK-47. I was the object of his intentions! That really pissed me off! I immediately called my wingman. Because we had already gone by and the ceiling was too low for turning around, we decided to continue. I really do not think the Marine Corps would have been too happy with us blowing away the "ville," even though I was convinced that's where the attack on LZ Ross had originated.

On my debrief I pinpointed on the map the exact house from which we had received fire. Hopefully, the grunts got the information and acted on it.

July 19, 1970. Stand-by medivac, An Hoa, about 1600 hours. The day had been extremely dull. I was the flight leader of a flight of two CH-46s and Cobras. McKiernan was my wingman. Nothing seemed to be happening, and we had spent most of the day trying to find a piece of shade.

At Marble Mountain, headquarters of HML-167, the day had also begun uneventfully for 1Lt Richard "Dick" Dodd and 1Lt David "Dave" Geaslin. Members of HML-167, the two men had known each other since flight school. Both men had arrived in country about a year earlier and were roommates at Marble Mountain.

Not on the early schedule, the two men had awakened on their own. No duty officer had shaken them awake that morning. After leisurely showers, they proceeded to the O-club for a daylight breakfast. Following breakfast, they walked to the squadron ready room. 1Lt Lewis "Lou" Casner followed them. As they entered, the SDO pointed at Dodd, the first to enter. "Flight leader," he said without any explanation. "Copilot," he continued as Geaslin entered. "Wingman," he said when Casner entered.

Because of their close friendship, Dodd and Geaslin had agreed not to fly together. After Geaslin pissed and moaned, Casner volunteered to fly with Dodd. The men briefed for the mission to cover a "sniffer."

The flight departed. The mission was uneventful in the beginning, but the situation changed quickly.

Geaslin heard Dodd's voice. "On fire!"

"Taking fire?" Geaslin asked, knowing Dodd had not said "taking fire."

"I am on fire," Dodd responded, his voice excited but in control.

Dodd's aircraft came by Geaslin's. It was fully involved. He passed starboard, and Geaslin could see flames in the gunner's cabin. The whole engine compartment was engulfed in flames, and flames were streaming back along the tail boom. The tail separated from the fuselage, and, with the tail rotor gone, the fuselage spun under the rotor. Flames whipped through the cabin, and the mass accelerated toward the jungle.

Back at An Hoa, I heard the radio in the medivac shack. "Scarface Four Two. Scarface Four Two. This is Da Nang DASC. I have a mission for you. Are you ready to copy? Over."

Picking up the hand mike, I called back, "This is Four Two. Stand by." Grabbing my kneeboard, I called back, "DASC, this is Four Two. I'm ready to copy. Over."

"You are released from Mission 76. Proceed to coordinates . . . I shackle, Romeo over Victor, 954654. You are to provide assistance as required. Contact Hostage Duke on primary frequency. Do you copy? Over."

Complying, I answered, "Roger, DASC. I have good copy. Do you need Mission 76 Swift aircraft? Over."

"That's a negative. Swift flight is released to RTB."

We cranked up immediately and departed to the northwest heading to the west end of Elephant Valley. Once we reached 4,000 feet, I gave Hostage Duke a call to ask what was up.

He reported a UH-1E gunship had just gone down into heavy jungle. It was on fire as it went down. A CH-53 had just dropped in a rescue team and we were needed to provide cover while the team was on the ground looking for survivors. The wingman, still on station, was bingo fuel.

Hearing the wingman's call sign, I recognized it immediately. "Comprise 33" was Geaslin's call sign.

Together since flight school, he and I had come into county at about the same time. Even though we could not use names in our radio conversation, I learned that our mutual friend Dodd was the pilot of the downed craft.

Immediately, a lump grew in my throat; Dodd and I had been in the same platoon in OCS. He and I had spent most of our free weekends bumming around the Washington, DC, area while at OCS. Although we had gone our separate ways when we were assigned to different squadrons, we were still good friends.

The rescue team was inserted. After about thirty minutes they reported finding no survivors. Preparations were made for the extraction of the downed crew. Because of the dense jungle, the extraction was going to have to be with a ladder.

As the CH-53 hovered over the jungle, the seventy-five-foot ladder was dropped into a very small hole in the jungle canopy. The pilot had to hold his hover steady as the team attached body bags containing the crewmembers' charred remains to the ladder. After accomplishing the grim task, the team attached themselves for the ride home.

The Sea Stallion ascended vertically bringing the ladder out of the jungle. Reality set in. I could see the body bags dangling from the ladder. The radios were silent as we escorted our dead comrades home.

Cobra escorting CH-53 with marines. Photo by John Witsell.

XXIV

Dimmer

RESUPPLY. I really hated resupply. Chasing a CH-53 or CH-46 around all day was like walking a Saint Bernard and stopping again and again to pick up and drop off its loads. It seemed nothing else ever happened.

Picking up resupply for outlying units normally took place at An Hoa or Hill 55. We would go back and forth to field units all day. About all it was good for was building up combat missions. Each time we provided gun cover for a helicopter going into an unsecured zone it counted as a sortie or a combat mission. If we got shot at, it was counted as still another sortie. We did take fire on occasion.

The CH-53s were the big boys of marine helicopters. Maintenance hogs, they were expensive to buy and to fly. Consequently, the commanding general really did not like sending a CH-53 where it could be lost, but around May of 1970, he began to utilize them in more dangerous missions including SOG missions into Laos.

I was flight leader of two Cobras covering four CH-53s. 1Lt J.T. Lewis was on my wing. The day seemed routine. Nothing unusual had happened. Thuong Duc, 45 kilometers southwest of Da Nang was the last supply LZ. All four of the 53s had external loads.

Inbound, I called for a zone brief. "Black Jack Two Three, this is Scarface Four Two with some resupply. We're ten southeast. How about a zone brief? Over."

Black Jack replied immediately, "Hello, Scarface Four Two. This is Black Jack. Glad to see you coming. We're getting low on supplies. The wind is out of the west. There aren't any obstacles around the LZ. We have been taking some mortar rounds on and off all afternoon. We suspect they're coming from the cover to the north. We can tell when they're inbound and will let you know if we hear anything."

"Roger, Black Jack."

Dimmer Six confirmed he had good copy on the zone brief and would take the first load in. He called his flight and gave them their instructions. Dash Two and the rest of the flight were to follow him in at one-half kilometer intervals. If Six had to wave off, Dash Two was to continue in and drop his load as soon as he could after the mortar hit. The rest of the flight were to follow suit. He told them not to dilly-dally around on the ground. He asked the flight if they understood. They replied in the affirmative, but seemed less confident than their skipper.

It was obvious Dimmer Six had been in this situation before.

LtCol J.M. Moriarty was working in the area. I gave him a call. "Hostage Six, this is Scarface Four Two. I've got what might be a hot zone. I'm over at Thuong Duc. Can you give us a hand and have some fixed-wing handy if we need them? Over."

"Roger, Scarface. I've got two ARVN T-37s headed this way. I'll have them on station at 10,000 feet in about fifteen minutes. I'll be there in three minutes. I'll linger overhead when I get there. What's up?"

"I've got four Dimmers re-supplying Thuong Duc. They've been receiving mortar rounds in the compound. They think the mortar is located to the north of their position. I'm going to go down and take a closer look to see if I can find it."

"Roger, Scarface. I'll be hanging around."

Wanting to let Lewis know my plan, I called, "I'm going down low to see if I can find that mortar. Cover me."

"Roger." If I was going to be down on the deck at 100 feet or less making myself a good target for anyone with a slingshot, I wanted my wingman covering my six. I dropped down low level. Dimmer Six started his approach to the LZ with his wingman right behind him. The foliage on the north side of several rice paddies provided about 200 kilometers of open area between it and Thuong Duc. As I raced along the edge of the foliage at 140 knots, I set my armament hot. My copilot was ready to work over anything that moved with his turret.

I heard an excited voice over the radio. Dimmer Six was on short final for the landing pad when Black Jack called, "Incoming! Incoming!"

"Going around! Going around!" Dimmer responded.

A mortar hit about thirty meters south of the landing pad.

"They have the LZ zeroed in," I said to myself. I was hoping I could get an idea of the direction of the mortar site from the impact, but it did not give me any clues.

Dimmer Dash Two did exactly as briefed. Just after the mortar hit, he came in, dropped his load, and was out of there. Getting rid of the net holding the resupply was simply a matter of punching a button on his cyclic.

I hoped Moriarty had seen the flash.

"I didn't see any flash. Did you, Hostage?" I asked.

"That's a negative, Scarface."

The mortar had to be close, I continued searching the edge of the foliage. It was very thick. The shooters would need to be on the edge in order to see the helicopters making their approach to the compound.

Dimmer Dash Three started his approach as Dimmer Six made a three-sixty. As Three made his approach, it was a replay of the first drop off. He waved off, and Dimmer Six made the drop after the mortar impact. This impact was almost on target, even closer to the pad than the first one. I still did not see any flash, nor did Moriarty.

I heard his voice on Uniform, "That takes a lot of nerve. I just had a .50 cal tracer go across in front of me. Looks like it came from the west."

The rising terrain west of Thuong Duc had heavy underbrush turning to jungle on the higher terrain. Moriarty thought the fire had come from the higher ground.

That got my attention. A .50 cal machine gun was not anything to fool around with! We still had two more loads to deliver. Concentrated on finding the mortar, I low-leveled to the east of where Moriarty thought the .50 cal was.

The last two loads were delivered. When the final mortar round was fired after Dimmer Four dropped off his load, Dimmer Six, orbiting high above, called, "I saw a flash! I'm going to mark it with a smoke."

Looking up at the CH-53 orbiting, we saw a red smoke grenade as it was dropped. I watched as the smoke came down. It burned out just before it hit the ground. Dimmer Six gave me directions from where the smoke landed to where he had seen the flash.

I was still low level and had a good view. I turned and started my climb to get ready for a rocket run. Checking, I could not see my wingman. I made a call. I asked for his location.

"Four Two, I'm off to the west looking for that .50 cal."

"Get your tail back over here. Your job is to cover your lead!" I was pissed, I had just spent thirty minutes at 100 feet trying to draw fire, and my wingman was not covering me.

Hostage Six, wanting to get his fixed-wing in, called, "Scarface I'm going to bring in my T-37s. I've got the target. I'm going to mark it now. Over."

After spending thirty minutes looking for it, I wanted to get my two bits worth in. I called him back, "Hostage Six, let us get one or two quick runs in before the fixed wing moves in. We're done for the day and would like to expend our ordinance."

"Okay, Scarface, but make it quick. My guys are running low on fuel."

Lewis joined up on me. I made my first pass shooting two rockets and adjusting my sight. I told Lewis to salvo on the next pass. Rolling in, we each put our rocket selector to "salvo." In rapid succession all fifty or so rockets we had left in our pods fired. The helicopter seemed to stop in mid-air when we let loose, and the area erupted following the blast of 100 rockets.

Leaving the area, Hostage Six's T-37s rolled in, dropping what looked like 250-pound bombs on the area.

I do not think they had any more trouble with mortars at Thuong Duc that day. I never could figure out how they knew there was incoming—perhaps Black Jack could hear the thump from the mortar tubes as they fired.

XXV
Pickens Forest

JULY 15, 1970. I had just walked into the club for evening chow when a sergeant from Operations came over. "Lieutenant, you're flight leader for an insertion tomorrow. There's going to be a briefing at 1900 at the CAC bunker."

"Thanks, sergeant. What's going on? A Kingfisher?"

"I really don't know, Sir," he replied.

After having a hearty meal followed with a cold beer at the club bar, I wandered back to my hootch and gathered some writing materials. Figuring I would probably need my maps, I caught a ride down to the flight line and grabbed them out of my helmet box.

Silva and Gallo were looking over the "frag" orders and working on the flight schedule for the next day.

"What's up? We have a Kingfisher mission tomorrow?" I asked, seeing them.

"Nah. It looks like the 7th Marines are going to be moving the whole damn division tomorrow. Actually not the whole division, but at least three battalions. Looks like a big dog and pony show to me," replied Silva.

Looking over the "frag" order, I decided I had better take my copilot to the brief so he could get the LZs plotted on his maps. I was happy to see 1Lt Kevin Kuklok was my copilot. He was probably the smartest man I had ever flown with. Though a master at map reading and situational awareness, he was going to get a workout the next day. I hustled back to the club and found Kuklok. We headed off to the CAC.

We showed up at the CAC on time. Once again, we were the only lieutenants there. *Here we go again*, I thought. *This must be something big. All the 'heavies' are here.*

LtCol McCauchey, the Commanding Officer of HML-167, came to the front of the room and called the brief to order. As the Airborne Command and Control, he would fly a UH-1E. He told us the next day would be a busy one. We would start a new operation called "Pickens Forest." This mission, regimental in size, would be a 7th Marines operation. Six Cobras, eight CH-46s, and six CH-53s would be launched at 0600.

Suddenly, he had my complete attention. We would be airlifting two battalions of troops along with three artillery batteries. We listened intently as he spent the next hour going over his maps explaining how we were going to carry out the task.

Pickens Forest was what the marines called a Category III operation. Category III operations were designed to locate and destroy NVA forces, supplies, and installations before they could interfere with the pacification process.

The area of operations would be in the VC's two principal mountain refuges located about twenty kilometers southwest of An Hoa along the Thu Bon River in Quang Nam province. The area served as a collection point for supplies brought in from Laos.

The maneuver's plan centered on a triangle of three fire support bases (FSBs), Defiant, Mace, and Dart. Dart and Mace had been used earlier in army and marine operations and could be reopened quickly.

The operations would begin with the insertion of one company of marines at Defiant to secure the site. They would be followed closely with a battery of 105 mm howitzers.

Because the element of surprise was critical, there would be no zone preps in this operation. 1ˢᵗ Reconnaissance had already sent several teams into the area to check out all landing zones. They felt the zones were secure of booby traps. Both Mace and Dart would have a battalion command post with two rifle companies and a 4.2-inch mortar battery. After the insertion, rifle companies would work south in search and destroy missions.

After the initial insertion at Defiant, two rifle companies would land along the banks of the Thu Bon river to sweep the area and provide a blocking force for activity created by the rifle companies moving south. The plan sounded good to me.

The next morning, after a thirty-minute brief, we were cranked up at 0600. I called my flight, "Scarface flight, Fox Mike, radio check." Numbers two through six checked in with good radios. We followed with a check on Uniform and Victor radios.

We were ready to launch. The CH-46s would load at An Hoa and the CH-53s would load artillery at LZ Baldy.

I split my section into three flights. My number two section would stay with the Ch-46s for the rifle company inserts on the FSBs. My number three flight was to stay with the CH-53s and cover them as they delivered artillery. I would take my flight to cover the two rifle companies that were going to be the blocking force. With high hopes of having a good "shoot-em-up" day, I was ready to blow things up and kick ass.

After launching, we joined up with Swift Six and his flight of CH-46s. My number three flight joined up with Dimmer Six and his flight of CH-53s headed for LZ Baldy. We landed at An Hoa where the troops were loaded on the CH-46s before heading out. I joined up with Swift Six's flight of four. Comprise Six had launched about five minutes ahead of us. I could see we were catching up.

Seeing the CAC Huey ahead of us, I checked in, "Comprise Six, this is Scarface Four Two. We have a flight of six on your tail. We should be with you in a couple of minutes. Over." Comprise Six responded.

He told me to make a low pass and mark the LZ. Swift was to follow right on my tail and drop his troops in if I did not see anything.

As we got closer, I passed the Huey. Kuklok was on the maps.

My concentration was interrupted by a radio call from my number five wingman. "Four Two, I'm heading for An Hoa. I have a hot engine oil light."

"Roger, stay up this frequency until you're close in to An Hoa."

"Roger." He called back about three minutes later. "Four Two, I'm over the Arizona. I may have to put this thing down. My temp is rising fast and pressure is going down . . . I'm putting this thing down!"

"Switch over to oil bypass! Right now!"

After a long thirty seconds, he called back saying that the temperature was going down and pressure was normal. He was going to continue to An Hoa and have another aircraft flown down.

I felt like the hero of the day! Sad to say, I could not take the credit. The same thing had happened to me while returning from a SOG mission in Laos a few days earlier. Roland Scott was on my wing and, just as I was in the same situation and about ready to put it down, Scott called and told me to do just that. I had written up the problem, but apparently it had not been fixed.

With that problem solved, my concentration returned to the mission at hand.

"Our LZ is straight ahead, Robby, about two klicks. Do you see that brown spot up there in the elephant grass?"

Looking ahead and spotting the grass, I answered, "Yup, I see it. What do you think it is?"

"You got me. I can't tell from here."

As we closed in, I saw what looked like a pile of boxes. "It looks like we caught them with their pants down. See that cache down there, about fifty meters north of the LZ?"

"I got it, looks like a cache all right," Kuklok answered.

Looking over the zone as I made my pass, I called the lead 46 following me in. "Swift Six this is Four Two. The zone looks good. I don't see any signs of enemy activity. The wind looks calm. A 'straight in' behind me should be good. Advise the troop CO there is what looks like a cache of something about fifty meters north of the LZ. I don't see any personnel around, but we will keep a good eye out for you. Scarface, out."

The '46 called back. He was right behind us.

Passing the LZ, I climbed and joined my wingman in an orbit as the CH-46s landed and the troops scurried out the back of the squatting "Phrog."

"We got gooners running. I see three of them running through the grass, just west of the cache," Kuklok said just as the last '46 was airborne and headed back to An Hoa to pick up the next load.

Spotting them, I called my wingman, "This is Four Two. I've got three gooners in the open. They're running just west of the cache. Do you have them?"

"That's affirmative Four Two."

"Roger. I'm in hot, going east to west." As the nose of our Cobra dipped into a 30-degree nose dive, guns went hot. "Kook, I'm going to put a sighting round in," I said. "If it looks good, I'll punch out a couple. You work out the turret after the second sct. Okay?"

"You betcha," Kuklok replied as he unhooked the turret sight and got it ready for action.

As the airspeed increased, I adjusted the trim making sure everything was right. I could see two of the VC thrashing through the elephant grass with nowhere to go or hide. The first rocket went straight, but the calibration had the sight slightly high and the rocket went in front of them. I readjusted my sight and punched off two more. They flew straight and hit just behind the two VC.

"Take them, Kook!" I said with my two salvos finished.

Kuklok opened up with the mini-gun laying down a barrage of 7.62 bullets. One VC fell and it looked like the other was hurt. I started my pull-up at about 500 feet when I heard my wingman call in hot.

"I see one down and one running. What happened to the third? Over."

"I don't know," I replied. "He must be laying low in the elephant grass, or he's in gooner heaven. What I can't understand is where the rest of them are. There must be more than three."

As he made his gun run, I saw the second VC, mortally wounded by the mini-gun, fall down. The third guy was right behind him. "Kook! There's our third guy. He just got up behind the last run." Calling our roll-in, I said, "Four Two is in. I have the third gooner!" The first two rockets went true. The VC had just lived his last day on this earth.

The grunts looked like they were all in a fighting position. They must have wondered what was going on with all the commotion we were making. Comprise Six was talking with them on the Fox Mike, so I assumed he had filled them in.

"Comprise Six, this is Swift Six back outbound with another load. Over."

The CH-46s had already gone back to An Hoa and loaded up again. Each aircraft carried fourteen marines so each flight carried fifty-six marines. They needed to carry about 300 to this position. After that, they would have to help carry troops to the other areas. As the second '46 was making his approach, I discovered I could not move my cyclic to the left.

"Kook! Take the controls and try and move your cyclic to the left! I can't move mine past center! You've got the controls." I was concerned. Checking my controls again, I found I could put my aircraft in a right-hand turn, but, when I came to wing's level, I could not get the cyclic to move left.

"I've got the controls," Kuklok said. After checking his controls, he called back, "I can't get it past center either."

"Check and see if there is a pencil or something making it stick. I can't find anything back here. Maybe we took a hit."

"No, I can't see a thing that could be making it stick. Now what, Boss?"

"Well, as long as we can make right-hand turns and can fly straight and level, I guess we're okay. I'll give Comprise a call and tell him we're heading back to An Hoa. We need gas anyway."

Comprise Six had been roaming around the area keeping an eye on the whole operation. I had not heard anything that would indicate that there was much excitement anywhere, so I gave him a call, "Comprise Six, this is Scarface Four Two. Over."

"Go ahead, Scarface."

"Roger, Six. We're going to head back for some petro. Over."

Comprise Six called back immediately, "That's a negative, Scarface! You promised me gun cover at all times. I don't see any other gunships around here other than you. Do you?"

Not about to let this guy get to me, I called back, "Stand by, Comprise." I called my wingman and asked his fuel status.

"I've got about 400 pounds."

"Okay, I'm about the same." We had about forty minutes each and An Hoa was only ten to fifteen minutes away, but that did not solve my control problem. About that time, I heard my second section leader talking on UHF. I gave him a call.

"Four Two, go ahead."

"Roger. I'm down south by Area One. I would like you to relieve me. I'm having some control problems I need to take care of and to refuel."

"No problem, Four Two. We'll be there in about one-five. Over."

"Roger. Comprise Six, this is Scarface Four Two. I'm experiencing a control problem and am departing for An Hoa at this time. My wingman will stay on station. Scarface One flight is one-five minutes out and will be on station. Over."

Sounding satisfied, Comprise Six answered, "Okay, Scarface. It sounds good to me. Comprise out."

"Kook, do you remember anything in the briefing about us saying we would give one hundred percent coverage?" I asked wondering if I had missed something.

"Nope, I think it just conveniently came to him."

I felt a little better. Now my concern was my control problem. "Okay, I guess we will have to make right-hand traffic at An Hoa. I had better give them a call."

"An Hoa tower, Scarface Four Two . . . single Cobra for landing. Eight south. Request right traffic. I'm experiencing control problems. Over."

"Roger Four Two, clear to land, right traffic. Are you declaring an emergency?"

"That's a negative, tower. I don't think it will be a big problem." I did not tell him I had no idea as to how I was going to hover with only fifty percent cyclic. On downwind going through the landing check list, I briefed Kuklok. "Okay, Kook, I'm going to take this approach right to the ground. We can figure out what to do when we get there." Kook nodded in approval.

I entered a right down wind, made nice and easy right turns, and came out on a good final approach. Rather than stopping at a hover which was our normal procedure as I got near the ground, I took it right to the ground as briefed.

We sat there momentarily before I told tower we needed some time in place to investigate our problem. Reluctantly, he gave me clearance.

"Okay, Kook, I'm going to put a little oomph behind the controls and see what happens," I said, searching for a solution on how to get my cyclic to move left-of-center. I gave the cyclic a good movement to the left and we both heard what sounded like a snap. "That sounded like a pencil to me," I said.

"Yeah, could be," Kuklok replied.

Moving the cyclic full motion in all quadrants, I did not feel any more binding. "Lets see what happens when we go to a hover. I think we will be okay. The controls feel fine now," I said wanting to continue our mission. I pulled the collective up slowly, getting the Cobra light on the skids. Everything felt good. I added a little more collective, and we rose to a hover. After doing some turns, dips, and dives, I was satisfied all was well.

"Let's go refuel."

CH-53 resupply for operation Pickens Forest.
National Archives photo by Sgt R.V. Hawkins.

We hovered over to the refueling pit and soon had the company of my wingman. While we refueled, I did a good check for bullet holes. I was not totally convinced my problem was a pencil stuck somewhere in the controls. After finding no holes and having a discussion with Kuklok about we should do, we launched and went back to the war.

The rest of the day was totally uneventful. All the inserts went as planned. The lack of action was my only disappointment. Each aircraft ended up with over nine hours of flight time for the day. Over 600 troops and three artillery batteries had been moved.

Col Derning, the Regiment Commanding Officer, was delighted. He had spent most of the day observing the move from the CAC Huey. He called the initial insertion "a beautiful example of air-ground team work."

"I've never seen school solutions work quite that well," he said.

A medivac package was to be assigned daily at An Hoa. The package would consist of two Cobras and two "Phrogs." About the third day after the operation began, I was unlucky enough to be assigned standby. After nine hours of sitting on our duffs in the scorching heat, our dispositions were hardly pleasant. A call finally came, "Scarface Four Two, this is Da Nang DASC. Over."

Eagerly grabbing the microphone of the VHF, I answered, "Da Nang DASC, this is Scarface Four Two. Go ahead. Over."

"Roger, Four Two. Your relief has just checked in with me and will be on station in one-five mikes. I have a mission for you. Are you ready to copy?"

"Stand by one, DASC," I said as I walked over to a table where our flight gear was heaped in a pile. I grabbed my kneeboard and maps. Captain John Arick, my copilot, heard the conversation about the mission and came over with the same. Paper and pencil in hand, I answered, "DASC, this is Scarface Four Two. I'm ready to copy. Over."

DASC came back with a mission to provide overhead gun cover for a unit located along the Song Vu Bon River about fifteen kilometers southwest of An Hoa. It looked like we would be supporting the unit we had put in next to the river several days earlier. We were to contact Gulf Maid Two on their tactical frequency, 40.1.

My wingman was 1Lt Mark Byrd, call sign "Scarface Four Seven." Arick, my copilot, was a career marine on his second tour. He had only been in country a matter of weeks this tour. I could tell he was not happy about flying as my copilot. Most of the second tour guys expected to jump right in and be designated HAC and flight leader. Normally, they made HAC as soon as they got a feel for the Cobra and the working area.

Our flight launched and headed west. Enroute, I called, "Tiger One, Tiger One. This is Scarface Four Two. Over."

"Scarface, this is Tiger One. Go ahead, over."

"Roger, Tiger. I've got a flight of two guns inbound to your poz. Should be there in five mikes. What can we do for you today?"

"Roger, Scarface, glad to have you. We need to make a river crossing and would like you to give us cover. Over."

"No problem, Tiger. We would be glad to help. Do you have us in sight yet? Over."

"That's affirmative, Scarface. We have you to the northeast. We are located along the river, about one-half klick south of our base camp. Over."

As we got closer, I could see the unit. They had just come out of the cover of the embankment and were walking along the sandbars of the river looking for a crossing site.

Once overhead, I called, "Tiger One, I have a unit just below us now. Verify. Over."

"That's affirmative, Scarface. We are right below you."

Looking down, the unit appeared to be platoon-sized with about thirty-five to forty marines. The lead element of the unit was just beginning to walk into the water. From above, I could see the water was going to be deep where they wanted to cross.

"Tiger One, this is Scarface. The river looks like it gets pretty deep right there where you are starting to cross. I would recommend you move north about another one hundred meters. It looks considerably shallower there."

"Thanks, Scarface. We'll take a look."

The platoon moved north. It looked like they had decided my spot was better and started to cross. The river, about sixty meters across with heavy vegetation all along the far bank, was the perfect spot for an ambush. Concerned, I called, "Tiger One, this is Scarface. You guys are really exposed down there. I'm going to lay some mini-gun fire down along the east bank. Okay?"

"Thanks, Scarface."

Making sure my wingman had the plan, I called, "Three Seven, did you copy what we're going to do? Let's work it mini-gun only. We will be 'danger close.'"

Rolling in, Arick worked his mini-gun all the way through the run. His tracers were showing the bullets hitting foliage along the edge of the river bank. Contrary to normal operations, I decided I would come around and make my run in the same direction as my first.

As I was about to roll in on my second run, Byrd came up on the radio, "I've got gooners in the open!"

I could see him doing a pedal turn and starting another gun run.

"Roger. I've got you covered." I set up to cover him. "I'm searching to see the VC." I did not see movement anywhere.

Hoping Arick had them, I said, "Captain, I don't have them. Do you?"

"That's affirm. They're running right by that trail."

I looked all along the river searching for a trail, but could not see anything.

"I still don't have them." I just could not see them.

"Give me the controls," Arick said with a bit of 'give me the God-damned controls' tone in his voice.

"You have them." He grabbed the controls and turned the aircraft a bit left and pointed it more to the south. There, about 150 meters in from the riverbank, were fifteen to twenty NVA running like hell down a trail.

I grabbed the controls. "Okay, I've got them. Thanks."

Arick had set the aircraft up perfectly for a run right down the path. I checked . . . ball centered . . . airspeed good.

I sent six rockets headed true on course toward the VC.

With rockets exploding, NVA were diving for cover along the sides of the riverbank when Arick fired a volley of 40 mm grenades, blanketing the entire area.

Pulling out, I remembered the river crossing. I imagined the troops were wondering what all the shooting was about. I gave them a call, "Tiger One, this is Scarface. We have gooners on the run about 150 meters in from your position. Be advised there may be more in your area. Looks like they were planning an ambush on you guys. There is a north-south trail that starts about eighty to 100 meters in from the river. I hope the fires our rockets started don't cause a problem. We're going to work the area. Stand by for a bit."

"Roger, Scarface."

By the time we rolled in for the second run, the VC had all moved to the cover off the path. I knew they had not gone far and were probably hiding in the tall grass and brush. I decided it was time to blanket the area.

"Four Seven, let's salvo the rockets on the next pass. Hold your Willy Pete. We don't need any more fires for the troops to contend with."

"Roger that."

Rolling in, I set the outboard pods to salvo. I figured I had thirty high explosive rockets left, fifteen on each side. My inboard pods were all Willy Pete.

The gun run started at 1500 feet. With our airspeed passing through 140 knots, I mentally checked my list, *Check ball. Target in the sights. Squeeze.*

As I squeezed the red button on the left side of my cyclic, the rockets started coming out two at a time with only a split second between. The Cobra shook as all thirty rockets departed toward the trail, exploding right where I wanted. Arick still had some turret left. We made another pass to expend his ordinance.

With our ordinance gone, it was time to hand control of the area back to the grunts. "Tiger One, you got it from here. It's all yours. We're RTB. It looks like you made a good call asking for cover. Scarface Four Two out."

"Thanks, Scarface. I think you saved some butts today. My actual [Commanding Officer] says thanks also. Tiger One out."

Two days later while standing in line for noon chow, I heard, "Robinson, what's your call sign? Are you Four Two?"

"That's affirm, why?" I answered, wondering what I was in for.

One of the guys from my squadron answered, "We were just down south and Tiger One said he had a message for you."

"Oh. What've you got?"

"Apparently you guys worked out for them the other day. They said you got eight confirmed and six surrendered. The guys that surrendered were wounded pretty bad and wanted medical attention.

Tiger One was pretty happy about it and wanted me to pass it on. Sounds like you guys did a pretty good job for them."

"Thanks for the info."

He had just made my day! Later, I spotted Byrd in the chow hall and could not pass on the good news fast enough.

At the safety meeting later that day, the Skipper went over the significant events since the last meeting and talked about improvements he would like to see before spending a few minutes going over pass procedures, emphasizing that MP's were getting tough on pass signatures.

The subject of passes made me think about talking to Byrd about dinner in Da Nang. I thought we deserved to celebrate a little. I cornered him after the meeting. "Mark, lets borrow the old man's jeep and hit Da Nang tonight. I heard of a restaurant that has great seafood."

"Sounds good to me. Only if you ask the Skipper for the jeep. You know what happened last time you borrowed it. Remember the drive shaft?"

With a chuckle, I agreed to do the dirty work and headed off to the Skipper's office and made my request. He looked at me with steely eyes. I knew he was thinking "I know better than to do this." Despite that, he handed me the keys.

A cloud of dust rose behind me as I scampered down to the S-1 office, got two passes and hustled back to the Skipper's office for his signatures.

We put down our first beer about 100 yards outside the gate at Marble Mountain. A few beers later, we found our restaurant. It was right down town Da Nang. A lot of security was in the area, so we were not too concerned about trouble. The food was as good as we had heard it would be. We were definitely in good spirits.

At about 2100 hours, we left. Walking out the front door, we were greeted by an airman MP.

"Hello, lieutenants. How are you guys tonight? Looks like you are having a good time. Mind if I check your passes?"

"No problem. Here's mine," I said handing it to him.

He gave it a good looking over. "Sir, you have not signed it."

"What! Let me see. Oh . . . well, the CO signed it."

"But, Sir, you needed to sign it to make it a valid pass. This pass is not valid."

"Well, give me a pencil and I will," I said getting irritated.

He made no comment and proceeded to check Byrd's pass. He found the same discrepancy. Apparently, this guy was going to be a real asshole. "I'm sorry, Sirs. But I'm going to have to take you two into the station."

I exploded. "What! Are you crazy? Give me a God-damn pencil and I'll sign it and be out of here." I was pissed. Watching, Byrd wisely kept his mouth shut, but I had had enough. I grabbed my pass out of his hand and began walking away. "Bull shit!" I said, alcohol making me much braver than usual.

I had not gone ten steps when I heard the MP's voice. "Sir, come back here!" I continued with my back to him. Again, I heard his voice. "Sir, I'm only going to tell you once more. Come back here."

Two steps later I stopped dead in my tracks as I heard him slide the pump, inserting a shell into the chamber of his shotgun. I was being dumb, but I was not totally stupid. I turned and humbly came back. Byrd, still standing next to him, snickered at me as I came back.

I raised my hands. "Okay, Sergeant. I give up. You had better take us two desperados off to jail.

By this time, help had arrived for the MP. I likely would have been one sorry S.O.B. had I not stopped. We told the MP about having the jeep. We did not want to leave it where it was. He accompanied us as we drove it to the station. Once inside the station, we were put in a room off to the side and left there. Alone. I looked around the room. "Mark, do you see any pencils lying around here?"

Finding one on a table, we promptly signed our passes.

We waited in the room for a good fifteen minutes and nothing happened until, suddenly, everyone was running out the front door with weapons in their hands. The MP we had had the confrontation with ran into the room.

"We just had a bomb go off downtown. You guys just get the hell out of here." We were gone! We chalked it up as just another tough day at war.

XXVI
Tailwind

IN EARLY SEPTEMBER OF 1970, the SOG commander received a communication requesting an insertion of a "Hatchet" force near Chavane. The insertion was needed to provide a diversion for Hmong mercenaries engaged in an operation to recapture an enemy strong point in northern Laos. They had been taking heavy losses.

"Operation Tailwind" was approved. Company B was placed on alert. In preparation, an aerial reconnaissance was conducted. Several suitable landing areas were selected. Because of the distance to the LZ, it was decided a combined force of four United States Marine Corps CH-53 Sikorsky Sea Stallions would be best suited for the main insertion. HMH-463, a United States Marine Corps squadron that flew CH-53Ds out of Marble Mountain near Da Nang, was selected to fly the mission. HML-367 would fly gun cover. This was going to be a big mission for the Marine Corps.

The Cobra section leader would be the squadron commander, LtCol Harry Sexton; 1Lt Pat Owen would be his copilot. The army would supply UH-1Ds for the initial Pathfinder insertion with army Cobra gun cover. The package consisted of five CH-53s, call sign "Gnat," four marine AH-1G Cobras, call sign "Eagle Claw," six army UH-1Ds and six army AH-1G Cobras, call sign "Dragon Fly." Four of the CH-53s would carry troops and one would be search and rescue. The SAR bird was equipped with a special extraction ladder mounted at the rear ramp. All marine crewmembers would wear parachute harnesses as well as their normal flight and survival gear. The harnesses had D-rings which could be rapidly connected to the ladder during the rescue of wounded or dead.

On September 7, 1970, Sexton and the nine marine helicopters departed Marble Mountain Air Facility. They arrived at the Special Forces camp in Kontum in the central highlands for the initial briefing by Command and Control Central (CCC). The G-2 portion of the briefing indicated threat ranging from small arms to anti-aircraft weapons.

Following the CCC brief, Sexton briefed the entire package as to the conduct of the mission, its procedures, tactics, emergencies, and SAR operations. The mission would launch the following morning.

That evening, the marine and army aircrews and the Green Berets gathered at the club at Kontum. Sharing a few beers and swapping stories, they got to know each other.

While at the club, Georgia, a large rock python, made her appearance. She belonged to one of the Green Berets who happened to be in the bush at the time. He had left her behind. She slithered into the club and headed toward Sexton. Sitting at the bar with his back to the door, he had not seen her enter. Slithering over

1Lt Barry Pencek with Georgia. Photo provided by Barry Pencek.

to Sexton's chair, she climbed up and reached the top with her head next to his ear. Feeling something odd, Sexton turned his head and found himself eyeball to eyeball with Georgia. The colonel was ass-holes and elbows as he leapt over the bar.

That was not the end of Georgia's night-time visits. A cold-blooded creature, she had the habit of crawling into her master's bed while he slept. With her master in the bush, his bed was occu-pied by a marine pilot. During the night, Georgia slithered into the warm bed. A blood-curdling scream penetrated the early morning air, waking Barry Pencek, a Cobra copilot, sleeping in the next bed. Jumping up, he turned on the lights and saw his roommate hanging on the stud rafters. The snake was snuggled in his bed below.

On September 8, the mission was declared a "go." Following the CCC brief, Sexton again briefed the entire package. The inser-tion package departed Kontum and headed for an airstrip located at Dak To, approximately forty-two kilometers northwest of Kontum. Dak To was going to be the primary forward re-arming and refueling point for this mission. Reaching Dak To, the package was given a "hold" because of inclement weather in the LZ.

While standing by, Joe Gallo, Gary Thiry, "Smokey" Norton, and Joe Driscoll eyeballed the re-arming point stocked with 2.75 flechette rockets. Having talked one of the CH-53 pilots into taxiing to the ammo dump, they proceeded to load the flechettes.

All four were in the cargo bay when the field came under rock-et attack. The CH-53 being loaded was running. The pilot 1Lt Greg Simpson, having no desire to get hit by incoming, pulled pitch to get the hell out of the area. The four bandits had another brilliant idea. Wanting to get out of the aircraft and back to their own, they ran out the back of the CH-53 just as Simpson pulled pitch and found themselves airborne. Gallo was the first to hit the ground, with the other three close behind. He suffered a broken arm and a blow to the head as the other three piled on top of him.

The crews scrambled for their Cobras, launched and began searching the area expending ordinance on suspected rocket sites.

Army Cobra hit during rocket attack at Dak To. Photo by 1Lt Barry Pencek.

Others, not close enough to their aircraft, took cover. One army Cobra on the ramp took a direct hit.

Shortly after the rocket attack subsided, the mission was cancelled for the day and the package returned to Kontum.

On September 9, inclement weather continued in the insertion area. The forecast showed no improvement and the marine package returned to MMAF.

On September 10, the package departed for Kontum only to return again to MMAF because of continuing adverse weather conditions.

On September 11, the package once again launched for Kontum. Once there, Sexton briefed the crews for the third time. Army Pathfinder Hueys, escorted by the six army Cobras, were to precede the marines by twenty minutes. The CH-53s were to follow with the main insertion package. After refueling at the staging area at Dak To, a "go" was received at 1130 hours. The package departed for the insert area some 100 kilometers to the northwest.

Enroute to the area the weather consisted of low-lying clouds forcing the aircraft to fly at 200 to 500 feet AGL.

Approximately fifteen minutes out of the insertion LZ, Sexton contacted Dragon Fly Lead. He was informed the Pathfinder inser-

Remains of Cobra hit by rocket at Dak To. Photo by 1Lt Barry Pencek.

tion had been completed and that they had taken enemy fire during the insertion. Spotting Dragon Fly Lead, Sexton informed him the insertion package was on station and ready. Sexton instructed Gnat Lead to hold his package east of the zone while he proceeded in and identified the landing zone. The second section of marine Cobras held with the Gnat flight.

Gunner's view from front cockpit of rockets being expended. Action taken during Tailwind. Photo by 1Lt Barry Pencek.

After identifying the LZ, he determined the zone could handle only one CH-53 at a time. Returning to the holding area, he led in Gnat Lead. As the aircraft began its approach, the Eagle Claw flight laid small bursts of protective fire around the zone. While in the zone, Gnat Lead reported taking fire from his six o'clock. The Cobras stepped up their suppressive fire and, just as Gnat Lead cleared the zone, Eagle Claw Lead reported taking hits.

1Lt "Sid" Baker, Eagle Claw Three, rolled in firing rockets. His aircraft took a burst of bullets. One bullet came through the floor and passed about an inch behind his left foot. Another smashed through his Fox Mike control box shattering its casing. Some fragments hit Baker in the face.

Gnat Two was cleared in. He, too, reported taking fire from all directions while in the zone. Baker's wingman, Eagle Claw Four, also reported being hit. Almost simultaneously, Sexton's wingman, Eagle Claw Two called stating he was taking hits.

Just as Gnat Two came out of the zone, Sexton felt a loud thump under his aircraft. He had just taken another hit. With enemy fire becoming intense, the Cobras stepped up suppressive fire with high explosive rockets and turret. Sexton cleared Gnat Three into the zone. As he started his approach, the Sea Stallion mistook the smoke from the HE rockets for the LZ and started his approach to the area where the heavy enemy fire was coming from. Spotting the error, Sexton redirected him to the landing zone. Gnat Three made his insertion. Gnat Four was cleared in.

The intensity was increasing. Sexton's experience and knowledge as a flight/strike leader was invaluable. Having led Kingfisher missions since taking over the squadron, he was experienced in large multi-aircraft missions. With all four insertions completed, Sexton ordered all assets to move east of the zone. Not hearing Sexton's instructions, Baker was still over the insertion zone. Seeing the rest of the packet leaving east of the insertion area, he followed suit. After Baker re-joined the flight, Sexton completed radio checks and made battle damage assessments. Determining Cobras numbers two and three had lost all radios, Sexton realized it was time to get his people home.

Sexton gave Gnat Lead a departure heading. Because they had no radios, Baker's wingman was instructed to join up on his leader's wing. Sexton would join his wingman and proceed out the exit route.

After landing they discovered the marine Cobras had taken a total of twenty-three hits. The CH-53s had taken thirteen. A seventeen-man maintenance team they had brought along from MMAF made repairs to the damaged aircraft at Kontum.

At 0800 hours on September 12, Sexton held a debriefing. The package returned to Marble Mountain and was put on one-hour standby. At approximately 1500 hours. a "Prairie Fire" emergency was declared. All available aviation assets in South Vietnam were to be available for a sensitive mission. The marines assembled an extraction package and departed for Kontum.

Upon reaching Kontum, all army assets were again turned over to Col Sexton. The extraction flight team under his command remained the same as previously. Sexton was briefed that the Hatchet force was on the move and being pursued. Heavy enemy fire was to be expected during the extraction. They prepared for a launch the following day.

At 0730 hours on September 13, Sexton briefed the entire package. Because of inclement weather, they were again placed on "hold." At 1045 hours they received a "go." After refueling at Dak To, the package departed for the extract zone. An OV-10 was on station. When the package was twenty-five minutes out, he received a call from Sexton requesting a zone prep.

Upon reaching the area, Sexton again had the package hold to the east of the extract zone. His section of marine Cobras proceeded to the area and identified the zone. The OV-10 then marked the zone. After Sexton assessed the zone, he determined it would be marginal for the CH-53 aircraft, but decided to give it a try. Sexton called in Gnat Lead, piloted by Major J.E. Carroll with 1Lt "Bill" Beardall as copilot, for the first pick up and led them to the zone.

The big helicopter turned left after spotting the zone. Beardall took the controls for the landing. As he approached the LZ located in a bowl of trees seventy-five to 100 feet high, he realized he was too fast. He had to wave off. After coming around again, he came to a hover above the hole in the jungle. He began his descent into what he described as going "from daylight into darkness to the middle of a fireworks factory that had blown sky high." Tracer rounds were going off in every direction. As the ground got closer, the zone grew smaller. About five feet from touch down, the zone got too small. A bump on the controls caused the aircraft to move only a few feet and the massive blades made contact with a tree in the surrounding jungle. It was a bad blade strike, but the pilots still had control. Beardall raised the collective. The aircraft ascended out of the zone and turned to the east.

Sgt G.J. Follin, the crew chief, assured the two pilots the aircraft could fly even though the tree strike had caused a bad rotor beat.

Shortly after commencing their eastward flight, the aircraft lurched as two B-40 rockets struck it, blowing out the first-stage hydraulic line. Immediately, they called stating they had taken hits and were in trouble. They were "going in."

Sexton called in the SAR bird and shot two Willy Petes near a probable landing area. Following Follin's instruction to get the aircraft down immediately, the Sea Stallion descended toward an open area with tall elephant grass. The Cobras were now with the aircraft delivering suppressive fire as the CH-53 came in for a landing. Beardall and Follin spotted NVA running along a nearby ridgeline toward the clearing.

Despite a damaged rotor blade, the aircraft made a successful landing. The crew immediately departed the aircraft and ran toward the approaching SAR aircraft. The extraction ladder was being lowered from the rear ramp.

As the SAR bird came in for its approach, the Eagle Claw Cobras laid down a smoke screen on both sides of the aircraft. Just as they came to a hover, the right door gunner on the starboard side, Sgt Larry Groah, heard a "bam-bam-bam" about twenty-five yards from the aircraft. He spotted a .51 cal shooting at them. Instinctively, he opened up firing his M-60. He fired until the anti-aircraft gun crew was silenced.

Looking around, he saw that the pilot, 1Lt Mark McKenzie, and his copilot, 1Lt Raoul Bustamante, were okay. They had their hands full keeping the aircraft in the air as it was becoming difficult to control because of damage from enemy fire. The gunner on the port side, Sgt Ron Whitmer was still firing. Capt "Chip" Cipolla, the squadron maintenance officer, and the crew chief, Sgt Spalding, were at the back ramp still lowering the ladder.

The Scarface Cobras were now pumping in their 40 mm grenades and shooting rockets along the ridgeline. Everyone hooked on to the ladder with D-rings. Immediately they were flying through the air looking down at their crippled bird. Its rotors were still turning. Moments later an AD-1 Skyraider was called in. The Skyraider dropped its ordinance and destroyed it.

Not five minutes had passed when Sexton received a call from the SAR bird. They were having problems and did not know if they were going to make it. Sexton instructed them not to take a chance. They would have to land. An excellent landing area was spot-

Downed Tailwind CH-53 crew on rescue ladder. Photo From HMH-463 Cruise Book.

Ordinance crew, L. Cpl B.C. Sanders(l.)and unidentified crewman loading 40mm grenades. Cruise Book photo.

ted directly ahead. Sexton marked the spot with two Willy Petes and instructed Gnat Three to be ready to act as SAR.

After landing, the rescued crew detached from their ladder. The new SAR bird elected to make his approach to the ground and board them into the aircraft. The initial SAR aircraft crew exited their aircraft and did a quick visual inspection for damage. The aircraft commander reported the damage was not as bad as initially thought. The aircraft appeared flyable.

Both SAR birds departed the LZ and joined up with the rest of the package. Arriving at Kontum, Sexton informed MAG-16 that because of the loss of one CH-53 and damage to another, additional parts and aircraft were required to complete the mission. The request was approved. The items were delivered within hours.

During mission debriefing, the CCC commander stated the following day would be critical. Severe weather was forecast to move in. Conditions would likely prohibit any further extract attempts.

Feverishly, maintenance crews worked late into the night to get the wounded aircraft back to "up" status. Two additional CH-53s and crews arrived making five Sea Stallions available.

At 0800 hours on September 14, the aircrews were again assembled and briefed. It was agreed fixed-wing assets would be available to do a zone prep prior to extraction.

A "go" was given. The package departed for Dak To, refueled, and immediately received a "hold" from CCC.

Prior to shut-down, Sexton contacted a marine OV-10 pilot assigned to the mission and asked him to scramble all available marine fixed-wing assets.

An air force OV-10, Covey had spent two hours over the extraction area. Landing at Dak To, he met with Sexton and the pilot of Gnat Lead, LtCol Robert R. Leisy. He explained the reason for the delay was that the team had not reached the extraction LZ. Also, the pre-scheduled USAF Phantom jets had not arrived and were not available for the mission. Sexton asked Covey for an ETA for the team so he could plan accordingly.

After the brief from the Covey pilot, Sexton and his crew returned to their aircraft. A few minutes later, they received a visual launch signal. In response, they started up, assembled the package, and departed with all twenty-one aircraft. Already airborne, the

CCC commander informed Sexton the visual signal was intended for aircraft start-up only.

At this point Sexton had had enough delays. He could hear the TACA Fox Mike transmissions with the Hatchet team and could tell the team was near the LZ. He made the decision to keep going and informed CCC control they were proceeding to the extract area. Enroute, he called the TACA giving him a twenty-five-minute ETA for the zone prep.

Arriving in the general area, Sexton found that Captain McCarley, the company commander, had elected to bypass the first LZ. The team was now near the second zone, but not ready for pick-up. Sexton held the package to the east and proceeded to the zone with his wingman.

Within minutes the team reported ready for extraction. The two Cobras returned to the package and led Gnat Lead to the LZ. As Sexton came to the zone, he radioed the team and asked for a smoke, but received no response. After telling the extract CH-53 to hold high, he again tried to establish radio contact. After five minutes of trying with no success, he fired a Willy Pete near the zone and gave Gnat Lead directions relative to the smoke. Finally, the team leader came back on the air. Sexton's assessment had been correct. They were having radio problems. The team popped a smoke. As Sexton led Gnat Lead into the zone, the remaining marine Cobras laid down a smoke screen and put in a stream of suppressive fire. The first platoon, consisting mostly of wounded, scrambled aboard. The huge helicopter completed the extraction and departed. Sexton called in Gnat Two. They loaded and made a clean getaway, receiving only moderate fire.

Shortly after the second extraction, the team leader told Sexton he thought only one more Sea Stallion was needed to get everyone out. About that time, Sexton felt a kick in his rudder pedals. He thought they had taken a hit.

As Gnat Three, piloted by 1Lt D.N. Persky, was in the zone, the Cobras increased their smoke screen and suppressive fire. When the

'53 departed, Sexton asked if all members had been extracted. He received no reply. Sexton again tried to contact the team. Again, he received no reply. Thinking all members were out of the zone, Gnat Four was ordered to abort his approach and return to the holding area to the east.

Further attempts to contact Gnat Three proved unsuccessful. Sexton assumed the CH-53 had developed radio failure and might have aircraft damage. Asking the OV-10 to check out the zone for any additional troops, he proceeded outbound from the zone to join up with the rest of the package. The OV-10 reported no troops remained in the zone. Finally able to reestablish radio contact, Persky called and reported they had taken hits and had lost an engine.

Sexton gave him a departure heading and closed in to check him over. Minutes later, Persky called again and reported he was losing his second engine and was auto-rotating. The SAR bird, piloted by 1Lt R.R. Arnold, was called in.

Because the marine Cobras were near ammo exhaustion, Sexton directed the army Cobras to provide low cover while he stayed high and coordinated the extract.

As the wounded monster descended, only one possible landing site remained. The second engine had failed over a large canyon with rugged jungle on all sides. Persky maneuvered the aircraft to the available zone near a river and completed his auto-rotation on the rugged riverbed. After touchdown, the aircraft rolled to the right and settled on its side.

While the army Cobras laid down suppressive fire, Arnold made his approach. From above, Sexton spotted a mirror signal indicating some of the crew had exited the aircraft. Arnold landed the SAR bird near the downed aircraft and picked up the crew, team members, and PAX. After the rescue, the package joined up and proceeded to Dak To.

At Dak To, the army Cobra leader informed Sexton radio contact with the OV-10 had been lost and they thought he might have

1Lt Penchek having a good time socializing with Montagnyards.
Photo by 1Lt Barry Pencek.

been shot down. They were going to return to the area. Sexton decided the marine Cobras would re-arm, refuel, and return as well. A few minutes later radio contact was made with the OV-10. Relieved, the package proceeded to Kontum.

Near Kontum Sexton received a chip light warning on the 90-degree gearbox. Inspection conducted after landing revealed a direct hit to the gearbox. Loss of tail rotor control was imminent had he flown much farther.

Following repairs and debriefing, the marine package departed for Marble Mountain concluding a mission that was, without a doubt, one of Scarface squadron's most intense. As for SOG, Tailwind proved to be one of their most successful missions. An abundance of intelligence documents containing NVA records and codebooks was obtained. The diversion accomplished what they had intended.

1Lt E.D. "Dink" Crowe having fun with Georgia at the party. Photo by 1Lt Barry Pencek.

Two weeks after this mission, the men of the 5th Special Forces invited the marine crews to Kontum for a party. The marines were made honorary members and were given green berets with the Special Forces emblem. They made sure no marine paid for a single drink all night.

Epilogue

ON AUGUST 11, I was flight leader of two Cobras on night medivac standby. The night was quiet until 0600 when we received a call for an emergency medivac about twenty kilometers northwest of Da Nang. Scrambling, we turned up our aircraft. Shortly after the engines were running, my wingman called and reported his aircraft was grounded because of a mechanical problem. After I called for taxi and take-off clearance for myself and the two CH-46s, our flight departed. Outbound I contacted Da Nang DASC. I was told to contact Bluebill 14.

The sun was just coming up as we passed Elephant Valley and headed toward bad man country. Patches of fog filled the low-lying areas in the jungle below. Here and there I could see smoke coming up through the trees from campfires where who knows who was probably cooking up some rice. The radios were silent and everything seemed tranquil.

The serenity was short lived. Five klicks out I called for a zone brief, "Bluebill One Four, this is Scarface Four Two, inbound for medivac. Over."

"Scarface Four Two, Roger. We have two emergency medivacs. Our unit came under attack about an hour ago. We are not taking fire at this time. Puff is overhead and has been working out. The wind is calm. The zone is a large open area with no obstacles. If you take fire it probably will be from the west. Over."

"Roger, One Four. I have a copy." Looking ahead I could see the huge C-130 gunship. Swift Lead was ready to come in. Puff called to say he was moving out of the way.

Swift Lead made a right spiral approach. As he slowed for landing and was about fifty feet from touchdown, his starboard gunner started firing his .50 cal to the west. I called in hot. I had the area he was firing at in sight. I set my rockets for Willy Pete and rolled in laying down a blanket of smoke. During my pull-out Puff called stating he was in position to fire. I did not waste any time getting out of his way.

The two medivacs were loaded and Swift Lead was out of the zone in short order.

With the medivac complete, Puff called. He had another mission and would be departing. Bluebill called and asked if I could expend the rest of my ordinance to the west of their position while they moved to a better defensive position. I agreed and told the Swift Flight to head back without me.

I had my copilot expend his mini-gun and grenade launcher first and I set my rockets for "salvo." My final run blew up a good chunk of countryside.

As I headed back, my mind started playing with me. I was flying my last flight in Vietnam, a lone gunship with no ammo out in bad man country. I was definitely too damn short for this crap!!

As Da Nang came into sight, my thoughts turned to how I had just flown over 1,140 combat missions and nothing had changed … the war was the same as the day I got in country. I still wonder today if it was worth it.

I do not feel that it is my place to judge the wisdom of the politicians who ran the war from their desks Washington. I do know that too many brave men and women lost their lives when the call came to serve their country. I also know that when they came back they experienced a homecoming that should not have happened and should never ever again happen to any American in the service of our country.

Too many of my brave, heroic friends lost their lives for our country. Their courage and actions are what makes this county the great country it is.

My comrades in arms were the best of the best, and I developed lifelong friendships. The camaraderie developed among soldiers, sailors, marines and airmen who depend on each other for survival is known only to those who have walked the walk.

Bibliography

BOOKS

Hodgins, Michael C., *Reluctant Warrior: A Marine's True Story in Vietnam*. New York, Ivy Press. Published by Ballantine Books, 1997.

Kelley, Michael P., *Where We Were In Vietnam*. Hellgate Press, 2002.

Moriority, J.M., *Ground Attack Vietnam: The Marines Who Controlled the Skies*. New York, Ivy Books. Published by Ballantine Books, 1993.

Plaster, John L., *SOG: The Secret Wars of America's Commundos in Vietnam*. New York, Simon & Schuster, 1997.

Stoffey, Bob, Col USMC, Ret., *Cleared Hot!* New York, St. Martin's Press, 1992.

Byrd, Mark, *HML-367 Cruise Book: Phu Bai*. 1970.

Byrd, Mark, *HML-367 Cruise Book: Marble Mountain*. 1970.

Smith, Charles M., *U.S. Marines in Vietnam: High Mobility and Standdown*. 1969, Washington D.C., History and Museums Division, Headquarters United States Marine Corps.

Cosmas, Graham A. and Murray, Terrence P., LtCol, USMC. *U.S. Marines in Vietnam, Vietnamization and Redeployment, 1970-1971*. Washington D.C. History and Museums Division, Headquarters, United States Marine Corps.

COMMAND CHRONOLOGY

HML-367 Command Chronology 01 September 1969.

HML-367 Command Chronology 01 October 1969.

HML-367 Command Chronology 05 November 1969.

HML-367 Command Chronology 01 December 1969.

HML-367 Command Chronology 01 January 1970.

HML-367 Command Chronology 03 February 1970.

HML-367 Command Chronology 01 March 1970.

HML-367 Command Chronology 05 April 1970.

HML-367 Command Chronology 01 May 1970.

HML-367 Command Chronology 01 June 1970.

HML-367 Command Chronology 05 July 1970.

HML-367 Command Chronology 01 August 1970.

HML-367 Command Chronology 01 September 1970.

HML-367 Command Chronology 01 October 1970.

MVA(aw)-225 Command Chronology 08 October 1969.

MAG 16 Command Chronology 12 April 1970.

MAG 16 Command Chronology 09 July 1970.

MAG 16 command Chronology 12 August 1970.

MAG 16 Command Chronology 12 September 1970.

MAG 16 Command Chronology 12 October 1970.

ANNEX B: Appendix VIII, Pages 7-8 Operation TAILWIND, MACV COMMAND HISTORY, 1970—ANNEX B (Studies and Observations Group.)

AFTER-ACTION REPORTS AND STATEMENTS

HML-367 AAR, 05Sept69, 1Lt John Upthegrove.

HML-367 AAR 13Sept69 1Lt Perry Unruh.

HML-367 AAR, 21Sept69, 1Lt John Rhodes.

VMO-6 AAR 21Sept69, J.M. Miller.

VMO-6 ARR, 21Sept69, G.L. Medford.

HML-367 AAR 08Oct69, 1Lt John Upthegrove.

HML-367 AAR, 09Oct69, 1Lt John Upthegrove.

HML-367 AAR. 10Oct69, LtCol B.R. Wilkinson.

HML-367 AAR, 10Oct69, 1Lt John Rhodes.

HML-367 AAR, 31Oct69, 1Lt Perry Unruh.

HML-367 AAR, 10Nov69, 1Lt John Rhodes.

HML-367 AAR, 10Nov69, LtCol B.R. Wilkinson.

VMO-2 AAR, 12Nov69, 1Lt M. Bartlett.

VMO-2 AAR, 12Nov69, 1Lt Paul Dumas.

VMO-2 AAR, 12Nov69, 1Lt D. Huffman.

VMo-2 AAR, 12Nov69, Maj D.W. Johnson.

MAG-16 After Action Statement, 16Jan70, Col H.R. Smith.

HML-167 After Action Statement, 16Jan70, LtCol K.W. Andrus.

HML-367 After Action Statement, 16Jan70 Maj H.F. Stroman.

HML-367 After Action Statement, 16Jan70 1Lt Mark Byrd.

HML-367 After Action Statement, 16Jan70 1Lt J.T. Lewis.

HML-367 After Action Statement on actions 11Sept70-14Sept70. LtCol H.E. Sexton.

HMH-463 After Action Statement on actions 11Sept70-14Sept70. LtCol Robert R. Leisey.

HMH-463 After Action Statement by 1ˢᵗ Lt W.H. Beardall on action 13Sept70.

HMH-463 After Action Statement by 1ˢᵗ Lt W.H. Beardall on actions 07Sept70-13Sept70.

Electronic interview, David Geaslin, 23Feb97

Electronic interview, Ted Soliday, 17Jan99.

Electronic interview, Ted Soliday, 18Jan99.

Electronic interview, Ted Soliday, 21Mar99.

Electronic communication, David Geaslin, 15Mar97

Electronic communication, Mark Byrd, 23Oct99.

Electronic communication, James W. Rider, LtCol USMC, Ret., 10Oct99.

Electronic communication, John Rhodes, LtGen United States Marine Corps (Ret.) 17Jun04.

Electronic communication, John Rhodes, LtGen United States Marine Corps (Ret.) 28Apr05.

Electronic communication, Pat Owen, LtCol United States Marine Corps (Ret.) 26June99

Mission statement, Col H.R. Smith, action on 16Jan69.

Mission statement, LtCol K.W. Andrus, action on 16Jan69.

Mission statement, Maj H.F.Stroman, action on 16Jan69.

Mission statement, 1Lt J.T. Lewis, action on 16Jan69.

Mission Statement, 1Lt Mark Byrd, action on 16Jan69.

Mission statement, 1Lt Robert. W. Robinson, action on 16 Jan69.

Activity report, R.L. Tucker, Bell Helicopter representative, Phu Bai. 21September 1969.

AWARDS

Medal of Honor. PFC Ralph E. Dias for action on 12Nov69.

Silver Star Award Citation. 1Lt John Rhodes for action on 21Sept69.

Distinguished Flying Cross, LtCol Warren G. Cretney for action on 16Jan69.

Distinguished Flying Cross, Capt Ron Fix for action on 16Jan69.

PUBLICATIONS

Whitaker World, Vol. No. 8, April 1970.

WRITINGS

Operation Tailwind by Bill Beardall, 12Oct1998.

Glossary

A-4 Skyhawk— U.S. attack single engine jet. Top speed 680 knots. Manufactured by Douglas Aircraft.

A-6 Intruder—U.S. All-weather fighter-bomber aircraft. Top speed 545 knots. Manufactured by Grumman Aviation.

AA—Anti aircraft weapon.

AAR—After Action Report.

Aboard—On base; with us.

AC-47 Gunship—"Puff." Twin-engine C-130 and C-117 transport configured as a gunship. Also known as "Puff the Magic Dragon."

AGL—Above ground level.

AH-1 Huey Cobra—U.S. helicopter gunship. Top speed 190 knots. Manufactured by Bell Helicopter.

AK-47-Standard weapon for Viet Cong and North Vietnamese regulars.

Arc Light—Code name for a B-52 strike.

ARVN—Army of the Republic of Vietnam.

Assholes and elbows—a hurry.

ATC—Air Traffic Control.

Avn—Aviation.

AWOL—Absent without leave.

B-52 Stratofortress—U.S. eight-engine bomber. Top speed 575 knots. Manufactured by Boeing Aircraft.

Basketball—Call-sign/codename for C-130 flare ship.

Battalion—Military unit usually consisting of about 500 Marines. Commanded by a lieutenant colonel.

Bingo fuel—Point in a flight where only enough fuel remains to return to base.

Bird Dog—designation for a Cessna single-engine O-1 observation aircraft. Top speed 115 knots.

Boondocks(boonies)—Rugged isolated area.

BOQ—Bachelor Officers' Quarters.

Brig—Jail.

Bronco—OV-10 twin-engine reconnaissance and ground support aircraft. Top speed 280 knots. Manufactured by North American Corporation.

Bullet bouncer—Chest protector (body armor) worn by helicopter crews.

Burp gun—.45 cal automatic weapon M3 sub-machinegun. Also called "Grease gun."

C-130—Hercules-four-engine turboprop cargo plane with short take-off and landing capability. Also used as flare ship and gunship.

CAC—Command and Control.

CCN, CCC, and CCS—Special Operations Command and Control North, Central, and South.

C-Rations—field rations for combat troops.

CH-47 Chinook—U.S. twin-engine heavy lift helicopter. Top speed 130 knots. Manufactured Boeing Aircraft.

Chatterbox—call-sign, United States Marine Corps Helicopter Squadron HMM-364.

CO—Commanding Officer.

Cobra—Nickname for the AH-1 Bell Huey Cobra gunship.

Company—Army or Marine Corps unit normally commanded by a captain. Unit consisted of three or four platoons of approximately forty soldiers each.

Chopper—helicopter.

Covey—Call sign for Air force O-2, forward air controllers flying support for special operations in Laos and Cambodia.

Crew chief—Helicopter crewmember on flying status who maintains the aircraft.

CS gas—Standard tear gas mixed with vomit inducing agent.

DASC—Direct Air Support Center.

DMZ—Demilitarized zone separating North from South Vietnam.

ETA—Estimated time of arrival.

F-4—Phantom-Fighter-bomber. Top speed 1500 knots. Manufactured by McDonald Douglas. Commonly referred to as "Fox-4."

FAC—Forward air controller.

Fast mover—Slang for a jet.

Feet dry—Pilot talk for the transition from flying over water to over ground.

Feet wet—Pilot talk for the transition from flying over ground to over water.

Fire Support Base (FSB)—Ground installations designed to house artillery units supporting outlying friendly troops.

Firefight—exchange of small arms fire between U.S. Forces and enemy.

Flare ship—any aircraft or helicopter supporting ground units by dropping illumination flares.

Flechette rocket—2.75 rocket containing several thousand of 1.5-inch finned "nails."

FM—Medium frequency radio.

FNG—Fucking new guy.

FO—Forward observer.

FOB—Forward operating base.

Fox Mike—Reference to the medium frequency radio.

Forty Mike—Mike-forty millimeter.

Gooner—U.S. Marine slang for the Viet Cong and North Vietnamese Regulars.

Grunt—Non-derogatory nickname for ground troops.

Guard Channel—VHF and UHF radio emergency channel.

Gunny—Gunnery Sergeant.

Gunship-Armed helicopter or adapted fixed wind aircraft.

Ho Chi Minh Trail—series of trails designed to funnel troops, weapons and supplies from North Vietnam to the war in the south. The trails ran mostly through Laos and Cambodia.

HAC—Helicopter Aircraft Commander

Hootch—Living quarters.

Huey—UH-1 utility helicopter. Top speed 120 knots. Manufactured by Bell Helicopter.

Huey Cobra—See AH-1 Huey Cobra.

I Corps—Northernmost region in South Vietnam. One of four major military regions.

Incoming—receiving enemy mortar or rocket fire.

KABAR—Marine combat knife with a six-inch blade.

KIA—Killed in action.

Klick—Kilometer.

LZ—Landing zone for helicopters.

LCpl—United States Marine Corps Lance Corporal.

Little People—Slang for Vietnamese.

Lt—Lieutenant.

LtGen—Lieutenant General, three star.

M-16—Primary weapon of U.S. and RVN forces during the Vietnam war.

M-60—7.62 air-cooled belt-fed machine gun.

M-134 minigun—7.62 six-barreled Gatling gun. Used in the AH-1G Cobra gunship turret. Fired 2000-4000 rounds per minute.

SOG—Special Observation and Studies Group. Commonly called Special Ops.

MAG—Marine Air Group.

MARS—Military Amateur Radio Service.

MAW—Marine Air Wing.

Medivac Air evacuation of wounded or injured personnel.

MGySgt—United States Marine Corps Master Gunnery Sergeant.

MMAF—Marble Mountain Air Facility.

MP—Military police.

MSL—Mean sea level.

Nail—Common term for Flechette rocket.

Napalm—Bomb filled with highly flammable jellied gasoline. Capable of producing intense heat.

NCO—Non-commissioned officer.

NVA—North Vietnamese Army.

O-dark-thirty—Pre-dawn; early.

O-2 Super Skymaster—USAF reconnaissance aircraft. Twin engine push and pull.

OCS—Officer Candidate School.

OIC—Officer in charge.

Package—Term used to describe the various aviation assets assigned to a Special Ops. mission in Laos or Cambodia.

Plot—Known enemy anti-aircraft sight.

Platoon—Approximately forty-five men belonging to a company.

POL—Point-refueling point.

Pop smoke—To mark a target location or landing zone with a smoke grenade.

Prairie Fire—Code name for sensitive and secret joint operations in Laos.

R&R—Rest and recuperation. An out-of-country seven-day leave given to each soldier.

Recon—reconnaissance.

RTB—Return to base.

SAM—Surface to air missile.

SAR—Search and rescue.

Scarface—call sign of HML-367 aircraft.

SDO—Squadron Duty Officer.

Shiney—Signal mirror.

Skipper—Commanding Officer.

Slick—Unarmed UH-1 Huey.

Sniffer—machine capable of smelling the ammonia emitted from human beings. Normally mounted on a low flying helicopter to detect enemy personnel movements.

Squadron S-2—Intelligence Officer.

Squadron S-3—Operations Officer.

Squadron S-4—Logistics officer.

Stabo rig—A harness-belt system enabling hands-free hookup to an extraction rope.

Standby—Waiting and ready for mission.

UH-1—Iroquois helicopter, a.k.a. Huey Slick. Most used helicopter of the Vietnam war.

UHF—Ultra high frequency radio.

Uniform—Reference to UHF radio.

VC—Viet Cong.

VFR—Visual Flight Rules.

VHF—Very high frequency radio.

Victor—reference to a VHF radio.

Victor Charlie—The Viet Cong or any enemy force. Slang derived from the military phonetic alphabet.

Viet Cong—South Vietnam communist guerrilla forces.

VMF—Marine fighter squadron.

Willy Pete—White phosphorous rocket used for marking a target or to provide smoke cover for ground troops.

World—term referring to the U.S.A.

Index